MW00678226

WITH THE CHILDREN ON SUNDAYS

Through Eye-Gate and Ear-Gate
into the City of Child-Soul

By Sylvanus Stall, D.D.

Author of "What a Young Boy Ought to Know," "What a Young
Man Ought to Know," etc., "Methods of Church Work,"
"Faces Toward the Light," etc., etc.

Christian Classics
P. O. Box 1585
220 W. Parkway St.
Denton, Texas 76201
1.800.969.0911
Fax 940.891.3334
Email: classics1928@aol.com

With the Children on Sundays
ISBN 0-9743426-0-2

First published in 1893
Reprinted 1995
© 2003 edition reprinted by permission
of Need of the Times Publishers

No part of this publication may be
copied, stored or reproduced electronically
or by any means without prior written
permission of the publishers except for
brief quotes to be used in sermons,
magazines, or periodicals. Non-profit use for
church services, Sunday school classes, and
Bible studies is encouraged.

PUBLISHER'S PREFACE

With the Children on Sundays is as unique as it is wonderful. It was first published in 1893 as a series of children's sermons and then was brought back into print in 1995. This new edition is an evidence of the consistent desire to have it available to the Christian public.

Please allow us to walk you through its content and usefulness. The book is perfectly designed to be a weekly book for family worship, as well as a ready-made Sunday school curriculum for children from the ages of five to eleven. Each chapter uses an object lesson that teaches a biblical truth, as well as wonderful illustrations that can be copied and used for coloring. Each chapter then closes with a series of questions that can be used to review the contents of the chapter.

If a father, mother, or a Christian children's worker is looking for the perfect year long study for a family or group of children, *With the Children on Sundays* is the book. This is, as the book cover says, `delightful reading for the family on Sunday afternoons." Another has said that it is `the finest book for family worship with children I have ever seen."

Perhaps the most encouraging aspect of the book is that very little preparation is needed for its use. You just open the book and begin using it. May you find it to be of great benefit with those you love in communicating God's truth in an interesting and systematic way.

Mack Tomlinson
Christian Classics
Denton, Texas
2003

CONTENTS

PREFACE.

SUNDAY ought to be the most cheerful, sunniest, happiest and best day of the week in every home. In most homes it is the dullest and most dreary day of the week to the children, and the most taxing and the most wearying to the parents, especially to the mother. It not only ought to be, but it can be made, not only the brightest and happiest but also the most influential in the character-building and religious training of the children. In some households Sunday is looked forward to with anticipations of pleasure throughout the entire week. In these homes, the father does not come down stairs on Sunday morning and say: "Now, children, gather up those flowers, throw them out of the window, pull down the blinds, get down the Bible and we will have an awful solemn time here to-day." Neither is the day given to frivolity or the home to demoralizing influences. From morning until night there are two great principles that govern; first, the sacredness of the day, and second, the sacredness of the God-given nature of childhood. The day is not spent in repressing the child nature by a succession of "don't do that," "now stop that," etc., that begin in the morning and continue throughout the day, and end only when the little ones lose consciousness in sleep on Sunday night. In these homes, the parents recognize the fact that the child nature is the same whether the day is secular or sacred. On Sunday the child nature is not repressed, but the childish impulses are directed into channels suited to the sacredness of the day. In such homes the children, instead of being sorry that it is Sunday, are glad; instead of regretting the return of the

9

day with dislike and dread, they welcome it as the brightest, the cheeriest and the best of all the week.

The purpose of the author in the preparation of this book in its present illustrated and slightly changed form, is to afford all parents a valuable aid in making Sunday not only the brightest, happiest and best day of the entire week for both parents and children, but also to aid the parents to make Sunday pre-eminently the day around which shall cluster throughout the entire life of each child the sweetest, tenderest and most sacred recollections of childhood, of father and mother and of brother and sister, and especially of their knowledge of the Bible and of everything sacred.

Did it ever occur to you, as a parent, that between the birth and the age of twenty-one years there are three solid years of Sundays—an amount of time almost equal to the number of years given to an entire course of college training? The Creator has not laid upon parents the responsibilities of parenthood without giving them ample time and opportunity to discharge these obligations to Him, to themselves, and to their children.

The idea which has been successfully demonstrated in hundreds of homes, where the impulses and natural inclinations of childhood have been turned into sacred channels on Sundays so as to enable the parents to teach spiritual truths in the most effective manner, is the method which is suggested by the author to the parents in the use, on Sunday afternoons, of the fifty-two little sermons given in this volume.

The parent who fails to use wisely the opportunities of Sunday afternoons for impressing the children with spiritual truths, loses the greatest opportunity that family life affords. Among the different instances known to the author, the following three may serve as illustrations of what may be found in many communities:

I knew a mother who regularly on Sunday afternoons gathered her children about her and read them religious books and literature. In her considerable family, every child became eminently useful. One, who was a university professor, told me that those Sunday afternoons with his mother in the nursery embodied the most formative influences of his life.

I know another family, of some seven or eight children, where Sunday was always used for religious instruction with the children. With the reading and other things, they always "played church", and the experience of those early childhood days made the boys splendid public talkers, and the girls were also very capable in the same direction. No better school of oratory was ever organized.

I know another family of four children, where the entire family looked forward throughout the week to the special and larger pleasure which Sunday always brought. They grew up naturally into a religious life, and developed that ability for public address and service which could not so well be gained in any other way.

Sunday is about the only day in most of households where the father is home with his family. It adds greatly to the pleasure and impressiveness of the day and its services if the father, with the mother, enters heartily into the spirit of that which will be all the more enjoyed by the children. It will enable him also to stamp his personality deeper into the character of his children than possibly any other opportunity which may be afforded him in life.

These brief object talks grew out of the necessities found in the author's own parish. When called to the pastorate of the Second English Lutheran Church, of Baltimore, I found a depleted congregation, while at the same time the Sunday-school was one of the largest and most flourishing in the city. It was then for the first time that I introduced regularly the preaching of "Five-minute object sermons" before the accustomed sermon on Sunday morning.

In a very brief period, about one-fourth of the infant department and two-thirds of the main department of the school were in regular attendance upon the Sunday morning service, and, even after this particular form of address had been discontinued, the teachers and scholars continued regularly to come direct from the morning session of the school to the services of the church.

These sermons were preached without notes, were subsequently outlined and then spoken into the phonograph, put in manuscript by a phonographer, and, that the simplicity of style and diction might be preserved, were printed with only slight verbal changes.

The objects used in illustrating these talks have been chosen from among the ordinary things of every-day life. Such objects have the advantage of being easily secured, and on account of their familiarity also prove more impressive, and being more often seen, more frequently recall to mind the truths taught.

To any thoughtful student who has marked the simple language and beautiful illustrations used by that Great Preacher and Teacher who "spake as never man spake," it will be unnecessary to say a single word in justification of this method of presenting abstruse truths to the easy comprehension of the young. Upon all occasions Jesus found in the use of the ordinary, every-day things about Him, the easy means of teaching the people the great truths of divine import. The door, the water, the net, the vine, the flowers which sprang at His feet, the birds that flew over His head, the unfruitful tree that grew by the wayside, the wheat and the tares that grew together in the field, the leaven which a woman hid in three measures of meal, the husbandman pacing his field engaged in sowing his grain, the sheep and the goats which rested together on the slopes waiting to be separated each into their own fold, the old garment mended with a piece of new cloth, the mustard seed, the salt—anything that chanced to be about the Master was used as an illustration, that He might plainly and impressively teach the people the saving truths of redemption and salvation. May we not also reasonably suppose that if Jesus were upon the earth to-day He would still exercise this same distinguishing wisdom in the use of the common, every-day things by which He would now find Himself surrounded?

Let it be distinctly understood that this book is not a substitute for the regular services of God's House. I believe in "the Church in the house," but I also believe that the entire family, including the children, should also be in the Church on the Lord's day. The absence of the children from the services of the sanctuary is one of the alarming evils of our day. There are but few congregations where children can be found in any considerable numbers. No one will attempt to deny the sad consequences which must follow as the inevitable results of such a course. The children at eight years of age who have not already begun to form the habit of church attendance, and are not quite thoroughly established in it at sixteen, will stand a very fair chance of spending their entire life with little or no attachment for either the Church or religious things. The non-church going youth of this decade will be the Sabbath-breakers and irreligious people of the next.

Who are to blame for this state of affairs, and to whom are we to look for the correction of this existing evil?

Manifestly, first of all, to the *parents*. That parental authority which overcomes the indifference of the child and secures his devotion to the irksome duties of secular life, should also be exercised to establish and maintain a similar fidelity to religious duties and spiritual concerns. If left to their own inclinations, children will invariably go wrong in the affairs of both worlds. Attendance upon the church should be expected and required, the same as attendance upon the secular instruction of the schools; for the best interests of the child are not more dependent upon the discipline of the mind than upon the development of the heart. In the formation of the habit of church attendance, it would be well to remind parents that example will be as helpful as precept. They should not send, but take their children to church. They should make room for them in the family pew, provide them with a hymn-book and see that they have something for the collection. Parents owe it to their children to teach them to be reverent in God's house, to bow their heads in prayer, to be attentive to the sermon; and while requiring these things of their children, they should also see well to it that after service, at the table, in the home, or elsewhere nothing disparaging of God's house, message or messenger should fall from their lips upon the ears of their children.

As these little talks were originally used before the main sermon on Sunday morning before a mixed audience of adults and a large number of children, it has seemed best, in order to carry out the idea of preaching, that the manner of speaking as though to an audience should be retained in this book. It is better suited than any other method for use also by the parent when reading these pages to the children in the home.

The earlier issues of these talks under the title: "Five Minute Object Sermons to Children" and the second volume: "Talks to the King's Children" were accorded a place of usefulness in nearly every land, and the author now sends forth this volume in its present illustrated and slightly revised form for a place in every home, trusting that it may be as influential in the lives of the children of to-day as it has proven in the lives of the children of yesterday.

SYLVANUS STALL.

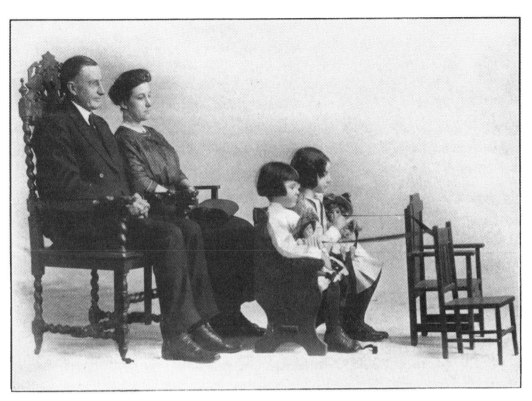

DR. STALL WITH HIS DAUGHTER AND HIS GRANDCHILDREN DRIVING TO CHURCH

THE LITTLE PREACHER AND HIS INTERESTED AUDIENCE

LITTLE BILLIE TAKING UP THE COLLECTION

DR. STALL READING TO HIS GRANDCHILDREN

SUGGESTIONS TO PARENTS.

HELPFUL METHODS FOR MAKING SUNDAY AFTERNOON WITH THE CHILDREN THE MOST PLEASANT AND PROFITABLE DAY OF THE WEEK.

The idea of "playing church" is by no means an innovation. What is shown in the pictures upon a preceding page has been actualized in many homes. Let me quote from a single letter which lies before me:

"The writer was one of a large family of children and well remembers the Sunday afternoons spent in his village home. 'Playing church,' was one of its features. The chairs were placed in regular fashion, imitating the seating arrangements of a church, every one of us took his or her turn as preacher, hymns were sung, a real collection was taken and one of us, as preacher, took his text and preached the sermon. There wasn't a dull moment in those good, old Sunday afternoons in our home. Occasionally, the preacher would provoke a smile by his original way of handling the text and of emphasizing some point in his discourse.

"We have all grown up since those happy days; some of us attained to a degree of efficiency as public speakers, and we attribute much of our efficiency and character in life to those profitable Sunday afternoon hours."

From the experiences of the children as narrated above, the suggestion occurs, why not use these object talks in like manner? "Play church" Sunday afternoons, read an "object sermon," show the illustrations, ask the questions at the end of each chapter and then follow it up with a discussion from the children, giving their ideas and experiences.

You will find that you will get as much benefit and entertainment from these Sunday afternoons "playing church" service as the children will. You will be surprised at their interest and the originality that they will display in these discussions. You will be quickening their faculty of observation and stirring their imaginations, in a manner that will surely make observant, thoughtful and considerate men and women of the children, and consequently, affect their entire destinies in the years to come. Then, too, you yourself will be helped mentally and spiritually, because it is absolutely true that in the devotion that we exhibit and the time and attention that we give to our children in this companionship, we will ourselves be receiving large blessings in the development of our own character and the finer characteristics that make for good people.

PLAYING CHURCH.

The following suggestions will be helpful, to which original ideas may always be added.

1. Make the "Afternoon Church" a real, not frivolous, occasion. The time it requires to make careful, pains-taking preparation on the part of the parent, is always profitably employed.

2. The afternoon church should always be a regular, fixed engagement. It adds to its importance.

3. Do not postpone nor omit it for any trivial reason. Treat it as any other important engagement.

4. When visitors are in the home, invite them to be present and to participate. It will help them as well as the juniors.

5. The fact that there is only one child in the family does not preclude the idea of playing church; for the dolls can be brought to church and even chairs can be converted into imaginary people.

6. Never permit the realness of the occasion to be questioned. Always avoid embarrassing the child and *never* ridicule. Refrain from laughing at any mistakes that may be made in speech, thought or conduct of the child, unless he first sees the mistake and invites you to join in his mirth.

7. Ask any additional questions pertinent to the subject besides those suggested at the end of each sermon. It will develop wider thought and increase the interest.

8. Encourage the child to ask questions, but always lead in directing the thought.

9. Adults present should always enter seriously and earnestly into the whole program or plan with the child's spirit. Where adults enter upon the execution of the plan with this spirit it adds much to the enjoyment of all. If they cannot do this, they should not participate.

10. A bell can be slowly rung as the time for church approaches.

11. Use the brightest and most cheerful room in the house for the afternoon church. Add to the furnishings on Sunday anything which may make the room even more than ordinarily attractive.

12. Chairs may be suitably arranged and a child can drive the others to and from church in an imaginary carriage, as shown in one of the pictures upon another page.

13. When the church is held in another room, an older child or person can receive the attendants and usher them to seats.

14. Open the church service with singing. Select several simple devotional hymns or songs, such as are used in the primary department of Sunday-schools. Have all the children learn the tunes and teach a verse of each song to any child that cannot read.

15. A collection can be lifted by one of the children. A toy bank may be used in which to save the money received at this child's service, and subsequently contributed through the Church or Sunday-school for missionary purposes.

16. Teach the children the importance of saving from their own spending money, or earning what they wish to give in the collection.

17. This money should always be regarded as sacred, and care should also be exercised lest this little fund might become a source of temptation to the children during the week.

18. At some time during the service a brief prayer should be offered. This may consist of a sentence prayer by each in rotation or by all uniting in the Lord's Prayer, or in some brief selection from the Prayer Book.

19. When a child is willing or wishes to do so, have him preach the sermon in his own way of expressing the thought, using the text or object of the day for his subject. Always give the same interested attention to him that is expected from him when another leads.

20. Some of the objects mentioned in the sermons can be easily and cheaply obtained for use at the church. When such an object is secured, it should not be shown to the children in advance of being used.

21. Do not prolong the service too greatly so as to weary the children. Effectiveness and pleasure usually terminate at the same time. Lend animation to the service and interest will not so soon flag. It is well also to impart interest by having the parent enter heartily into every part of the service.

22. A social period after "returning home" from the "children's church" should be introduced.. If the children have played driving to church before the service, the idea should be continued and completed by driving home in the same manner.

AFTER CHURCH.

23. After the conclusion of the church service, additional exercises or games suited to the sacredness of the day may be appropriately used to enter-

tain the children and continue their happiness. By methods of this kind, Sunday may be made not only the most profitable, but the brightest and best day of the week.

24. Some light refreshment may be introduced, as fruit, cake or candy. This refreshment should be something very simple and inexpensive, and also something not calculated to spoil the appetite or injure the digestion of the child. In recognition of good conduct, close attention or special help at the church service, one of the children may choose what the refreshment is to be for the next Sunday. This choice should be kept a secret during the week.

25. Pictures and illustrations can be cut from magazines, and these can be pasted in a scrap book or on blank paper to represent Bible characters and scenes, or those used in the sermons.

26. Many acting games and tableaux can be arranged by the children from the sermons and Bible stories. Chairs can be arranged so as to represent a pit or tent, and the children within them may be "Joseph in the Pit" (Genesis xxxvii) or "Daniel in the Lion's Den" (Daniel vi). See illustrations on pages 80 and 91.

FOR OLDER CHILDREN.

27. Let one child represent an idol. He must stand motionless and give no sign of life. The others are to ask him questions and for favors. If the "idol" laughs, moves or speaks, he loses and another takes his place. Idols are lifeless things that cannot move, see, hear or speak.

28. Children's blocks are useful in building a well, altar, castle, temple, chariot, etc. Have the children give a text or verse from the Bible referring to the objects builded. A Bible story may be told about the object, its history, use, etc.

29. One child, or more as may be needed, can pose to represent a character or scene. The others are to guess the character represented. For example: A child can sit with hands upheld. A child on each side of him hold up the extended arms. They represent Moses with Aaron and Hur during the battle (Ex. xvii: 12).

30. Charades, or words and scenes may be represented by the children in motion. The children may be divided into groups. One group will select a word and represent it in the presence of the others by motions. For example: Children come into the room and go through the motion of sowing ("Seeds"), reaping ("Harvest"), threshing with a flail ("Wheat and Chaff"), picking flowers ("Weeds and Flowers"), taking pictures ("Eye and Camera"). Many of the sermon subjects may be used in this manner. Cutting stone, measuring, eating husks, washing dirty face, etc. The other groups are to guess the word and have their turn.

31. Children are always fond of riddles; especially when they are able to guess the answer. The suggested review questions at the close of each object sermon for afternoon church, may often be effectively used with slight changes. For example: "What is it that cannot see nor hear, but always knows when danger is near?" The answer is—"The Oyster."

What is it which no boy or girl can see or hear, and the approach of which can not be made known by any of the natural senses? (Sin.)

What is it which tells us when sin is near? (Conscience.)

Have the children try to make up their own riddles from the objects shown and their uses, or lessons learned from the sermons.

SLATES AND CRAYONS.

32. Provide slates, or paper and pencils may be provided, and the children draw the object or something suggested by its use. Always have blank paper and pencils on hand for some of the games or exercises mentioned below.

33. Cheap colored crayons can often be used with added value.

34. Each Sunday appoint one child to take charge of the slates, papers and pencils, which are to be kept in a safe place and not disturbed during the week, and then to distribute them on the following Sunday.

BUILDING AND WORD GAMES.

35. Word building games are always interesting. Cut small squares of cardboard and plainly mark each with a letter. Many more vowels than consonants will be required. (These little squares with printed letters can be purchased at any toy-store.) Mix up the squares on a table, and the child who spells the largest number of names of places or objects mentioned in the sermons, using the letters on the squares, wins the game.

36. This can be played in a variety of ways. For instance: Select the name of an object, person or place, and the one who first picks out the necessary letters to spell it, is declared the winner.

37. Each child is given the same number of assorted letters and all try to make up the largest list of names from his portion of letters in a given time.

BIBLE GUESSES.

38. Tell a Bible story, or review one of the object sermons, omitting the names of characters or objects. Without warning, the one reciting the story stops, and the next player carries on the story if he has been able to guess the omitted names, without mentioning them. If he has not discovered or guessed

the right story, the next player takes it up, and so on until the story is completed and everyone knows it.

39.   One of the children goes out of the room and the others decide on some object used in a sermon, or a certain thing mentioned in the Bible, which is to be described.   For example: A watch, telescope, or the Ark, Joseph's coat of many colors, etc.   Upon entering the room, the child may ask all manner of questions which can be answered by "yes" and "no".   When the right thing is guessed, another goes out of the room and the game is repeated.   Two or more children, or groups, may be the guessers at the same time.

40.   The game of thinking is equally interesting.   The leader thinks of some character, place or object in the sermons or mentioned in the Bible. The "thinker" then says—"I am thinking of some thing (person or place) and the name begins with 'C' (or the initial letter)."   Each of the other players asks a question in turn, that can be answered by "yes" or "no".   The questions are continued until some one guesses the name.   The one who first guessed the name becomes the leader.

41.   Make word pictures by describing persons and scenes without mentioning names.   The others are to guess what it is.   For example: The leader may say—"I see some ladies walking beside the water.   Suddenly they stop and listen.   Then one of them wades into the water and finds something," etc. If the picture is not promptly guessed, the story or picture of Pharaoh's daughter finding the baby Moses (Ex. ii: 3) is further described, until the picture is made known.   Other stories may be used in the same manner.

42.   One or two players go out.   The others sit in line and choose a well known proverb, Bible verse, or sentence from the object sermon, having as many words as there are players.   Each player having made certain what his word is, the others are called in.   It is their duty to put the sentence together. They ask each player in turn a question on any subject, and in answering the player must use the particular word given him.   The questions may be continued, and the word must always be used in the answer, until the one guessing has discovered the particular word that player has, and so on until all the words in their order are guessed and the sentence or proverb discovered.

In the same way, instead of the questions, the particular word may be acted, as charades, until the person guessing has discovered each word and at length composed the complete sentence.

43.   Distribute paper and pencils.   Let a single letter be selected and have each child write down the names of characters, objects and places mentioned in the sermons, or the Bible, that have the same initial letter.   For example: The letter "A" may be selected, then would follow "Apple", "Adam", "Apostles", "Angels", "Army", "Asia", etc.   Other initial letters may be selected and the game continued.

44. Have some one call out and write down a Bible name beginning with "A", as "Abram". The next one is to think of a name beginning with "B", as "Benjamin". "C" would come next, as "Caleb", then "David", "Eli", etc. The object is to see how many letters of the alphabet can be used and how often without repetition. Also names of places, objects and titles may be used.

45. Ask the children to write down as many as they can of trees, or stones, flowers, birds, instruments, animals that are mentioned in the Bible.

46. Bible geography can be made interesting and profitable. Get a shallow box and fill it with fine sand. Cities and countries may be wonderfully made. A small pile of the sand will represent a mountain, strips of blue or white paper can be used for rivers and lakes. Use small blocks and spools for houses and temples, small pebbles for roads. The people can be represented by matches and trees by tiny branches or leaves. When Palestine, for instance, is to be studied, small pieces of paper may be laid on the sand for the cities; the names or initials of the cities should be written on the pieces of paper.

47. Maps may be drawn and colored crayons used to show the roads, water, cities, buildings, etc.

48. From one of the sermons or a Bible story, select the name of a person, place or thing. Have each player write a sentence with the selected name embodied in it. When the sentences are read aloud, it will show quite original uses made of the name.

49. To supply missing letters is an easy, simple game. Write names of sermon objects or Bible characters with letters omitted. The children will enjoy supplying the missing letters necessary to complete the name. Sentences and Bible verses may be used with missing words for the children to supply.

BIBLE DRILLS.

50. Bible drills are entertaining and especially valuable to children old enough to read and commit the lessons to memory. By a simple method the children can figure out the books in the Bible and their classifications. By pursuing the studies, the names of the books will soon be learned and in their regular order.

51. Have the children count the letters in "Old" (3) and "Testament" (9). Place them together (39) and it gives the number of books in the Old Testament.

52. Now multiply these two figures (3 × 9) and the result will give the number of books in the New Testament (27).

53. Add together the two sets of figures (39 plus 27) and you will find the whole number of books in the Bible (66).

54. The figure "6" is found in the number of books in the Bible (66), the

number of known authors or writers of the books (36), and the number of years during which the Bible was written (1600).

Thus we have 36 authors, 66 books, 16 centuries.

55. The books of the Old Testament may be divided into five groups: as the Pentateuch (Books of Moses), History, Poetry, Major Prophets and Minor Prophets. Have the children trace the outline of a hand on paper and the thumb and fingers will represent the groups. Thus, the thumb will represent the Pentateuch; the first finger, the History; the second finger, Poetry; the third finger, Major Prophets; and the fourth finger, Minor Prophets.

56. The New Testament may also be divided into five groups and represented by the other hand in the same manner. The five groups are Biography, History, Pauline Epistles (or Paul's Letters), General Epistles (or letters), and Prophesy.

57. The number of books in each group of the Old Testament are: 5 plus 12 plus 5 plus 5 plus 12—equals 39 books. In the New Testament, the five groups are made up of 4 plus 1 plus 13 plus 8 plus 1—equals 27 books.

58. The name of each group with the number of books in the group, may be written on separate cards. The cards are shuffled and the children sort them and place them together in their proper order, forming the Old Testament, then the New Testament.

59. The names of the different books which make up the groups are looked up and written under the name of the group. Take the groups in their regular order. Thus, group one would be Pentateuch, 5 books: Gen'e-sis, Ex'o-dus, Le-vit'i-cus, Num'bers, Deu'ter-on'o-my. The second and fifth groups, where there are twelve books each, may be subdivided into threes and fours for greater ease in committing to memory.

60. If the proper spelling of the names has also been committed to memory, or learned, then a regular spelling-bee may be held and the names of the Bible books used for the test words. The same tests may be made with the spelling of names of persons, places and things mentioned in the Bible.

61. After the books of the Bible, in their order, have been learned, open the Bible and call out the book at which it is open. Name another book and ask which direction (toward the front or back of the Bible) shall he pages be turned to find that book. Many other test questions may be asked, such as: "What book is between Job and Proverbs?" "In which group is Lamentations to be found?" "Between what books is that of Luke?"

62. Arrange the children in a row, or let them take their places in tents as shown on page 60, and then, as in a spelling-bee, ask the preceding or the following questions, or any other Bible questions that would be suited to the age of the children. When one fails to answer he loses his place and the child who gives the correct answer moves forward. The element of play is thus maintained.

BIBLE QUESTIONS AND ANSWERS.

63. Who was the first man? Adam.

Who was the first woman? Eve.

Who was the first murderer? Cain (Gen. iv: 8).

Whom did he kill? His brother Abel.

Who went to Heaven without dying? Enoch and Elijah.

How old was Enoch "when God took him"? 365 years (Gen. v: 23, 24). The same number of years that there are days in a year.

Who was the oldest man? Methuselah.

How old was Methuselah when he died? 969 years (Gen. v: 27).

Who built the Ark? Noah (Gen. vi).

How many persons were saved in the Ark? Eight (Gen. vii: 7). Noah and his wife, his three sons and their wives.

How old was Noah at the time of the Flood? 600 years (Gen. vii: 6).

Who had the coat of many colors? Joseph (Gen. xxxvii: 3).

How many brothers did Joseph have? Eleven (Gen. xlii: 3, 4).

What did they do with Joseph? Cast him into a pit and afterwards sold him to the Ishmaelitish merchantmen (Gen. xxxvii: 28).

Where did the Ishmaelitish merchantmen take Joseph? To Egypt.

To whom did they sell him? Potiphar (Gen. xxxix: 1).

Who lied about Joseph and had him cast into prison? Potiphar's wife.

Who were in the prison with Joseph? The king's chief butler and chief baker (Gen. xl: 1, 3).

Who was King of Egypt at the time Joseph was in Egypt? Pharaoh.

Why did Pharaoh make Joseph ruler? That he might gather the grain during the seven years of plenty to lay up in store against the seven years of famine.

What did Pharaoh dream? About seven fat kine, or cows, and seven lean cows (Gen. xli).

What did Joseph do with the grain he gathered during the seven years of plenty? Put in great store houses.

Why did his brothers come to Joseph in Egypt during the famine? That they might get food (Gen. xlii).

Did his father, Jacob, and family go to live in Egypt? Yes.

How old was Joseph when he died? 110 years (Gen. 1: 26).

How long did Jacob's descendants remain in Egypt? A little more than two hundred years.

Why did they desire to leave Egypt? Because of the oppressions and cruelty of Pharaoh (Ex. i: 8, 14).

Whom did God raise up to lead the Children of Israel out of Egypt? Moses.

How long did they wander in the wilderness? Forty years.

Was Moses permitted to enter the Promised Land? No.

Who led the Children of Israel into the Land of Canaan, which was the Promised Land? Joshua.

How did the Children of Israel cross the Red Sea and the Jordan? The waters were divided and they crossed "dry shod."

Who was the strongest man? Samson.

Who was the meekest man? Moses.

Who, as a ruler, was a man after God's own heart? David.

Who built the Temple? Solomon.

Who went to Heaven in a chariot of fire? Elijah.

On whom did the mantle of Elijah fall? Elisha.

Who was swallowed by the great fish? Jonah (Jonah i: 17).

Who destroyed the Temple and Jerusalem and carried the Children of Israel into captivity? Nebuchadnezzar (2 Kings 24, 25).

Where did he take them? To Babylon (2 Kings 25).

How long were they captive in Babylon? Seventy years.

Who interpreted Nebuchadnezzar's dream? Daniel.

How did Nebuchadnezzar reward Daniel? Made him ruler over Babylon (Daniel ii: 48, 49).

What were the names of Daniel's three friends? Hananiah, Mishael and Azariah.

What heathen names were given them instead? Shadrach, Meshack and Abednego (Daniel i: 6, 7).

What befell the three friends of Daniel? They were cast into the burning fiery furnace.

Why were they cast into this furnace? Because they refused to fall down and worship a great golden image which Nebuchadnezzar, the King, had set up in the plain of Dura.

Were they consumed in the furnace? No, God delivered them (Daniel iii).

What befell Daniel years later, when Darius was King? He was cast into the den of lions (Daniel vi).

Why was he cast into the den of lions? Because he prayed to the true God.

Did the lions harm Daniel? No, God stopped the mouths of the lions and delivered Daniel.

Through Eye-Gate and Ear-Gate Into the City of Child-Soul

THE OYSTER AND THE CRAB.

CONSCIENCE.

SUGGESTIONS TO PARENTS:—It will awaken the curiosity and add greatly to the interest of the children if the parent will have them secure during the week preceding a couple of oyster shells. In most of cities and towns, these can be easily obtained. It is better for the children themselves to secure them, because it makes them participants and important factors in what is to be done. Do not tell them in advance what use is to be made of the oyster shells; simply say that they are for use in connection with Sunday afternoon.

Introduce the play idea from the beginning. Let the children arrange the chairs to "drive to church," as shown in the preceding pictures. If there are two children who both want to do the driving, suggest that one can drive to church and the other can drive when returning from church—and a third may drive from the house to the stable when the horses are to be put away.

At the church service let everything be done reverently, and make it a matter of real worship. One of the children can act as usher, and if there is but one child, this one can usher her dolls to seats; or imaginary people may be shown to seats. All of this will appeal very strongly to the child. Select hymns suited to the children's tastes and such as they can sing. Do not sing too many verses. Children like variety.

The service ought to be such as is in harmony with that regularly attended by the parents, and such as the children are familiar with. It may be as informal as the Salvation Army, or a greatly abridged form of the "Episcopal Service" can be used. The Lord's Prayer may be repeated in unison, or sentence prayers used, or a brief selection from the Prayer Book. The preaching by one of the children should precede the reading of the Object sermon.

After carrying out the idea of the church service, the other ideas presented may be introduced, and after the imaginary drive home some simple refreshments can be served, as also mentioned in the chapter of "Suggestions to Parents" on page 17.

MY DEAR YOUNG FRIENDS: I want to speak to you to-day about "Having a good conscience." (I Peter iii: 16.) This is rather a hard subject, but I desire to make it plain by the use of a familiar object. "What's this I have in my hand?" I rather expected that you would say an oyster; but, really it is nothing but an oyster shell. I suppose you have all eaten stewed oysters, or oyster broth. I remember, when a little boy, that one day when we had stewed oysters

Oyster and Shell.

for supper, I found a little yellow something in my broth. I did not know whether my mother had put it in purposely, or whether it had fallen in by accident; whether I should push it aside of my plate, that it might be thrown with the crumbs to the chickens, or whether I should eat it to discover what it was.

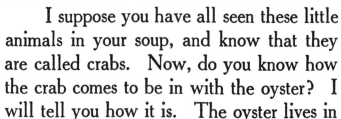

Little Crab.

I suppose you have all seen these little animals in your soup, and know that they are called crabs. Now, do you know how the crab comes to be in with the oyster? I will tell you how it is. The oyster lives in the water at the bottom of the bay, and some bright day, when the sun is shining down genial and warm, just the same as in the summer, we open the doors, and sit out on the porch to enjoy the cool of the day; so the oyster opens his shells and lets the cool currents of water move gently through his house. But while lying there with his shells wide open, along comes a great hungry fish. He sees the oyster, but the oyster cannot see him. The oyster cannot see, for he has no eyes. He cannot hear, for he has no ears. Of the five senses which each of us have, hearing, seeing, smelling, tasting and feeling, the oyster can only tell of the presence of his enemy when he feels himself being dragged out of

Fish Going to Eat the Oyster.

his house, and being quickly swallowed by the fish. But his knowledge of what is happening only comes when it is too late.

Now, with the little crab, who also lives in the same neighborhood with the oyster, it is quite different. The crab has eyes, and can see the hungry fish that comes to eat him up. He has legs, with which to try and run away; but the fish can swim so much faster than the little crab can run that he is sure to be devoured before the race is half over. So what do you think the little crab does? He crawls along quietly, and creeps into the shell with the oyster, and the oyster and the crab enter into a kind of partnership for mutual protection. After this, when the oyster opens his shells, the little crab uses his eyes very diligently to look around, and watch for the approach of any fish. As soon as he spies any sly fish coming near, he pinches the oyster, and immediately the oyster closes his shells very tightly, and the oyster and the crab are both within, safely protected from the fish.

Now, boys and girls, we are something like the oyster. We are constantly exposed to the danger of being destroyed by sin. We cannot see sin, we cannot hear sin, we cannot perceive it by any of our senses. So God has given us a conscience, which means "to know with God." When you are tempted to do a sinful act, it is conscience that quickly whispers, "Now that is wicked," "If you do that, God will be displeased."

Let me illustrate this thought. One real pleasant day, when the birds are singing, and everything is attractive out of doors, Johnnie thinks how hard it is to be studying his lessons in what he calls a prison of a school-room. He knows that papa and mamma will not give him permission to stay at home; so a little before nine o'clock, as he saunters towards the school, Satan suggests to him to play "hookey," and when he comes to the corner of the street, looking back to be sure that no one sees him, he turns the corner to remain out of school, intending to come home at the regular time for dinner and escape discovery. Just as soon as he turns the corner, and even before that, conscience has seen the danger, and whispers strong and clear, "Johnnie, this is wicked; you will surely get into trouble, and you will make papa and mamma sad, and also displease God." Now, if Johnnie does not turn right back when conscience warns him, he is sure to go on without having any pleasure all that forenoon, because his conscience continues to warn and reprove him.

Or suppose that Willie goes down the street and sees Mr.

"Willie is more frightened than the dog."

Brown's dog a little ways off. He looks around quickly for a stone, and immediately conscience says, "Now, Willie, don't hit the poor dog, for the stone will cause him pain, just as it would if some one were to hit you with a stone." But Willie does not listen to conscience. He throws the stone with all his might. It strikes on the pavement, just by the side of the dog, glances and breaks in many pieces the large plate glass in the window of the drug store.

Willie is more frightened than the dog, and without a moment's forethought he runs around the corner, to get out of sight. And after concealing himself for a time in the alley, he steals quietly into the house at the back door. How he dreads to meet his father and mother. Every time the door bell rings he thinks surely that it is the druggist or the policeman. Oh! how this sin pains him; just like the oyster would be hurt if he does not heed the little crab, when he warns him that the fish is coming to destroy him. If Willie had only listened to conscience, what sin and trouble it would have saved him. So, boys and girls, God has given each of us a conscience, and if we want to be saved from sin and suffering, we should always be quick to obey our conscience. Let each of us try and "keep a good conscience."

QUESTIONS.—Can the oyster see or hear? Can it feel? What often destroys the oyster? What lives down under the water near the oyster? Can the little crab see? Can he get away from the fish? How does he assist the oyster? How does he warn the oyster of danger? Can boys or girls see sin? What has God given each of us to warn us of danger when sin is near? Does every boy and girl have a conscience? Does conscience always give warning? Do boys and girls always obey their conscience? Should conscience always be obeyed? Will you always try to obey conscience in the future? The parent may ask additional questions or make application in any other manner they deem best.

Next Sunday the sermon will be about the worm in the apple. Let one of the children get a nice, large, perfect apple, and also another apple which has been dwarfed and deformed because of a worm inside the apple. These will be the objects which we shall use next Sunday.

THE WORM IN THE APPLE.

SIN IN THE HUMAN HEART.

SUGGESTIONS TO PARENTS:—The objects used to-day are a large perfect apple and a stunted, wormy apple. Have also a knife with which, at the proper time, to open the wormy apple. With these preparations made, let the children "drive to church" after the manner suggested for last Sunday.

After the singing of a hymn or two, prayer and collection, let one of the children, in the manner of the preacher speaking to his audience, tell in his own way of the "Oyster and Crab" and of God's purpose in giving us a conscience, and let him or her draw the moral lessons and impress the spiritual truths. Even if it is done in but few words, or a faltering way, do not embarrass or discourage by criticisms. Speak words of encouragement. If preferred, the little sermon may be a presentation of the sermon preached by the pastor in the morning, or one child may present the object sermon of last Sunday and another child the sermon by the pastor in the morning. The more who take part, the better, as variety adds to the interest.

Then gather the children around close so they can see the pictures as you read the following sermon. Have the apples at hand also for demonstration.

THE object which I have chosen to-day, is one with which I am sure every boy and girl is thoroughly familiar. The moment you see it you recognize it. This large and beautiful apple is one of the most perfect of its kind, large in size, beautiful in color, and one which tempts the appetite of any one who is hungry.

Now, boys and girls, I have here another object. Can you tell me what this is? I expected that you would say that it was an apple, and that is true. But you have not told me the whole truth concerning it. This is not only an apple, but it is a wormy apple. It did not grow as large as the other, and, by looking at the outside, I see that it is defective. It is stunted, like wormy apples quite universally are. You might think that the worm went into this apple because it was not full grown and strong and large, the same as it is sometimes thought that boys who have never improved their advantages, but have failed to become noble and good, therefore sin has entered their hearts. The truth is just the reverse; wickedness first possessed their hearts, and that has been the cause of their failure to improve their opportunities, and to become manly, and noble, and good, and kind. If they had first got the evil and sin out of their hearts, they would surely have stood a much better chance. They would have become Christians, and have grown up more and more like Christ, to be good, and kind, and generous, and useful.

I want to ask you a question concerning this worm. But to be sure that we are not mistaken, let me take a knife and cut this apple in two, and see whether or not there is a worm inside. Just as I said, this is a wormy apple. It has evidently had two worms in it. Here is one of them, and the other has taken its departure. Now, boys

Worm in the Apple.

and girls, I want to ask you, did this worm eat his way into the apple, or did he eat his way out of the apple? Quite as I anticipated. I expected that you would say that he ate his way into the apple; but the fact is, he ate his way out of the apple. I am sure that you will ask immediately, at least in your minds, how then did he get in, if he ate his way out? I will tell you how it was. Early last spring, just after the apple trees had been in blossom, and when this apple had just begun to form on one of the branches, there came along a bug and stung this apple, and deposited in the inside the germ of the worm. As the summer grew warmer, and the apple grew larger, the germ began to develop, until finally it grew into a worm. When it began to grow strong, it discovered that it was confined in the interior of something, and soon it began to eat, and continued until it ate its way out of the apple. This other

Insect Stinging Bud.

worm, which still remained in, had continued to eat in the various portions of the apple, and possibly because of having less bodily vigor had concluded to remain there for a time, but you can see from the inside of the apple that it has done great injury, at the very core or heart, and I suppose that if it had been left to itself, in the course of a few days, or a few weeks at most, it also would have eaten its way out of the apple, in order to escape from its confinement.

Now, boys and girls, this worm represents sin in the human heart, or wickedness possibly presents the thought better, and when you see a boy or girl doing wrong, they are simply giving outward expression to the wickedness which exists in their hearts. Boys are bad, not so much because the influences by which they are surrounded are bad, but because their hearts are sinful, and wicked, and bad. But I am sure that you will want to know how wickedness gets into the human heart. I will tell you how it is. Way back in the spring-time of the history of the human race, way back in the Garden of Eden, soon after God had created Adam and Eve, Satan came and inspired in the hearts of these first people the desire to disobey God. God told Adam and Eve that they should not eat of the fruit of the forbidden tree, and that when they did they would die, that is, they would be separated from God. Satan came and told them that they would not die, but that when they ate of the fruit of this tree they would become very wise. They believed Satan rather than God, and they did that which was wicked and wrong. And so throughout all the generations since, there has been that willingness to believe Satan and to do what he wants us to do, rather than to believe God and do what God would have us to do.

Boys and girls who find themselves inclined to disobey their father or mother, to be disrespectful to those who are older than they, to do wrong on the Sabbath, to remain away from the Sunday-school and church, and to enjoy the beautiful spring-day, by strolling through the fields or wandering through the woods, do so, not alone because the day is pleasant or because of the opportunities from which others turn away, but because there is wickedness in their hearts. So when boys quarrel and fight, or steal, or do any other thing that is wrong, it is not so much the influences by which they are surrounded, the temptation from without, but the wickedness and the evil and the sinfulness which there is in the human heart, eating its way out through their heart into their lives, and deforming their lives, which otherwise would be upright, honorable and manly and Christ-like. I trust that when you are tempted to do wrong you will recognize the fact that there is evil in your heart, and that you will go to Jesus and earnestly pray Him to take away this evil out of your heart, and to give you a new, clean heart. Just the same as with these apples, if you had the privilege of choosing, I am sure you would prefer the large one, which has not been spoiled because of the destructive worm inside, so I trust you will choose to have the good heart, which God can give you, rather than the heart that has wickedness and sin within. If you will go to God in prayer and ask Him, He will give you a good heart, a true heart, one that has no sin and no wickedness within.

QUESTIONS.—Which is nicer, a big, red apple or a little stunted one? What prevented the little apple from growing big and beautiful? When did the little worm get into the apple? If it had not been for the worm in the apple, would the apple have grown large and well formed? What causes boys and girls to desire to do wrong? Who tempted Adam and Eve to do wrong? Did they listen? Did they believe God or did they believe Satan? Are boys and girls still tempted to do wrong? Are they likely to yield to temptation? To whom should we go when we are tempted to do wrong? Who alone can cleanse our hearts from sin? Should we always go and ask God for strength when we are tempted? Which would you choose, a good heart or a wicked heart?

Suggest to the children (or better still select one or have them select one) to procure for next Sunday some weeds that grow by the wayside and also a few cut flowers or potted plants.

After "driving home" from church and after putting the horses away, which little action gives the children a few moments' diversion, then other methods contained in the chapter of "Suggestions to Parents" can be selected according to the age, intelligence and interest of the children. After this, refreshments or whatever is best suited to the thought of the parents and the conditions of the household may be introduced.

WAYSIDE WEEDS AND GARDEN FLOWERS.

NEGLECTED VERSUS CHRISTIAN CHILDREN.

SUGGESTIONS TO PARENTS:—The objects to be used to-day are a bouquet of flowers or some potted plants and a bunch of weeds that grow by the wayside. These will illustrate the difference between neglected, untaught and undisciplined children, and the children of a well trained household. Make the lesson impressive, so that the children will appreciate that the restrictions and discipline which are imposed upon them are all for their own good—that without these careful attentions they would grow up like the children in the slums. The neglected character of the clothing of undisciplined and uncared for children is only indicative of the minds and hearts and character of these children.

Arrange the chairs, "drive to church"; let the ushers show the different real or imaginary persons to seats. Then let the hymn, prayer or "opening service" precede the "preaching" of the object sermon of last Sunday or the regular sermon at the morning church service by one or more of the children, after which a hymn may be sung, and the parent gather the children close so they can see the pictures, and read the following sermon on "Wayside Weeds and Garden Flowers." During the reading, or before, or after, let the children gain the impressive lessons from the colored picture which so beautifully illustrates the sermon.

THE land of Palestine, in which Jesus lived, has always been noted for its flowers. They grow everywhere in great abundance, and oftentimes in very great perfection and beauty. One time, when Jesus was preaching on the mountain, He used the flowers which were growing on the side of the mountain, to preach an object sermon to the multitudes about Him. He said, "Consider the lilies of the field; how they grow; they toil not, neither do they spin, and yet I say unto you that Solomon, in all his glory, was not arrayed like one of these." (Matt.

Copyrighted, 1911, by Sylvanus Stall.

Wayside Weeds and Garden Flowers

vi: 28, 29.) Let us to-day take the same object lesson, to set forth to our minds a clearer understanding of some truths, which are very important to every father and mother, as well as every boy and girl.

As you see, I have here two bouquets. This, which I now hold in my hand, is indeed very beautiful. Here are some lovely roses, some tulips, some peonies. Here is a dahlia and heliotrope. Here are some tube roses, and a great variety of other flowers, which together constitute a very beautiful bouquet.

Now, here is another bouquet. I see you smile, but indeed it is a bouquet. I spent a great deal of time gathering these flowers, at which you laugh. I sought them in such places as would afford the best varieties of these several kinds.

Now, boys and girls, I want to ask you where these flowers grew? I will hold up this beautiful bouquet and ask the question. I know what will be your answer; you will say that I bought it from a man who keeps a hot-house, or that I gathered them in some flower garden which was very carefully tended; and such, indeed, is the case.

Now, I will hold up this other bouquet. Can you tell me where I gathered these? I did not think that you would have much difficulty in determining. I gathered them along the road-side, in the fields and in the woods. These flowers are what the farmer calls "weeds." Here is a rose with a single leaf that grew in a neglected corner, along the outskirts of a woods. It is a genuine rose, but it is by no means pretty, or at all to be compared with those in the other bouquet.

I will tell you why there is such a difference in the appearance of these two bouquets. One grew in the garden, where it was protected by a fence from being tramped upon. The weeds that grew about it were all pulled out of the ground, and the stalk upon which this flower grew was given a fair chance, so that it might

grow successfully.   The roots of the plants were carefully nourished, and whenever there was not sufficient rain the flowers were
all watered, and thus the plants and flowers grew to their greatest
perfection and beauty.

Now, these other flowers which I gathered in the fields and
along the roadside and in the woods, have had a hard time of it.
In their growth they had to contend with other weeds.   They
have been tramped upon by the cattle.   They have been scorched
by the sun.   And year after year they have grown in these
neglected quarters with great difficulty, consequently they are
stunted and have never attained any perfection or beauty.

Do you know that these very beautiful flowers in this bouquet
at one time grew just the same as the flowers in the other bouquet?
But they were removed from the roadside, and from the fields and
from the woods, and placed by themselves where they could be
properly cared for and cultivated, and they grew more beautiful
from year to year, until we have this present satisfactory result.

Boys and girls are very much like flowers.   Those who are
neglected, who are permitted to walk the streets, to stroll along the
roads and over the fields, to go along the streams fishing on Sunday, instead of being in Sunday-school and in church, those who
are permitted to run out at nights and play with all kinds of company—these are the boys and girls who are like the flowers which
grow by the roadside.   Nothing very beautiful, or very good, or
very perfect can reasonably be expected from them.

This beautiful bouquet represents those boys and girls who
have Christian fathers and mothers, who surround them by influences which are well calculated to make them pure in thought and
upright in life, so that they may grow up to be good Christian men
and women.   These flowers represent the boys and girls who grow
up in the Sunday-school and in the Church, who give their hearts

to the Lord Jesus Christ, and grow up into His likeness, and into His image, and into His stature, and become noble Christian men and women.

When parents permit their children to run wild, they cannot expect them to grow up Christians. It is only by culture and education and Christian influences that they can be improved, so as to become honorable and upright.

Nearly all the products of the field have been improved by cultivation, just the same as these flowers have been improved. Wheat in its native state, as it may still be found in France and Italy along the shores of the Mediterranean, was a stunted and straggling plant, with a small and inferior seed, but after long years of patient and continued cultivation, it has grown to its present plump and prolific proportions. All the beautiful fruits which now grow in our orchards were at one time unsightly and undesirable. The apple was small and sour, and unpalatable; but by pruning and grafting and fertilizing, it has grown to be not only beautiful to the eye, but delicious to the taste. The acrid and unwholesome berries, which formerly grew on the mountain ash, have been developed into the sweet and juicy pear. By cultivation, the acrid and bitter sloe has grown into the beautiful plum. The same is also true of the potato, the turnip and the cabbage.

Boys and girls can only be developed into useful men and women by the influence of the week-day and Sunday-school, the Christian home and the Church, by reading and studying the Bible and other good books.

When you are restricted or corrected by your parents, you may oftentimes feel very much irritated and may feel rebellious, and may think that you do not have as many privileges or as much freedom as some of the other boys and girls whom you know. But you must remember that all this is done by your parents for your good, and later on in life you will see the value of it all and be very grateful to your parents for what they have done for you.

When I was a boy, in the little village where I lived they organized a cannon company of six or eight boys, who were to accompany the men who went to other villages to listen to political speeches before elections, and then to march in a torch-light procession. I was at that time a boy about twelve years old. I was asked to join. The boys were all to wear red blouses and red caps, and to my thought just then, nothing in the world was so much to be desired as the torch-light procession and the red blouse and cap, and to be permitted to march behind the drum and the fife, hauling the little cannon after us.

I shall never forget how I cried and how ugly I felt toward my father when he would not let me be one of the cannon boys and wear a red blouse and a red cap. He said that at night I ought to be at home and in bed, and not be exposed to possible bad influences, the danger of catching cold and of other bad results which he could clearly see, but which I, at that time, thought were only imaginary.

When I grew to be a man, I saw that my father was right, and later when at intervals I journeyed back to my boyhood home and visited the cemetery, I frequently placed one elbow on the tomb-stone of my father and the other elbow on the tomb-stone of my mother, and with my face buried in my hands thanked God that He had given me Christian parents who were wise and judicious enough not to let me have my own way in all things when I was a boy, but who had restricted me and guided me wisely and well.

So, boys and girls, it will be with you when you have grown to the estate of manhood and womanhood. You will be, oh, so thankful again and again that father and mother have oftentimes denied you things which you have most desired to have.

QUESTIONS.—Which are the prettier, flowers which are neglected by the roadside, or those which are cultivated in the garden? Are boys and girls like flowers? Which boys and girls are the best, those who are neglected and not taught, or those who are cared for and carefully trained? Is it more pleasant for boys and girls to have their own way in everything, or would they prefer to be taught and trained by their parents? Which kind of flowers are the heathen boys and girls like? Can wild flowers be made more beautiful by care and cultivation? Can the boys and girls in heathen lands be made like Christian boys and girls? What is necessary to effect this change? How can Bibles and missionaries be sent to them? Did the writer of this book want to have his own way when he was a boy? What did he want to be? What kind of a cap and blouse did he want to wear? When he became a man, was he thankful to his father for not allowing him to have his own way at that time? Will all good boys and girls, when they become men and women, be thankful to their parents for right training?

"The Cannon Boys."

NUTS.

GOD MEANS THAT WE MUST WORK.

Suggestion :—The objects used are some nuts of various kinds.

If the parent has not already familiarized himself with the different methods of entertainment in connection with the reading of the object sermon to the children, he would do well to turn to the chapter on "Suggestions to Parents" on page 17 and introduce some one or more of the play ideas which have accomplished so much of pleasure and profit in many homes.

Arrange chairs and "drive to church," let the audience, both real and imaginary be shown to seats, and after the opening service let one of the children in his or her own way present the lessons remembered from the sermon of last Sunday, or recast what was said by the pastor in his morning sermon. After the collection and singing, let the children "drive home" and let refreshments or some one of the Scriptural entertainments previously suggested round out the pleasure and profit of Sunday afternoon.

NOW, boys and girls, I have here some hickory nuts, walnuts, butternuts, chestnuts, and filberts, or hazel nuts as they are sometimes called, and I want to tell you something that I suppose God means to teach us by these nuts.

Nuts.

Many people remember that when Adam and Eve were driven out of Eden, God told them that "In the sweat of thy face shalt thou eat bread" (Gen. iii: 19), and also that God drove them out of the garden to "till the ground from whence man was taken." (Gen. iii: 23.)   On this account some people suppose that if Adam and Eve had not sinned it would never have been necessary for us to work, but that is a mistake.   If you turn to the second chapter of Genesis, in the fifteenth verse, you will find that it says, "The Lord God took the man, and put him into the Garden of Eden to dress it and to keep it."   So you see that Adam was required to work, even before the fall.   Of course his work was not as severe as it was after he was driven out of Eden and his labor brought him a richer fruitage.

Now, what do these nuts teach us?   I think that most all boys and girls like to eat hickory nuts and butternuts, and chestnuts and filberts, and indeed all kinds of nuts.   But did you ever stop to think that God has made it necessary that we should crack the shell before we can eat the kernel that is inside?   God has purposed to teach us that labor is necessary before we can eat even of that which He gives us, so on the outside of this desired food he places the shell, in some instances hard and difficult to be broken, in order to teach us that labor is necessary before we can eat of His gifts.

Now the same thing is true with regard to the grain that grows in the field.   No one ever saw potatoes grow without being planted and cultivated.   Rye and oats and wheat do not grow wild.   Weeds will grow without being sown or planted, but grain and vegetables not only have to be planted, but have to be taken care of.   Possibly you might think that my statement was not wholly correct, because we go out into the orchard and gather apples and pears and peaches, and other kinds of fruit which have no hard shells on them, and which do not have to be planted in the spring of the year.   But do you know that we could not gather this kind of rich fruit from the trees unless trees of these kinds had been cultivated for long centuries, grafted and developed so as to produce the rich fruit which is now placed upon our tables? So you see that even this has cost labor, and if we were to neglect the trees in the orchard, it would only be a few years until they would produce only a very small variety of fruit, and even that would be sour and have an unpleasant taste.

But God means to teach us this lesson also in another way. Man has found it very necessary to use the different kinds of metals,

Apple Tree.

iron and copper, silver and gold. God has not laid these metals on top of the ground, but has made it necessary that we should dig down into the earth and secure these metals at the cost of a great deal of labor. The same is also true with regard to the coal and the oil, and all the rich mineral products with which God has blessed us. None of them can be secured without labor.

We are all naturally lazy. I have oftentimes thought that we are all born lazy. Some learn to be industrious with less effort, but all have to be taught to work. God means that we should work. Have you ever thought that God could feed us without our labor if He chose to do so? He could rain down our food from heaven, just the same as He gave manna to the Children of Israel, while they were journeying to the promised land. He could not only feed us, but He could also clothe us from heaven. I am sure that if God gave us our clothing from heaven, He would not make such foolish fashions as wicked people over in Paris invent, and which all the rest of the world seem to think they have to imitate. Not only our food and clothing, but God could also have made it necessary that there should be no preachers. Instead of giving us His Word in the Bible, and then asking us to go into all the world and to preach it to all creatures, He might have used the stars at night, just the same as the printer uses the different kinds of type and prints the letters and words upon the page; so God could have used the stars in order to write His law upon the heavens in a universal language that would be known by all peoples, and so at night, and even in the daytime, people could look up into the heavens and read God's law. Thus it would have been unnecessary ever to have printed Bibles, or to send preachers to preach. The cost of building churches and supporting ministers would thus have been unnecessary, but God does not do things in that way. Lazy people might desire that things were arranged in this way, but God has seen fit to make it very different.

But why do you think that God means that you and I should learn to work? There are two or three good reasons which I can think of. We are so constituted that no one can be in good health for any considerable period without physical exertion, and so you see that if we want to be well—and no one can be happy who is not well—it is necessary that we should learn to work. You will always find that lazy people who eat a great deal suffer many physical ailments. They are always complaining, and I think you will always find that they really are sick, but they could be well if they would only go to work as God meant they should.

Then there is another reason. An idle man is always a dis-

4

satisfied man.   A boy or girl with nothing to do is sure to
be unhappy.   If we desire to be happy and contented we must learn
to work.

But there is also another reason.   Our spiritual well-being also
renders it necessary that you and I should have something to do.
Work is really one of God's greatest blessings, and we are told that
those who are idle tempt Satan to tempt them.   I do not believe that
an idle person can be a good Christian.   An idler is of no use either
in the world or in the church.   God can make no use of him, and
Satan must surely despise him also.

So if you desire to be delivered from sickness and to remain
well and strong, if you desire to be contented and happy, if you
desire to be good and useful, if you desire to be helpful in the great
purpose for which God has created you and placed you upon this
earth, you must learn to work, and the best time to learn to work is
when we are young.   We are to learn to labor with our hands, with
our minds, always remembering that whatsoever we do, we are to do
all to the glory of God.

Now let us all join in singing,

"Work, for the night is coming."

QUESTIONS.—Did God assign some work to Adam when he was first created?   What was he to do in the Garden?   Why does God place the kernel of
nuts inside of a shell?   Do vegetables and grain grow without being planted?
Will weeds grow without being planted?   Why did God place the metals, and
coal and oil down below the surface of the ground?   Are we naturally industrious or lazy?   Could God clothe and feed us without our labor?   Why does He
not do it?   How could God have printed His law so that it would not be necessary to have Bibles and preachers?   Are idle people healthy and contented?
Why not?   Whom do idle people tempt?   Can an idle person be a good Christian?   When is it easiest to learn to work?   What should we always remember
in our work?

BANKS.

GATHERED AND GUARDED TREASURES.

SUGGESTIONS:—Objects for use: A child's bank and a metal kettle of any kind to show how people used to place their money in boxes, kettles, etc., and then bury them in the ground.

Use the methods suggested in the preceding sermons. Examine the chapter on "Suggestions to Parents" and introduce new features from Sunday to Sunday. Children like variety.

MY DEAR YOUNG FRIENDS: What is this I hold in my hand? (Voices: "Bank, penny bank, money bank.") Yes, y o u are right, this is a bank, and I suppose many of you, perhaps all of you either now, or at some past time have had such a place to deposit your money.

In the time of Christ the children did not have little banks like these. Even the big people did not have banks where they could deposit their money. When they had jewels or money they would place them in a box, or a copper kettle, and bury them in the earth. They would hide them away

A Penny Bank.

from other people, and thus seek to secure them for themselves. In that period of the world, there were many thieves and robbers; Palestine was often invaded by hostile armies; there were occasional earthquakes, which destroyed whole cities, and so the people used to bury their money for safe keeping. After burying it, sometimes they were killed in war, or perhaps died suddenly, before they had time to tell anybody where they had concealed their money, and on this account all over that land there were buried treasures, or "hid treasures" as they are called, and to-day if you were to go to Palestine you would see many people digging here and there everywhere to find money or treasures that have been hidden away for long centuries. Even in the time of Job people must have dug for treasures, as they are doing in Palestine to-day, for Job says of the miserable and unhappy, that they often "long for death, and dig for it, more than for hid treasures." (Job iii: 21.)

It is altogether right for you to economize and save your pennies. I hope every boy and girl will have a little bank, but while you are learning to save, you should also learn to give to every good cause, to give in Sunday-school and to give for the support of the Church, for missions, and to give to assist the aged and the poor, and to contribute something for those who are in poverty and in distress. If you simply learn to save, or hoard up money, and do not learn at the same time to give, you will become what people call "a miser," and that word means miserable. Misers are always miserable, not because they do not already have sufficient, but because there is so much more that they desire. They always wish for more.

But while you are learning to save money and to gather treasures here upon the earth, you must not forget that the Bible says, that we are to lay up for ourselves "treasures in heaven, where moth

Hiding Treasures in the Earth.

and rust do not corrupt, and where thieves do not break through nor steal." It says, "Seek ye first the kingdom of God and His righteousness, and all these things shall be added unto you." God means that first of all you and I shall give our hearts to Him, and then afterward, in all our getting, we should constantly remember that we are only stewards of God—that is, that all the money and everything else we possess in this world belongs to God. He simply permits us to have it and to use it in His name, and we must honor and reverence Him by giving to help on every good work.

Now, after we have given our hearts to God, and have become followers of the Lord Jesus Christ, we are to lay up our treasures in heaven by living right, by seeking to be good, and by doing good to others. We are to lose no opportunity to do that which will be a blessing to those about us.

One of the boys or girls said this was a penny bank. That name is very suggestive. A bank is a place where you deposit money. Now, if you have a bank like this, do you only put into it silver dollars, five-dollar bills, ten-dollar gold pieces? If each boy who is here were to wait until he had a ten-dollar gold piece, or a five-dollar bill, or until he had come into possession of a silver dollar before he placed any money in his bank, I am sure his bank would always remain empty. The way to fill a bank is to put pennies in it—to save each cent and each five-cent piece. To-day a penny, and to-morrow a few pennies, and so on through the week, and through the year, and at the end of the year you will find that you have saved quite a goodly sum.

Now, there are some people who want to lay up treasures in heaven, but they do not want to lay it up there, little by little. They prefer to wait until some opportunity comes when they can do a great deal of good at one time. But the person who does not do good every day and every hour, little by little, will never have any treasure in heaven. It is the pennies that make the dollars; it is the "many mites that make the muckle." It is the constant doing of little things, for the glory of God and the good of others, that makes a man great. Great men are great in little things, and if you desire to be great men and great women, you must always use the little opportunities, and use them well. Lay up treasure in heaven, each and every day, just the same as, day after day, you would save your pennies, and thus fill your banks. If you want a large treasure in heaven you must constantly be engaged in laying up your treasure there. Never lose an opportunity to do good, and in this way you will have an abundant treasure in heaven.

QUESTIONS.—Where do people put money for safe keeping? Is it only silver and gold which is put into a bank? Do thieves ever break into banks? Can any treasure be laid up in the earth where it is absolutely safe? Where does the Bible tell us we are also to lay up treasure? When boys and girls are obedient, is that laying up treasure in heaven? Does being great in little things make a great man or a great woman? Should boys and girls learn to save their money? What would they be called if they spent all their money? What would they be called if they hoarded up all they could get? Should we always use all our money in the fear of God?

After the conclusion of the services and after "driving home from church", introduce some other interesting features so as to make the day sacredly impressive.

THE CHART.

AVOIDING THE DANGERS.

SUGGESTIONS:—Objects: A geography, or detached maps will serve to show that the portions of the earth which are under the water are quite like the portions of the earth which are above the water. Islands are only mountain summits or elevations.

"Drive to church", have the ushers show different real or imaginary persons to seats, have the little sermon and service precede the reading of the following object sermon.

MY LITTLE MEN AND WOMEN: We are all travelers. Now when a traveler starts out upon a journey he always desires to have in his possession one of these things which I hold in my hand. I know you will recognize it at once, and say that it is a map. This map tells you the name of the country; it shows you where there are mountains, where there are rivers, where there are valleys, where there are cities, and shows you the entire United States of America. In traveling through a strange country, if you do not have a map, you might be lost upon the mountains, or your journey would be obstructed by the rivers which you could not cross, and in various ways you would find it absolutely necessary to have a map.

Outline Map of the United States.

56

Now, when a traveler goes out upon the sea, it is just as necessary that he should have a map, or what the sailors call a chart, as it is for the traveler upon the land. The chart which the sea captain has, shows the mountains and the valleys and the rivers which are in the sea; for these exist in the sea, as well as upon the land. The rocks, against which ships are sometimes dashed to pieces, are simply the tops of high mountains that come very near to the surface of the sea; and the captain without a chart, not knowing where they are, is likely to run against them with his ship. The islands are simply the tops of these mountains, that rise higher above the water, and form a place of abode for man; and we call them islands, because they are very much smaller than the great continents on which you and I live.

A chart of the sea always locates the dangerous places. They show where other ships have been foundered, and oftentimes where hundreds and thousands of lives have been lost. It also shows what are really rivers in the sea, or great currents, one of which we call the Gulf Stream. When a ship is crossing the Gulf Stream the motion or current of this water might carry it many hundreds of miles out of its course, and if the captain had no chart he would not be able to allow for this distance, which the ship is being carried, either north or south.

Now, you and I are travelers in this world. We are out upon a great voyage, and it is necessary that we should have a chart, and therefore God has given us the Bible, which you and I can use greatly to our advantage. In the Bible, God has pointed out the dangers which lie like the hidden rocks under the surface of the sea. In the commandments God marks out the great dangers which beset you and me. There is the rock of Idolatry. Whole nations of the earth have been wrecked on this rock. Then there is another, Profanity, swearing: Oh! how many boys and men are ruined because they do not observe how God has marked this dangerous rock, against which no one can run without danger of losing his immortal soul.   Then there is Sabbath breaking, another rock; and there is reverence due to parents; and God marks another, "Thou shalt not kill"; and then there are others, against stealing,

Rocks and Mountains at the Bottom of the Sea.

against bearing false witness, against covetousness.   All these dangerous rocks God has marked in the Bible, in order that you and I may not run against them, and thus be shipwrecked in our voyage to the haven of everlasting rest.

God also marks the influences which you and I must come in contact with. Every boy who goes to school feels the influence of other boys, some of whom are very bad. If he permits himself to be moved by these things he will go wrong, just the same as the ship that is crossing the Gulf Stream is carried out of its course. So the Bible warns us against bad company.

Now the chart which the sea captain has, indicates also the ports of safety. It shows the location of these different ports, and the direction the captain must take in order to reach them. So the Bible shows us where you and I can find refuge in the day of storm, and in the day of trial, and in the day of sickness, and in the day of distress. To the sea captain, out upon the great ocean, there are ten thousand directions which are sure to end in shipwreck. There is only one safe way to go, in order to reach his desired port in safety.

Now what would you think of a captain out upon the seas who folded up his chart and laid it carefully away, and never looked at it, never studied it, never sought to know what is on the chart? Do you not see how he would go upon the rocks? His ship would go down to the bottom of the sea, just as surely as if he had no chart on board his ship. It is important that he should have his chart in constant use. So it is important, not only that we should have the Bible, but that we should use the Bible, that we should read it, that we should study it, that we should know what it says. I trust that each and all of you not only have a Bible, but that you study it daily, and that you seek to avoid the dangers which God has pointed out, and that you desire to know the will of God concerning you.

QUESTIONS.—What should a traveler always have in a strange country? What must a sea captain always carry with him on his ship? What does the chart show? Are we travelers? To what country are we journeying? Has

God given us a chart to show the dangers to which we are exposed in our voyage or journey? Should we read the Bible every day? What are two principal parts of the Bible? Do you know how many books there are in the Old Testament? Do you know how many books there are in the New Testament? Do you know who was the first man? Who was the first woman? Who was the first murderer? Who built the ark? Who had the coat of many colors? Who led the Children of Israel out of Egypt? Who was put in the lion's den?

After the entire service has been completed and after the "drive home from church", chairs can be arranged with their backs toward each other, set a little way apart, with a shawl, blanket, or even a sheet, thrown over them so as to form a little tent. A number of tents can be made to illustrate the Children of Israel camping in the wilderness. They were travelers tenting by the way, who forgot about their chart and fell into sin, and God had to turn them back in the wilderness for forty years of wandering. All this suggests important lessons to the parents.

A series of tents can be arranged like the one shown in the picture below (see also page 74) and then, with one child in each tent the questions can be asked. When a child fails to give the correct answer, he moves down to the last tent in the row, the other children move up, and the question is passed to the child next in order, the same as in a "spelling-bee" and other progressive plays. Questions like those given on this page and on pages 25 and 26 can be used; also questions such as are found in the chapter on "Suggestions to Parents," especially from paragraphs 50 onward.

The Children of Israel Camping in the Wilderness.

THE ANCHOR.

HOPE THAT LAYS HOLD OF CHRIST.

SUGGESTIONS:—Object: Anchor of any kind. One cut from paste-board would answer. During the week the little ones might be interested to cut out both anchor and the chain, using paste-board.

Before reading the following sermon, "drive to church" and after the audience has been shown to seats, begin the service with singing, have the regular prayer and have one of the children preach over the sermon at the church in the morning or the object sermon of last Sunday.

MY DEAR YOUNG FRIENDS: I want to talk to you to-day about a very important subject. The Bible speaks of hope, and says, "Which hope we have as an anchor of the soul, both sure and steadfast, and which entereth into that within the veil." (Hebrews vi: 19.)

I suppose most of you have been on board a ship or large boat. Very near the bow, or front end of the boat, you have doubtless noticed a chain, at the end of which was an anchor, made in the form of this one which I hold in my hand. Now, I would not care to go out to sea on any ship which did not have an anchor on board. In crossing the

The Anchor.

Atlantic you may sometimes be out for days and weeks, and sometimes even for months, and have no need of using the anchor. But
all the time, while the weather is pleasant and everything is moving
along prosperously, the fact that the anchor is on board the ship and
that it can be used in time of danger, gives a sense of security to all
the passengers. If it were not there you would constantly fear, lest
the storms or fog might come when your ship was near land or
dangerous rocks or shoals, and then your ship might be lost with its
many hundreds of lives on board, simply because it had no anchor.

Every man and woman, and every boy and girl, needs to have
hope as an anchor to his soul. We should have faith in God, and
then at times when all is well, when we are prosperous and blest,
and everything goes along like the ship in pleasant weather, we
will constantly have peace and rest in our minds and hearts, because
we know that our hope is staid on God, and that though the world
be removed, yet God will not disappoint us.

Some people seem to think that religion is a good thing to
have when they get sick, or when adversity or sorrow or great
affliction comes. But the fact is that religion is a necessary thing
at all times. We need it when we are well and strong, as well as
when we are sick and weak. We need religion in this world to
live by, as well as to die by, as well as for our salvation in the
world to come.

The anchor is very serviceable indeed in time of storm. Often
it has to be used in order to secure the ship and save the lives of all
who are on board. If it were not for the anchor the ship might be
thrust upon the rocks, or it might be dashed to pieces by the waves
that break upon the coast. The anchor is oftentimes very serviceable. So it is with the religion of the Lord Jesus Christ. When
trials and perplexities and adversities come, as they do in every life,
then it is that this anchor is a source of very great blessing, because

it saves from shipwreck, occasioned by unbelief and the perplexities into which those are cast who have no hope, or trust in God.

To be serviceable the anchor must take hold of something. If it simply drags along it will not hold the ship; but the ship may

Anchor Laying Hold of the Rocks.

go to pieces on the rocks, even though it has an anchor, which has already been cast over. Now in time of sorrow and perplexity or distress every one throws out an anchor. That is, he tries to take hold of something which will sustain him and keep him, just the same as a boy who falls into the water would grab after a board. They say that a drowning man will even grasp after a straw in order to help to support his body, so that he may save his life. So every one in perplexity reaches out to lay hold of something. But the text which I quoted in the beginning says that this hope which we have as an anchor to the soul lays hold of something, and that something is the Lord Jesus Christ. It is like the ship whose anchor goes down, far below the waves, deep down out of sight, and lays hold of the rocks which form the foundation of the earth. So the faith of the Christian is staid, not on things which are seen, but on the things which are not seen. As the text expresses it, it lays hold of those things "which entereth into that which is within the veil." That is, this figure refers to the Temple at Jerusalem, where the Holy of Holies was concealed from the rest of the Temple by a large curtain or veil, and no one was permitted to go into this Holy of Holies except the High Priest, and he but once a year. But when you and I have the faith of the Christian, although we may not be able to enter into the great mystery of God's grace and mercy, yet our faith lays hold of that which is beyond our understanding, and beyond our possibility to see or fully to comprehend, and thus our faith lays hold of that which is "within the veil." With our understanding, you and I cannot enter into the mysteries of God, but by faith we can enter into them. I trust that every boy and girl here will have that faith in God, which will be as an anchor to his soul, sure and steadfast, entering within the veil at all times.

I will tell you how this anchor of faith and hope can be of service to you. There are times when you see other boys and girls who have many more comforts and luxuries and possessions than you have. You may even be discouraged sometimes because you think your lot in life is more than usually hard and difficult.

When I myself was a boy, my father died, and only three

years later my mother died. I was left an orphan and without a home. I had to become an errand boy in a store, and for a number of years I had a hard struggle. I was a Christian boy, and I had this anchor of faith and hope. I trusted in God that He would make all of these things to work out eventually for my good. I could not at that time understand how. It was beyond my understanding, but later on in life I found how all the trials and struggles of my earlier years had worked together for my good. I understood that passage of Scripture which says: "All things work together for good to them that love God." (Romans viii: 28.)

So, when you see others who have it easier and who have more comforts and luxuries than you have, if you have this hope which the text speaks of as "laying hold within the veil" be sure that in God's own good time, in His infinite wisdom and love, He will work out for you also the blessing and the good which you can only hope for, but which at the present time you can neither see nor understand.

QUESTIONS.—What does every ship carry? Would a ship be safe without an anchor? When the anchor is let down into the deep water, must it take hold of something? When is the anchor used? If a ship did not have an anchor in time of storm along the rocky coast, would it be safe? Do men and women, boys and girls, also need an anchor? Can we have peace and happiness without hope? Is religion necessary only when we are in trouble? On what does hope lay hold? Can we see the things on which the Christian's faith lays hold? Can we always understand God's providences? Did the writer of this book have trials when he was a boy? Could he understand them then? Did he understand them later on in life? Do all boys and girls have trials? If received in the proper spirit, will they always work out for their good?

HUSKS.

THE DISAPPOINTED PLEASURE-SEEKER.

SUGGESTION :—If the children can obtain some of the pods which are called "husks" in the Scripture, which can be had in some towns and cities, and which the children usually call "Johnny-bread" they will be able to taste the husks which the prodigal fed to the swine and which he himself desired to eat. If these cannot be had, the pods from the sweet locust tree will be serviceable.

I HOLD in my hand what I suppose most of you have seen, and perhaps many of you have eaten. It is what boys oftentimes call "Johnny bread." It looks very much like the long pods which grow on the honey locust trees. It is sometimes called "Johnny bread," because some people mistakenly think that this was the kind of locust that John the Baptist ate when he came in the Wilderness, preaching that the kingdom of heaven was at hand and that men should repent. We are told in the Scriptures that he ate locusts and wild honey. The locusts which he ate were very much like our grasshoppers, such as are still eaten by very poor people in the East.

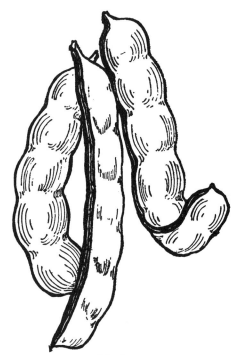

Husks.

In the 15th chapter of the gospel by St. Luke, we have a very

66

beautiful parable, called the parable of the prodigal son. In connection with the husk which I hold in my hand, I want to tell you something about this prodigal son.

In this parable Jesus tells of a very kind father who had two sons, but the younger son was dissatisfied and discontented. He was a boy very much like many who live in this country and at this time. He was a boy who wanted to have his own way. He thought that his father was an "old fogy." The son wanted gay company and gay clothing. He wanted to travel and see something of the world; so he asked his father to give him the money which would come to him at his father's death, in order that he might go immediately and have his own way, and have a good time, as he supposed.

His father was very sad, for he had tried to bring up his boy in the right way. But when he could not prevail upon him, and his son would not listen to him any longer. but insisted upon having the money, and going away from home, the father granted his request.

When the money had been counted out, the son gathered it all up, bade his father and brother and all his friends good-bye, telling them what a happy time he was going to have, and started out for a far country.

This same desire to see something of the world has induced many boys to run away from home. Many years ago, when there were numerous ships that went out on long voyages to catch whales, oftentimes boys who had run away from home went away to sea with these ships. Now, however, restless and discontented boys, who have read worthless and deceptive books, sometimes go to live a wild life on the plains in the West. Sometimes boys even become tramps. Scores and sometimes hundreds of them can be met any week by going to the Breakfast Association, in Philadelphia; or some of the Rescue Homes, in New York, where poor, wandering boys and tramps are given a free meal on Sunday morning or Sunday evening. Prodigals now, as in the time when Christ lived, have a very hard time of it. They start out with high hopes, sometimes with money in their pockets, with fine clothing and bright anticipations, expecting to have a good time in the far country which they are seeking. But their experience is always the same.

When this prodigal came to the far country, for a few weeks, or possibly a few months, he had plenty of money. He thought his money would always last. Bad men and women gathered around him, for they all wanted to enjoy what his money would secure for them. But it didn't take long; his money was soon spent, and when his money was gone his pretended friends were gone also. He soon found himself penniless, friendless and hungered. He had to go out and seek for work. Perhaps he had been too much indulged at home. He had never learned a trade, and possibly had never learned to do work of any kind, and so there was nothing for him to do but to accept the humblest and meanest kind of labor. He was a Jew, and for a Jew to tend swine or hogs was one of the meanest things in all the world. And yet he was willing because of his poverty and his want, to do even this most degrading service. This boy who wanted to be his own master, now became the most menial of slaves, even to the tending of swine. He wanted gay company, but he had only pigs for his companions. He wanted wine and feasting, but now no one even offered him husks to eat. He left his home to seek happiness, but he found only misery.

These husks which I showed you, which some boys call "Johnny bread," are exactly what this wayward, disappointed, disheartened, hungry boy was given to feed to the swine which he

The Disappointed, Hungry Prodigal Tending Swine.   69

was hired to tend. He was so hungry that he would have been glad to eat these husks with the pigs, but no one gave him any to eat.

When this wayward boy was thus brought down to poverty and hunger in that far-off country, while he was tending the swine, he began to think. If he had only stopped to think before he left his home, he would never have started away. He would surely have known that he was better off at home than anywhere else. But now that misery and want had come to him, we are told that "he came to himself." That is, he came to his senses. It was sentiment which led him from his home. It was sense that brought him back. The trouble with boys and girls, and with older people too, is that they do not stop to think. They follow their fancies and sentiments, and they are led astray in this way.

God wants us to stop and think, and He says, "Come, let us reason together." God does not ask any unreasonable thing of us. He simply wants to treat us as thoughtful beings, but we want to follow our own inclination and our own desire. God treats us very kindly. He gives us every needed comfort and every daily blessing, and yet oftentimes people are discontented and dissatisfied with God; they complain and think they have a hard time of it. Instead of being faithful and true to God, they turn away from him. They desire to forsake God and serve Satan. They desire to accept what Satan says, and so turn away from God and all that is good. But they have the same experience over and over again that this young man had. He went out with fine clothes and plenty of money, and with high hopes; but he returned home in rags, without a penny in his pocket, disappointed, penitent and ashamed.

But I must not forget to tell you, that when he had journeyed many a week, toiling wearily over the long road that had separated him from his father's house, at last he came near his old home. In going away he had nearly broken his father's heart. With sorrow

Copyrighted, 1911, by Sylvanus Stall.

The Returning Prodigal

he was bringing his aged father down to the grave. But his father still loved his wayward boy, and expected him home. As he sat watching at the door looking over the hills, he saw the returning prodigal when he was yet a great way off. This loving and forgiving father had compassion upon his son, ran and fell upon his neck and kissed him, and welcomed him back home again. The wayward boy's heart was all broken up by such kind treatment. He fell upon his knees at his father's feet and said to his father, "Father, I have sinned against heaven and in thy sight, and am no more worthy to be called thy son; make me as one of thy hired servants."

But the father called his servants and commanded them to bring the best robe and put it upon this boy who had given him so much sorrow; to bring the ring and put it upon his finger; and then to kill the fatted calf, so that they might make a great feast, in order that all might be made very glad, because this his son, who was dead, was alive again, he who had been lost was found.

So when we come back to God after we have sinned against Him, and are repentant and sorry for what we have done, in love and great tenderness He forgives our sins. And like the prodigal, in the time of his sorest misery, found in his father's heart the greatest mercy, so you and I may come to God knowing that in the day of our dire distress He is always willing to love us and to forgive us as His own dear children. Let us be careful not to sin against Him, and then we shall not have the humiliation and the sorrow of coming back, like this poor prodigal, when he returned in rags and poverty to his father's house. Never make the mistake of going away from your God and then you will not have the remorse which will bring you back in sorrow and shame.

QUESTIONS.—Who first told the parable of the prodigal son? Why did the prodigal leave his home? What did he do with his money? Did his pretended friends stay by him after his money was gone? In his poverty what did he do?

Did he have enough to eat? When he was in want and came to himself, of whom did he think? What did he resolve to do? What do boys who run away from home generally become? Are tramps happy? Was the father sad all the time the boy was away? How did he receive the returning prodigal? Does God love us even though we do wrong? Will God forgive us and accept us? Is God glad when we repent?

After "driving home from church" a series of tableaux could be arranged: (1) Showing the father counting out the money to the boy. (2) The boy bidding good-bye to his father and friends. (3) Surrounded by flatterers for whom he is spending his money. (4) In poverty tending swine. (5) In rags returning home. (6) Being welcomed by his father.

Or the children may arrange a tent in which the prodigal is presumed to live on the plains while tending the swine, which may be represented by a series of books, toys or any objects; for the imagination of the children will convert any object into any other object, person or thing.

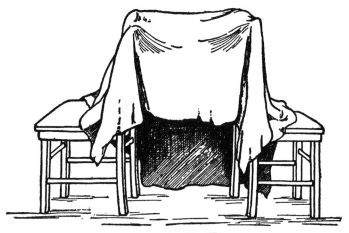

The Prodigal's Tent.

IRON—LOW GRADE AND HIGH GRADE.

CHARACTER AND WORTH.

SUGGESTION :—Objects used: A piece of old iron, some nails, broken clock and watch springs, and also a piece of native iron ore, if convenient.

M Y DEAR BOYS AND GIRLS: I want to show you to-day that there is a great difference in the value of things, even though they are made of the same material.

In the second chapter of Genesis we are told, "And the Lord God formed man of the dust of the ground." So, you see that all men and women are made of the same material, yet men differ greatly, both in character and works.

I have here some iron ore, some old iron, some nails; here are some clock springs, and here are some springs of

Iron Products.

watches. This iron ore is as it is dug from the earth. It is called the native iron, but mixed with it there is much earth and stone and dross, which must be separated from it in order to make it pure. This is done by casting the ore, together with limestone and other materials, into a huge furnace, where the fire is so intensely hot that all are melted and thus the iron is separated from the dross, or stone and earth, which is now mixed with the ore. When the iron is thus separated and molded into large bars, it is worth from a fraction of a cent to two cents per pound, according to quality and mar-

75

ket price. After it has been cast into great iron bars, and is known as pig iron, it is afterward bought and melted over again and molded into the form of stoves and wheels, such as are used in factories, and a variety of other forms for manufacturing and other uses.

Now, here I have some pieces of iron, such as boys call "old iron." They often find pieces of this kind of iron, which have been thrown away, and gather and sell them at a price varying from one-quarter to a cent or more a pound, according to circumstances. Then it is melted over again and made into stoves, or whatever the manu-

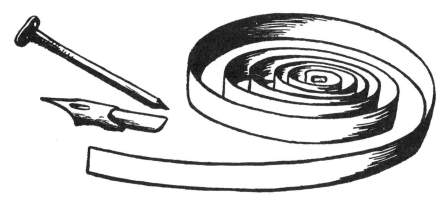

Nail, Pen and Clock Spring.

facturer may desire. Now, here are some nails, such as sell at five cents a pound, and here are some steel pens, which are worth from one to four and five dollars a pound. Here are some springs, such as are used in the construction of clocks. These are the springs which make clocks go. When you wind up the clock you simply tighten this spring, thus storing the power which is necessary to keep the clock in motion for twenty-four hours, for eight days, or even a longer period.

Now here are some springs, such as are used in watches. These springs are worth, according to their size and quality, from twenty to fifty or sixty dollars a pound. Here also are some little screws, such as are used in the construction of watches, and which are worth even a hundred dollars a pound.

While these different articles are all made of the same material, you see there is a great difference in their value. One is not worth a single cent a pound, and another may be worth one hundred dollars a pound. Now this difference in value is due to two things. One is, difference in quality, and the other is the use which is made of the article into which the iron is manufactured.

I suppose, if these different pieces of metal could think, and had the power of speech, this piece of old iron would complain to the other pieces which are of more value, and say to the watch spring, "I am just as good as you are, we

Watch Spring and Screws.

were both dug from the same ore bank. I remember the time when we were both cast into the hot fire and melted in the furnace; after that I was taken to the foundry, and made into a stove, and after a few years of use I was rejected and cast into the alley. I have had to lie about in the mud and in the cold and snow, and men have passed me by and scorned me as though I were of no value. But I want you to understand, Mr. Clockspring and Mr. Watchspring, that I am just as good as you are, and there is no reason why I should be cast out into the mud and cold, while you are placed in a gold case and carried in a gentleman's pocket."

The nail also would cry out, and say that he was just as good as the little screws which are used in the watch, and would complain against being driven violently into a board, where it is compelled, year after year, to hold a board on to the side of a building; to have putty placed over its head, and then paint over the top of that, so that nobody could even so much as see where it was, or know what it was doing.

Now, the old iron, and the nail, and the others have no right to complain. There is a vast difference of quality, and there is also a difference of work.

The higher grades and better qualities of metals are secured by refining processes. Again and again the metal is cast in the fire and melted. Sometimes it is beaten on the anvil into such shapes and forms as will render the metal of greater service, and consequently of more value.

Suppose this metal had feeling, and the power to express its wish. Do you not see how it would cry out against being cast into the fire, and being beaten with great hammers upon the anvil? I am sure the fire, the hammers, and the anvil bring no sense of pleasure to the metal while being refined and being beaten into such forms as render it of greatest value.

Just so, in some senses at least, are all boys and girls alike. If they were all permitted to grow up in neglect, without being governed by thoughtful parents, without being educated and refined, without being sent to school and required to attend church, without being taught at home and being instructed in the Catechism and in the Bible, and without being shown their duty to God and their fellow men, they would all be pretty much alike. It is the difference in the influences that are made to refine some boys that causes them to differ so much from others who are about them. The boy who has only been taught to pick stones, or sweep the streets, or dig ditches, may cry out against the boy who is gentlemanly, and obliging, and obedient, and truthful, and reliable, and who has a position of great responsibility in a bank, or in the office of some man who occupies a very responsible position; yet oftentimes, and quite universally, there is a very great difference in the merit and value of these two boys. One has been disciplined and governed and controlled, educated and taught, while the other has likely been neglected, and consequently has not learned the importance of these things.

God designs to refine all of us, and therefore He desires that all should be taught to study, should learn to read and write, should learn all they can from the schools, should be taught to work, should be taught to expect trials and self-denials, and should be led to expect sickness and disappointments, and all these things by which God designs to make us better from year to year. But, just the same as the iron would cry out against being cast into the fire and being beaten upon the anvil, so do boys and girls, and men and women also, cry out against the providences by which God is refining them and making them better for this world and fitting them for the world to come.

If we desire to be of largest service in this world, and to occupy a place of honor in the world to come, we must expect that God will deal with us, as He has told us in the ninth verse of the thirteenth chapter of Zechariah, in which He says, "I will refine them as silver is refined, and will try them as gold is tried." And in the book of Malachi He says that He, that is God, is "like a refiner's fire, and like fullers' soap, and He shall sit as a refiner and purifier of silver, and purge them as gold and silver."

When the gold and the silver is cast into the crucible to be purified, the fire is made very hot, and the metal is left in the crucible until the man who is refining it and who sits looking into the crucible can see his own image reflected in the metal. So we are cast into the fires of affliction, and God looks down upon us; but when we become like Him, so that God sees His own self reflected in our character, and in our disposition, and in our temper, then we shall have been refined as God desires, and He will then be ready to receive us into His own home on high.

QUESTIONS.—Can you name different things made from iron? Is a horse shoe as valuable as a watch spring? What makes the difference in their value? How are iron and steel refined, or made more valuable? Are unrefined and untaught boys and girls all quite alike? What makes them become different? Do some boys and girls become more useful and valuable in the world than others? What causes the difference? Would the iron cry out against being refined? Do boys and girls object to being taught and disciplined? How does the Bible say that God refines us? Can the refiner see his image in the melted metal? Does God want to see His own image reflected in us?

"Joseph in the Pit."

A POCKET RULE.

HOW GOD MEASURES MEN.

SUGGESTION:—Objects: A yard-stick, pocket-rule, tape-measure and any measure or scales convenient.

Use the measures and scales for measuring the height and weight of the different children, and explain to them that if they continue to grow, they will eventually become full grown men and women. So God measures them to-day in moral things, and if they will learn what God requires and be obedient to their parents, they will increase in moral stature as well.

MY DEAR YOUNG FRIENDS: I am sure you will be able to tell me what these are which I hold in my hand. This you would call a yard-stick; the other, because it folds, you would call a pocket-rule, and here is another, which you would call a tape-measure.

Now, if I were going to measure any of you, to tell how tall

Yard-Stick, Pocket-Rule and Tape-Measure.

you are, I would use one or the other of these rules; as each is divided into even inches, I could use any of these three I should prefer. I would say one boy is four feet two inches, another four

81

feet nine inches and another five feet four inches, and so on according to the height of each person. We speak of this kind of measure as feet and inches. When it is used in measuring cloth, or other goods in a store, we speak of it as yards and parts of a yard. Then

there are also other forms of measures, dry m e a s u r e—quarts, pecks, bushels; and liquid measure—quarts, gallons and barrels.   There is also a standard of weight—ounces, pounds and tons.

It is necessary to have standards of weights and

Farmer's Measures.

measures. This is absolutely necessary, or we could not tell in purchasing cloth or lumber, in buying sugar or molasses, or other things, whether we are getting the right quantity, or whether we are not getting the right quantity. So, everywhere you go in the United States we have the same size or standard of weights and measures, and the Government appoints men in each city to go about and examine whether the scales which the storekeeper uses for weighing sugar, and the measures which he uses when he sells vinegar and molasses—whether these are perfectly accurate, as the law requires.

Scales and Measure.

But, if you look on the other side of this tape-measure, there is a different standard of measure. This, on the reverse side, is the metric system, used in France and many other countries. If you were to go into a store in France and wanted to purchase cloth, you would not ask for a yard, you would ask for a metre of cloth, which instead of thirty-six inches, which makes our yard, would be a little over thirty-nine inches; so the standard of measures and values varies in different countries. There is a slight difference in the length of the English yard and the American yard. In this country we also speak of dollars and cents. In England they have the penny, shilling, pound or sovereign. And so in different countries there are different pieces of money, having a great variety of values.

I have spoken of these things simply to call your attention to the fact that God has a standard of measure, and a standard of value, as well as men. When the Government enlists soldiers into the army every man is measured, and he must be of a given height; if he is not as tall as the requirement, then he is rejected. When Napoleon chose his body-guard the men all had to be exceedingly tall.

God also has His standard of measure. He does not measure us according to the height of our body, but according to our moral character. He measures us to see whether we are good or bad. God's standard of the measure of our moral character is found in the Bible. You will find it, both in the Old Testament and in the New Testament. In the Old Testament we have the Ten Commandments, in which we are required to worship God, and to worship nothing else; to keep the Sabbath day holy; to honor our parents; and various other requirements. In the New Testament we have a great many principles for moral government which Jesus announced when He was upon the earth.

We have all broken some one or more of the Ten Commandments and the precepts which Jesus left for us to follow. If you desire to see how you should live, if you would keep the law perfectly, you will have to look at the life of Jesus Christ. He was the only perfect man who ever lived. He came to this world to set a perfect example for men to imitate. Just the same as you copy after the lines correctly written at the top of your writing book, so you and I are to copy after the life and character of Jesus Christ.

The moral law is a perfect law; the Psalmist says, "the law of the Lord is perfect, converting the soul." I showed you how in France they have a different standard of measure from that which we have in the United States, but with the moral law the standard is the same everywhere and at all times. It is wrong to lie or steal in America, and it is equally wrong to lie or steal in France, or in Africa, or in India, or on the islands of the sea, or anywhere in all of the universe. If it is wicked now to swear, or to commit murder it always was wicked. It was just as wicked three thousand years ago as it is to-day, and it never will be right to take the name of God in vain, or to destroy human life. God has but one standard of morality for all people and for all time.

What God requires of the young in order that they may be pure and holy, He requires also of grown-up people. If it is wrong for the preacher and the Sunday-school superintendent to go to the theatre, or to do anything else, it is equally wrong for every member of the church and for every member of the Sunday-school. Before God we must all be measured by the same standard of morality.

If I had one year ago measured the height of each of you and written it down, and then measured you again to-day, I would find that during these twelve months each of you had grown. You are taller to-day than you were a year ago. Now, God has given us a standard of moral character, right and wrong, and I want you all to study it very carefully, so that you may see how tall you are, how far you come short of the character of Jesus Christ. And as you grow taller in body, so you should grow in moral character, and if you will study God's word carefully, you will be able to discover what progress you are making in becoming more like Christ, in becoming better boys and better girls, and afterward better men and better women, from year to year, than you were each preceding year.

May God bless you abundantly, and may you grow daily "unto a perfect man, unto the measure of the stature of the fulness of Christ." (Eph. iv: 13.)

QUESTIONS.—How many kinds of measures can you name? Are the standards of weights and measures the same in all countries? How many standards of measure does God have? Where can God's standard of measure be found? Are God's standards the same for all persons in all countries, in all parts of the world? Is there any place in the world where it would be right to lie or steal, or murder? Who was the only perfect man? Does God's standard ever change? Should we constantly strive to become like Christ? How can we tell what progress we are making in becoming more like Christ?

THE MAGNET.

JESUS THE GREAT DRAWING POWER.

SUGGESTION:—A small magnet can be purchased in almost any hardware store at trifling cost. With this, also have some little tacks, nails both small and large, together with some old rusted and crooked nails, and a pocket knife.

Do not omit "driving to church" and the other play features suggested in previous sermons.

I AM sure that there is not a boy or girl here, who has not at some time felt a desire to be good and do right. When you have felt this way, it has been due to the fact that the Holy Spirit has come to you and has put these good thoughts and good desires into your heart.

There is not a person living who has not at some time felt this same drawing and desire to do right and to be good. The results, however, have been very different with different people.

I shall seek to illustrate this drawing power to you to-day, and to do so have brought this magnet.. I have also brought these tacks and nails of different sizes; and here are also some old, rusted,

Magnet and Tacks.

crooked nails. Let these several kinds represent the different kinds of people.

When I take this magnet, and move it around among these small tacks, and then hold it up, you will see that very many of these tacks cling to the magnet. They hold on by some unseen

86

power. Sometimes the tacks are even not able to touch the magnet, but are drawn through the influence which extends through other tacks, and so large clusters hang on to the magnet. If I shake the magnet you will see that some fall off. These small tacks represent the youngest children. In the early years of our lives we are more easily drawn to the Lord Jesus. It is then more easy for us to come to Christ and give ourselves fully to Him. It is much easier to be Christians when we are young. Yet many put it off till they are older, when it is much more

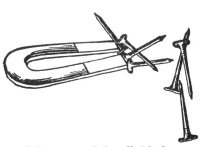

Magnet and Small Nails.

difficult and they are less likely to be successful in living a Christian life.

Now, if I remove these small tacks, and place the magnet among these small nails, you will see that several of the small nails cling to the magnet, and I can lift them up. There are not as many, however, as there were of the tacks clinging to it. In like manner, as boys and girls grow older, they find it more difficult to come to Christ.

Magnet and Larger Nails.

Here are some larger nails. When I place the magnet among them, but very few are attracted to it. And when I attempt to lift the magnet, most all of these large nails fall off. Only one, sometimes two, hold on successfully.

Here are some nails that are still larger. Now, when I attempt to lift one of them with this magnet, you see that I can only lift one end of the nail. That is due to the fact that while the magnet draws these nails, the earth also draws them. That is the reason why these smaller nails, when they fall from the magnet, fall to the earth; because the earth draws them. The earth draws with so much greater force and power upon these large nails than the magnet draws that I cannot raise them by the magnet. It is on this account that they continue to hold fast to the earth rather than to the magnet.

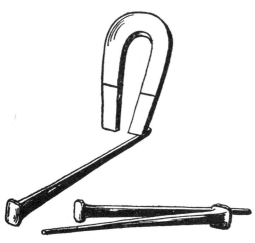

Magnet and Large Nails.

This represents the people who have grown old; who have large cares and responsibilities; who have become worldly-minded; who are drawn away by the "deceitfulness of riches and the lust of other things," and who, although they feel a desire to do right, yet have a stronger desire to do that which is not well-pleasing in the sight of God.

Now, here are some old crooked, rusty nails. Let us see what effect the presence of the magnet will have upon them. Just as we might have expected. These rusty nails do not seem to feel the power or the influence of the magnet's presence. If I place the magnet up against the nail, and attempt to lift it, it does not seem to be drawn at all. It simply lies still, unmoved. These old, crooked, rusty nails represent people who have grown very old and very wicked, and who have become greatly hardened in sin. Jesus Christ and His love seem to make no impression any longer upon them. They are joined to their idols. God's Spirit has taken His departure, and they are left alone. Let me warn you, both young and old, that if you feel the drawing of God's Spirit, you should yield to Him, so as not to become more corroded and rusted, and coated over by every sinful influence, so that at last the love of God shall fail to have any effect upon you.

If now we take these different classes of nails and mix them together, and then stir the magnet among them, you will see how the smaller nails, in larger numbers, cling to the magnet. These bright nails are also affected by it. Oftentimes the influence of the magnet is seen, as it is communicated from one nail to the other; but these rusty nails, not only do not themselves yield to the influence of the magnet, but they also fail to communicate that magnetic influence to any of the other nails around them. In like manner, wicked people seem to come between Christ and others who would be drawn to Him. Let me say to you, keep out of bad company. Avoid wicked companions—those who swear, or lie, or do anything that is wrong, for their influence over you will be bad, and they will prevent the good influences of holy things from acting upon you.

Suppose now that I take my knife blade and move it among these nails, you will see that it does not attract them like the magnet did. It has no magnetic power. If I draw the knife blade across the magnet a few times, it receives this magnetic power from the magnet. Now, when I move it among the nails you will see how these little tacks and some of the larger nails are drawn toward it.

Just so it is with each of us as individuals. Without coming in contact with Christ and receiving His Spirit, His drawing power, we will never influence others to do that which is right and good and holy. If we desire to have an influence for good in this world we must, first of all, come to Christ ourselves, and receive this drawing power from Him. You have doubtless seen those who have become Christians, and after they have given their hearts to Christ they have immediately begun to draw others. They go out and invite others to come to church, they invite others to go with them to the prayer-meeting, to come with them to the Sunday-school, and so in every way they seek to influence others that they may draw them to Christ.

When Jesus was upon the earth vast multitudes attended Him. Where He went they followed. But now when Jesus is no longer bodily present upon the earth, when we cannot see Him with our natural eyes, we speak of walking by faith, and you may be curious to know what is meant by walking by faith. I think that I can illustrate it in this way: Here is a sheet of writing paper. Now above the writing paper I will place this magnet, and then below it I will place this small bit of iron. The attracting power of the magnet holds the iron up against the paper. Now, when I move this magnet on the upper side of the sheet from place to place, you will observe that this little piece of iron on the lower side of the sheet goes in the same direction. It follows the magnet very closely. The paper is between them. Now, if this paper were enlarged so as to be as long and as broad as the ceiling of this room, of course you would not be able to see the magnet. It would be hidden from your view. But as you would move the magnet from place to place, the little iron below would continue to follow it.

So Jesus Christ is no longer visible; we cannot see Him with our natural eyes, but He draws the Christian who is in this world, and so the Christian follows Him. He walks in the footsteps of the Lord Jesus. And it is on that account that we say that the Christian walks by faith, and not by sight.

Just before Jesus was crucified He said: "And I, if I be lifted up from the earth, will draw all men unto Me." (John xii: 32.) So He draws you and He draws me. And so also by His love He would draw every person in all the world to Him.

Let us not resist the drawings of the Holy Spirit, but come to the Lord Jesus Christ and love Him with our whole heart.

QUESTIONS.—What can the magnet do? Can the power of the magnet be seen? Can the magnet lift as many nails as tacks? Are old rusty nails drawn by the magnet? Who are like the little tacks? Who are like the small nails? Who are like the rusty nails? Does everybody desire at times to be good? What draws them in the right direction? Can we see the power that causes us to desire to be good? What is the name of the power or force that causes the nails to fall from the magnet? What power draws people from doing right? Should we always yield to the power that draws us in the right direction? Does Christ have to be seen in order to accept His influence?

Daniel in the Lion's Den.

KEYS.

HOW TO UNLOCK THE HUMAN HEART.

SUGGESTION:—Objects used: Locks and keys of any form or size. If possible open the lock and show how the key fits into the different wards of the lock. Explain how other keys would not fit.

M Y DEAR BOYS AND GIRLS: I have here to-day quite a variety of locks. Here are also quite a variety of keys. You will notice that there are several more keys than there are locks. Now, I suppose that we would have no very great difficulty in selecting the keys that would be most likely to turn backward and forward the bolts in these different locks. We would naturally expect that these larger keys would fit these larger locks and the smaller keys would be adapted to lock and unlock the smaller ones.

Here is this large lock; I suppose it is very possible this large key may be suited to lock and unlock it. Yes, it just fits. You see how it turns the bolt in and out as I turn the key.

Lock and Key.

Now, here is another lock; let us see if we can find a key that will fit it. This key seems about the size, but after passing it into

92

the lock it seems to strike something that prevents it from turning, and consequently is of no service. Let us try another. That seems to work much better, and turns the bolt backward and forward.

Here is still another lock; let us try this key with this lock. That seems to work very well. Possibly we might be able to lock and unlock this other also. Let us try it. Yes, this key fits both these locks. This key is what the locksmith calls a skeleton key. It is so made that it avoids the obstacles which are placed in the different locks to prevent them from being opened by all

Lock and Key.

varieties of keys. Here is a still smaller lock. This lock has a very peculiar keyhole, and I know at once that there is no need of trying to unlock it with most of the keys which I have spread out here. I recognize it at once as what is called a "Yale lock." The key is thin, is bent in various ways, and along the edge has several notches. Let us try a couple of these keys. This one seems to fit very well to the grooves. It passes into the lock, but I

Yale Lock and Key.

cannot turn the bolt. Let us try another. Yes, this seems to be the one that was made by the locksmith to fasten and unfasten this lock.

A key then is simply something which unlocks the door or the gate, so you may open it and pass inside. Now, there are a great many kinds of keys. Sometimes a book is called a key to business. Perhaps another book is called a key to the study of medicine; another the key to the study of law. And so there may be a great many kinds of books which are called keys. When properly used or studied they open the way for a clear understanding of how to transact business, how to study medicine and how to study law. And so there are various books that are keys to the understanding of very, very many subjects. When you indicate to me the kind of difficulty that you have to overcome, it would be reasonably easy to indicate the kind of book you need in order successfully to meet that difficulty.

When I find a book that teaches a boy good business habits and helps him to become a good business man, I know that book was written with that object in view. When I find a book that teaches one how to understand the human system, the nature of disease and the character of the remedies which are to be used when people are sick, I know that book was written with a view to help people to understand the nature of disease and the character of medicine. Just so it is with every other book. Each is like the lock and the key, for the locks have inside a peculiar sort of winding way, and when I find a key that exactly fits into this winding passage I know immediately that the locksmith designed that the key should fit into that particular lock and turn back the bolt.

Now, God wants to get into the human heart, and I find that God has a key with which to unlock it. I do not think you would be long in guessing what book God has made the key with which to unlock the human heart. I think that every boy and girl would at once say that it is the Bible. Yes; it is the Bible. It fits exactly into all the wards and chambers, and winding passages which characterize each and every need of the human heart. The moment I bring this wonderful key of divine truth to the human heart, I find that the lock and the key were both made by the same infinite Creator. Some locks are very complicated and intricate, and the keys are also very peculiar. They are made especially for that particular lock, and no other key in all the world will unlock it. The moment I get that particular key and turn it around in the lock I know at once that both the lock and the key were made by the same person, and that the lock was made to be opened by no other key. So God has created the human heart and made it very difficult to be opened, and there is no key in all the world that can open it except the Bible.

As a robber or a burglar may try to get into a house by the use of a skeleton key, or by "picking the lock," so men have often tried to gain admission into the human heart by the use of various substitutes for the genuine and the real key. They have tried amusement, and wealth, and sinful pleasure, and very, very many things; but they never succeed in getting into the inner sacredness of the human heart. Unless the heart is opened by God's Word, and the Holy Spirit is admitted so that God can take possession, there is always a sense of loneliness, a sense of dissatisfaction, a desire for something that the person does not possess; he is at unrest, he is restless and dissatisfied, like a boy or girl who is away from home, and has a homesick longing to return to that home.

You never will be able to understand the hidden mystery of your own spiritual life and spiritual being until you use the Word of God to help you to solve the mystery. The Word of God is not only designed to unlock the human heart, so that God and the Holy Spirit may gain admission, but this key is also designed to lock the door against Satan and sin and keep them out of our hearts.

Unless we daily use our Bibles to lock our hearts against evil thoughts, and wicked purposes, and sinful desires, we will find that they will steal into our hearts; and like the evil spirit that had been driven out and afterward returned and brought seven other spirits more wicked than himself, so sin and Satan will again take possession of our hearts and lock them against God and all that is good.

QUESTIONS.—Are there many kinds of locks? Must there be as many kinds of keys as there are kinds of locks? Is the human heart like a lock? Does God desire to get into the human heart? With what key does He unlock it? Are the lock and its key made by the same man? Who made the human heart? Who made the key to unlock it? Can the Bible be used to lock the human heart against the entrance of sin? What are skeleton keys? Do men try false keys with which to open the human heart? What are some of the things with which they try? Is the human heart ever satisfied until unlocked by the Bible and possessed by God?

TRAPS.

UNSUSPECTING MICE AND MEN.

SUGGESTION:—An ordinary mouse trap will be serviceable. The trap can be set and instead of a mouse, a child can spring the trap with his finger. The parent had better try his own finger first, to see that the trap is not too strong. A rat trap should never be tried in this way.

M Y DEAR YOUNG FRIENDS: You may think that possibly there was a time when wicked men did not desire to destroy others, as is so often the case in this day. Hundreds of years ago, God said, "Among my people are found wicked men: they lay wait, as he that setteth snares; they set a trap, they catch men." (Jeremiah v: 26.)

I suppose you have all seen traps. There are a great many different kinds. Some are very dangerous, and yet you cannot see the danger until you are caught, or until you see some other person who has been caught in the trap.

Mouse Trap.

Now here is a trap. I suppose that you have all seen such traps as this, and possibly have them in your own homes, to catch the little mice which destroy your food, and oftentimes do much injury.

Now, this trap does not look dangerous to the unsuspecting mouse. The little wire, which is to be drawn up by a strong

97

spring to choke the mouse to death, is concealed, and he does not know that there is a wire there at all. He simply smells the piece of cheese. This tempts his appetite, and, as he is fond of cheese, he desires to obtain it, and so he attempts to crawl in through this small hole to get the cheese; but the moment he nibbles at the cheese, it disturbs the little catch which holds the spring, and when it is too late to escape, the little mouse finds that he has been caught. Then he does not think of the cheese, but struggles to get loose and escape out of the trap. But all of his struggles are in vain,

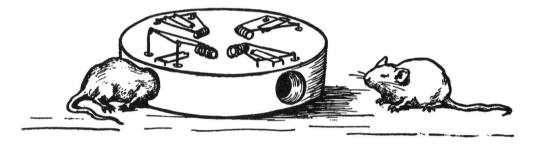

Mice and Trap.

and after a few moments he is choked to death. Then the man, or the housewife comes, takes the little mouse out of the trap, and with the same piece of cheese the trap is again set for another unsuspecting mouse. So people go on, day after day, catching one mouse after another, with the same trap and with the same bait.

Now, there are traps which men set for boys and girls, and men and women, such as story papers, bad books and pictures, that might be called pest papers, printed poison, moral leprosy. To the innocent, the unthinking and the unsuspecting these things may not appear very dangerous, but they are very deadly in their effects, and they result in the temporal and eternal ruin of thousands upon thousands of people every year.

Then there are also the saloons, with gilded signs, frosted windows, and showy looking glasses. Rooms which are made attractive only to catch men, to rob them of their money, and of their self-control, and of their reason, and of their homes, and of all temporal good, and of all hope of heaven—destroying men's souls and bodies, both for a time and for all eternity.

Then there is the theatre, with its glittering lights, with its tinseled show, with its corrupting play, with its scenes upon which no pure-minded man or woman can look without blushing; scenes which deaden the moral sense, pollute the mind, such as are calculated to rob the individual of virtue, and of integrity, and of faith in God, and of hope of heaven.

Then there are other dangerous traps which are set for young men and for older men—tobacco, cigarettes and cigars, and beer. These traps which are set for our money, which so often rob of health and strength, for no boy who uses tobacco in any form can be strong like the boy who does not use tobacco. Boys begin with the deadly cigarette, and then go on to the cigar, and then follow with drinking beer, and so, step by step, they go on down to ruin.

If you have ever gone fishing on a calm, beautiful summer day, and have looked down through the water, you have often seen the fish as they gathered around the hook, and then watched them as they nibbled at the bait. First they come up very shyly, and barely touch the bait with their nose. Then they come again, and possibly just bite a small trifle—barely taste of it. Then, again and again they nibble at the hook, until finally they undertake to get a large bite, when they discover that they have swallowed the hook. Then it matters not how much they flounder about, and struggle to get away, it is too late, it is impossible for them to escape. They are pulled into the boat or upon the bank, and a few hours later they are on the stove, being cooked for some hungry fisherman. Just so Satan comes to those whom he wishes to catch. He comes with money, and with pleasure, and with the thought of having a good time. He tempts people by presenting to their thought something which they desire. He leads them on step by

Fish Doing a Dangerous Thing.

step, and when they see others all about them who are being destroyed in the effort to obtain the same pleasure which they are seeking, Satan makes them think that in their own case the result will be very different.

You will notice that this mouse trap has four different places where mice can be caught, and is it not strange that when one mouse enters on this side, and is caught, and is lying there dead, that another live mouse should come along, and see the same trap and desire the same thing, and walk right in to the same danger, and the same sure death? You would think that when he saw the other mouse had been caught, and had lost his life, that he would turn away. But instead of that, he smells the cheese, walks right into the trap, and is caught, and in a few moments is as dead as his neighbor. So boys see others who have been ruined by smoking cigarettes, who have paved the way for their destruction by smoking cigars, by keeping bad company, by drinking beer, and by going on step by step. They see drunkards all about them who have squandered all their money and lost all their friends, and been forsaken by their own parents, their wives, and their children; who have become outcasts, and for whom no one longer has any respect. Men see these things daily, and yet they go on in the same way, beginning with beer and going, step by step, from social drinking, until they themselves become drunkards and outcasts, and go down to fill a drunkard's grave. The Bible says that no drunkard can inherit the kingdom of heaven.

I trust that none of you who listen to me to-day will be so foolish as to permit Satan to deceive you. Look about you and see the results of worthless story-papers, of card-playing, of theatre going, of social drinking, of round dancing, lying, swearing, cheating, and all forms of wickedness, and then remember that these same influences, if wrought into your life, will also produce the same result. Do not be like the foolish mouse, which sees its dead companion in the trap, and then walks up unthinkingly and pokes his head into the same inevitable death and destruction; but remember that Satan waits to destroy you, just the same as he has destroyed others.

In the book of Job (xviii: 10) it says, "The snare is laid for him in the ground and a trap for him in the way;" and in the 8th verse of the same book and chapter it says, "He is cast into a net by his own feet, and he walketh upon a snare." Satan has laid traps and snares all along your path through life, and you will need to be very, very cautious, lest you are ruined for time and destroyed for eternity. Remember the text for to-day, which says, "Among my people are found wicked men; they lay wait, as he that setteth snares; they set a trap, they catch men."

QUESTIONS.—What are traps for? Are there different kinds of traps? Is a trap a dangerous thing? Does a dangerous trap always look dangerous? Are there traps set for boys and girls, and men and women? Who sets these traps? What are some of the traps? How are fish caught? Who tries to trap and destroy boys and girls, and men and women? What does Satan sometimes use? When the mouse sees others caught, what should he do? Does he run away? Does he go and do the same thing? Does he suffer the same result? If Satan's traps destroy others, will they destroy us? Have you ever seen any persons who were caught in Satan's traps? Can anybody do wicked things without great danger?

7

BREAD.

UNIVERSAL SOUL HUNGER.

SUGGESTION:—Bread, rolls or biscuit can be used if thought necessary, and these can be used for refreshments later.

If the children are tired of "driving to church" in an imaginary carriage, let them drive in an imaginary sleigh, with imaginary bells, amid winter scenes.

MY LITTLE FRIENDS: I am sure that every boy and girl in this room knows what it is to be hungry. It is a part of our childhood experience to feel hungry almost every day. While the body is growing there is almost a constant demand for nourishment and food.

We have here a small loaf of bread; it is called a Vienna roll, and here is a small biscuit. Now, this is bread, only it is baked in small loaves. As people all over the world h a v e hunger, so bread in one form or another has become the universal food of

Loaf of Bread, Roll and Biscuit.

the world. When in the Lord's Prayer we ask God to "give us this day our daily bread," we mean not simply bread made of flour, but we mean necessary food, food of all kinds; and so the word bread has come to be used to signify all kinds of wholesome

102

food. God gives us our food day by day, just the same as each morning the manna rained down from heaven for the Children of Israel while they were journeying through the desert. God does not send it to us in just the same way, but each day He furnishes us a sufficient amount of food to sustain our bodies.

Now, as there is universal physical hunger, and as God has made provision to supply the food necessary to satisfy the hunger of the body; so there is a universal hunger of the soul, and God has also made provision to satisfy this universal hunger of our higher spiritual nature. In the sixth chapter of the Gospel by St. John, you will find much said about the food for the higher, the spiritual nature. Jesus said, "Verily, verily I say unto you, Moses gave you not that bread from Heaven; but My Father giveth you the true bread from heaven. For the bread of God is He which cometh down from heaven and giveth life unto the world."

The body is sustained by the food which grows up out of the earth, because the body is earthy. But to sustain the higher and spiritual nature of man, which is from heaven, the food is sent down from heaven, and therefore Jesus says of Himself that He is "The bread of God which cometh down from heaven, and giveth life unto the world," "I am the bread of life, he that cometh to me shall never hunger, and he that believeth on me shall never thirst." And in the forty-eighth verse of that same chapter He says, "I am the bread of life; your fathers did eat manna in the wilderness and are dead. This is the bread which cometh down from heaven, that man may eat thereof and not die. I am the living bread which came down from heaven; if any man eat of this bread he shall live forever, and the bread that I will give him is my flesh, which I will give for the life of the world."

Now, when you desire to be good, when you desire to live like Christ, you desire to know more concerning Him; and when

Plants Reaching Out Toward the Light.

you desire to read God's Word, and to learn of that which is holy and good and right, then you have this spiritual hunger. That is the kind of hunger of which Jesus was speaking in this chapter. The presence of Jesus in the soul and the knowledge of Him that is given in the Bible is the best kind of food for our spiritual nature. This was the kind of spiritual food upon which Joseph fed when he lived in the midst of idolatrous Egypt. It was upon these spiritual truths that David and Daniel and Paul and Luther fed daily, and this nourished their spiritual natures. I trust you all have this hunger for the bread of life. Jesus said, "Blessed are they which do hunger and thirst after righteousness, for they shall be filled."

Did you ever see a plant growing at the window in a crock and observe how it bends or reaches out toward the light? If you turn the crock around so that the plant bends inward toward the room, after a day or two you go to the plant and it will have changed its direction, and instead of bending into the room, it will be bending out toward the window. Now this plant feeds on the light from the sun, and on that account it reaches out toward the sun. So if you hunger after that which is good, you will reach out after God, just as the plant reaches out after the sun.

This kind of bread which I hold in my hand costs something. Flour costs several dollars a barrel, and bread from five to ten cents a loaf. In times of famine bread has sometimes been sold at many hundreds of dollars for one single loaf. But the bread of life is free; it costs nothing. Everybody can have spiritual food for the simple asking for it. Therefore it is that we go to God in prayer and ask Him for every good and helpful grace and blessing; that we ask Him for His presence in our hearts, and to make us good, and to help us to become like Christ.

But there are some who have this hunger after that which is good, but they do not know about God and about the Lord Jesus

Christ. They do not have any Bibles. Therefore it is my duty and your duty to send them the bread of everlasting life. It is for this purpose that we give our money for missions so that missionaries may be sent to them to tell them of God and His love, and of Jesus Christ the Saviour, and to take them the Bible.

In order that we may be strengthened by bread, it is necessary that we should eat it, and that we should assimilate it or make it part of our own bodies, in order that we may become strong, otherwise we would die of hunger in the midst of great store-houses of food. So men and women die spiritually in the midst of churches, in the midst of Bibles, Bible influences, and Bible privileges; yes, die without Christ. In order that our spiritual natures may be fed with spiritual food, we have every Christian influence in our homes, we have the Sunday-school and the Catechetical class, and the Church with its preaching service, and prayer-meetings and other services. If you desire to be good, you must study your Bibles, go to Sunday-school and to church, and seek to know all you possibly can concerning the Lord Jesus Christ, and receive Him into your hearts, and live a Christian life by His aid and the grace which God will grant you from day to day.

QUESTIONS.—Do all boys and girls get hungry? What food is most universally used in the world? Does the body require food every day? Why? Do we have a spiritual nature as well as a physical nature? Is there a spiritual hunger as well as a physical hunger? Will food which satisfies the physical hunger satisfy the spiritual hunger? Who does the Bible say is the "bread of life"? Can we obtain food for the body without buying it either with money or effort? Must Jesus, the spiritual food, be bought? Can salvation be purchased? If God did not give it to us could we ever pay for it? Where can we learn most about this spiritual hunger and about the "bread" which came down from Heaven? How shall we send the Bread of Life to the people in heathen lands?

THE STONE.

THE NATURAL AND CHANGED HEART.

SUGGESTION:—Objects: A small cobble stone and a larger one, to represent the heart of a child and the heart of an adult, and a pin with which to prick the stone and prick the hand.

NOW, boys and girls, I have here a stone, which because of its peculiar shape reminds me of the human heart. But if I take a pin and prick this stone it has no feeling whatever. If I take this pin and prick the back of my hand, I feel it immediately. It is very unpleasant. Indeed, I do not like to endure it, but this stone has no feeling. If I were to love this stone, the stone would never be conscious of it. I might bestow great gifts upon this stone, I might purchase fruit for it, and everything that you and I might love for food; the finest clothing also, the most costly l a n d s and houses, or we might even bestow upon it very great

Pricking a Stone.

honor, and yet this stone would know nothing of it. It would always be insensible of all that I might do for it.

107

Now the Bible represents the natural heart as being wicked. We are told in the Bible that our hearts have no feeling; that God loves us, and yet that we do not appreciate it; that God bestows upon us our daily food, and that He clothes us, and blesses us with every good, and has provided for us mansions in the skies, and that He desires to give us everlasting salvation. He loves us so much that He gave His only begotten Son, Jesus Christ, to die for us, and yet with the natural heart no one ever loves God, or appreciates anything that He has done for us. And so God desires, as He tells

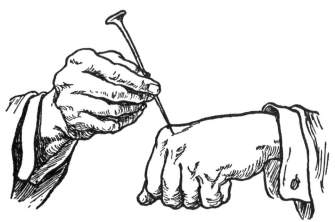

Pricking the Hand.

us in the Bible, to take away, out of our flesh this heart of stone, and give us a heart of flesh, so that we may appreciate and love Him in return for all that He has done for us.

The heart is spoken of in the Bible as the seat of the affections, and therefore it is that God desires us to have a new heart, a changed heart, a heart that can love Him. The Bible says that each one is to keep his heart with all diligence, for out of it are the issues of life. We are told also that "the heart is deceitful above all things and desperately wicked."

Many years ago in England there was a man by the name of John Bunyan. I suppose you have all heard of his wonderful book entitled the "Pilgrim's Progress." I hope that many of you have read it. All of you should read it, if you have not yet done

Assaulting the City of Child-Soul.

so. Get your mother or father to read it for you, if you cannot read it yourself.

This man Bunyan also wrote a book entitled the "Holy War." In this book he represents the human soul or the human heart as a city, and calls it the "City of Mansoul." This city has various gates, and at all these gates the enemy is trying to gain admission into the city, so that he may capture it. It is, indeed, a very apt illustration of the human heart. Do you know that your heart is like a city, and that Satan is trying to capture and to get possession of it? Indeed, he may already have possession of it. And when God by His grace shall come and cast out Satan and all his evil companions, they will come back and try to get into the city again. They will come to the various gates of the city; for your heart has various avenues of approach, which may be called gates. There is eye-gate. Satan comes and he appeals to you and tries to get into your heart through the eye. Bad pictures that are posted upon the bulletin boards along our streets, and wicked things upon which you and I ought not to look—worthless papers, bad books— these Satan desires to have us look upon, and in that way get evil thoughts into our minds and wicked purposes into our hearts, so that he can once more get possession of our hearts.

Then he comes to ear-gate, and tries to get into our hearts through our ears. There are wicked songs, and bad stories, and wicked words that men pour into our ears, even when we walk along the streets. And so Satan tries to get into our hearts through ear-gate, and he tries to get into our hearts through what I will call mouth-gate. He tempts our appetite, and would have us eat things which would injure us, or to drink that which would harm us. And so he tries to get a boy to smoke, or to drink, if at first only beer, or something else, until at last Satan makes a drunkard of him. So Satan would get into the heart through mouth-gate. And when he cannot get into the heart through mouth-gate, or any other way, he oftentimes approaches mouth-gate by way of nose-gate. By the smell of something that is pleasant he tempts the appetite, and thus would lead us astray.

And then he would also approach our hearts through the sense of feeling. There are many wicked things that Satan tempts people to do in order to give them pleasure, and so he seeks to get into their hearts, and to get entire control of them, and in that way to get God out of their hearts.

The best thing that you and I can do, is to accept of God's invitation, where He says, "My son, give me thine heart." I trust that you will give your heart earnestly and fully to the Lord Jesus Christ. He will take away this heart of stone out of your flesh, and give you a heart of flesh. He will keep your heart securely for you, if you will only give it fully to Him.

QUESTIONS.—Does the stone have any feeling? Are our natural hearts like a stone? Can a human heart that is insensible like a stone be conscious of God's love? Who offers to give us a heart that will be conscious of God's love? Who wrote the book picturing the human heart like a city? Who is trying to capture this city? Through what gates does Satan try to enter? How does he try to get into Eye-Gate? How does he try to get into Ear-Gate? How does he try to get into Mouth-Gate? Can you tell any other methods that he tries? To whom had we better surrender the city of our soul? If we commit the city of our soul to God, will He protect and defend it? Is there any other way of safety?

THE POLISHED STONE.

PERFECTION THROUGH SUFFERING.

SUGGESTIONS—A piece of polished stone, or a polished jewel, or piece of polished metal will answer for the object to be used.

MY LITTLE MEN AND WOMEN: I trust you are all trying to be good, and perhaps while you have been trying to be a follower of Jesus you have desired many things and hoped that God would give them to you, because you were trying to do right, and yet, perhaps, you have been disappointed because God did not grant your wish. You have been seeking to be faithful, and yet, perhaps, sickness has come to you, or disappointment and sorrow. Perhaps sickness and death have come into your family. Your papa or your mamma has been taken away by death, and you have been left very sad and lonely, and you have come to wonder how it is, if God loves you, that He does not grant you just what you wish, and that He permits sickness and sorrow and bereavement to come to you and to your home.

When you have looked about you, you have seen many good people who have been in much distress, oftentimes in poverty, afflicted with sickness, bereaved of their loved ones, and left in great sorrow and disappointment. When you have taken up your Bible you have found that the same was true many hundreds of years ago. David was greatly afflicted. Paul had his thorn in the flesh. The disciples were often cast into prison, and it is very

112

Copyrighted, 1911, by Sylvanus Stall.

Stones Being Prepared for a Great Building

likely that all of them were put to death, as their Master had been before them.

Now I want to illustrate to you to-day why God permits sorrow and affliction to come to us. I have here two stones, both taken out of the same quarry. This one is polished and has a very beautiful surface. It is very beautiful, not only to look at, but it would be beautiful in any place you might choose to put it. This other is rough and jagged, and not at all pleasant, either to handle or to look upon. This rough stone can be made useful, but it would be no more useful than any other rough and unsightly stone. It would do very well to place in the foundation of a building, to be all covered up with mortar and have other stones laid on top of it; to be built in the foundation down below the ground, where no one would ever see it. But it would be of no special value in its present condition for anything other than that.

I think this polished stone may very properly represent Christian people. For long, long years this stone had been lying peacefully and quietly in its rocky bed. But one day a man who purposed to build a very beautiful palace came along, and he found that the great rocks in a certain portion of the country contained stone that could be polished very beautifully. They could therefore be made very useful in constructing his palace or cathedral. So he sent a large number of men to the quarry and they began to drill great holes in the rock. Now, if these rocks had any feeling you can see at once that they would object to having such great holes drilled into their sides, because it would hurt a great deal. But after the men had the holes drilled they put powder in them and blasted off great pieces of these rocks. Then these great blocks were hauled away and placed in the hands of stone masons, who began with chisels and mallets to cut and carve. After that, with some fine sand or emery, or something of that kind, other men ground and polished the face of the stone until it became very beautiful.

Now, if these stones had had feeling, you can see at once that they would have objected to being chiselled and cut, and carved, and ground, and polished. This process would have hurt so much that the stones would have cried out, and asked to be delivered from such a painful process.

Stones Being Polished.

It is related of Michael Angelo, that one day he was passing a quarry where large blocks of beautiful marble were being taken out. In one large block he saw a beautiful angel. He ordered the block to be taken to his studio, or the place where he studied and worked. And then he put his men at work to chisel off the rough corners, and thus to deliver the angel out of the rough pieces by which it was surrounded. After many days and weeks, and perhaps months of working, in which this large block of marble had to submit to a great deal of chiselling and

"The Beautiful Angel Was Carved Out."

carving, and cutting, and polishing; lo! and behold, the beautiful angel was all carved out and stood complete and perfect. It was polished and was made very beautiful, and when it was set up, it was the delight of every one who looked upon it. But all this, you easily see, was only made possible by that cutting and carving, which would have been very painful to the marble if it had been possessed of feeling.

I think you will begin to see that these things which we call troubles and trials, after all, are well calculated by God to bring out that which is noblest and best in us.

When you grow older you will come to say like Paul, that you know that "tribulation worketh patience, and patience experience, and experience hope, and hope maketh not ashamed." You will then come to understand that these things "work out for us a far more exceeding and eternal weight of glory," and like Paul, you will learn to be "patient in tribulation." One time when Paul and Barnabas were at Lystra and healed a cripple, the people were moved against Paul by some wicked Jews from Antioch and Iconium, and they pursued Paul and threw large stones at him and hit him with such great force that he fell down, and they supposed that he was dead. But Paul was not dead, and afterwards when he met some of the Christian people at that and other places, when they talked to him about it, and thought that it was very hard that God should have permitted these wicked people to stone him, Paul told these Christians that "through much tribulation we must enter into the kingdom of heaven."

But I must not detain you longer. I want simply to say in closing that when St. John had been banished to the Isle of Patmos and was permitted to have a view of heaven, and looked into that glorious city, he saw a great company, and he inquired of the angel who these people were. The angel replied: "These are they which came out of great tribulation, and have washed their robes and made them white in the blood of the Lamb.   Therefore are they before the Throne of God and serve Him day and night in His temple; and He that sitteth upon the Throne shall dwell among them.   They shall hunger no more, neither thirst any more; neither shall the sun light on them, nor any heat.   For the Lamb which is in the midst of the Throne shall feed them, and shall lead them unto living fountains of water; and God shall wipe away all tears from their eyes."   (Rev. vii: 14-17.)

If in our sickness, or sorrow, or disappointment here upon the earth, we are sad or lonely, let us remember that in the happy home to which we go we shall be forever with the Lord, and that all tears shall be wiped away, and that we shall be happy forever and ever on high.   It is only through these tribulations that you and I can be prepared to enter heaven.   If God were to give us everything we want, like children who are indulged, we would soon be spoiled and would not be fit for the enjoyment of heaven or the companionship of the angels.

QUESTIONS.—What is rough stone used for?   Does the stone have feeling? If it had feeling, would it object to being cut and chiselled and polished?   Could it be used in a great building unless it was first quarried and prepared?   How can the rough stone be made beautiful?   Can it be polished so that you can see your face in it?   Who prepares people to be builded into His kingdom?   How does He do this?   Who composed the great multitude whom John saw in the glorious city?   What had happened to them?   What should we remember in times of sickness and sorrow?   Why are trials necessary to fit us for heaven? Will we be in the presence of God there and have angels as our companions?

ROPES.

HABITS AND HOW THEY BECOME STRONG.

SUGGESTIONS:—Objects to be used are a spool of thread, a piece of string or twine and a piece of rope.

After the sermon has been read, the thread and strings could be used to tie the hands and feet, and thus illustrate how impossible it is to break them when they are wound again and again around the hands and the feet, even though the thread be very fine. So with habits, seemingly insignificant.

M Y DEAR BOYS AND GIRLS: I have to-day a piece of rope, and also some different kinds of string. If I take this rope and try to break it, I find that it is impossible. I do not believe that any five or six ordinary men could pull with sufficient strength to break this rope. I am sure that no twenty boys and girls could pull hard enough to break it.

Here is a very strong string. Perhaps a couple of boys, possibly four boys, might be able to break it. But here is a thinner string. Possibly I may be able to break this. Yes, I can, but with great difficulty. It takes all the strength I have to break it.

Rope.

Now, here is some that is still thinner. It is about as thick as heavy thread. I can break it very easily.

But now, when I take this heavy rope and cut off a piece, if I

120

unwind these different strands, I find that this rope is made by twisting smaller ropes together. If I untwist this smaller rope, which I have taken out of the larger rope, I find that it in like manner is also made of smaller ropes, or strings. If I take these smaller

strings, and untwist them, I find that they are made of still smaller strings; if I take any of these smaller strings out of the rope, I can break them easily, but when I twist several of them together, I cannot break them.

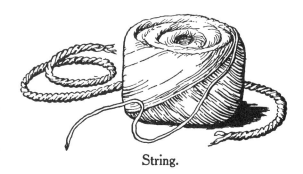

String.

I think that these smaller cords, out of which this rope is made, will very fittingly illustrate habits. It is a very dangerous thing to form bad habits. We should be very careful to form good ones, but bad ones are very dangerous. The boy who remains away from Sunday-school but once, thinks little of it. The boy who remains away from church, or stays at home from school, or disobeys his parents, or spends the evenings on the streets instead of in the house reading good books, or breaks the Sabbath, or does any one of many things, may think very little of it at the time; but do you know that when we go on repeating the same thing over and over again, the habit grows stronger and stronger until at last we are not able to break loose from that habit? There are men who think that they can stop smoking. They began with only an occasional cigarette or a cigar, until the habit grew upon them, and now possibly they think they are able to stop, but when they undertake to break off smoking, they find that it is a very difficult task, and very few smokers who undertake it succeed permanently. The old habit is likely to overcome them again and again.

So it is with swearing, and with telling falsehoods, and with being dishonest, and with drinking liquor, and everything else that men and boys often do. These habits at last become very strong, until they are not able to break loose from them.

Now, if you take one of these strong habits from which a man is not able to break loose, and untwist it, you will find that it was made strong by a repetition of small habits. Habits are made strong by doing the same thing over and over again. It is just the same as when I take this spool of thread and wrap it around the feet

Hands Bound.

of a boy. I can wrap it around and around, and while it would be easy for him to break the thread if it was wrapped once or twice, or three or four times around his feet; yet after I have succeeded in placing it ten or twelve, or twenty-five or fifty times around his feet, he is not able to walk at all.

I could tie his hands by wrapping this small thread around and around, just a few times. At first it could be broken, but after a little it becomes so strong that he is not able to break it at all. So it is with habits. When we do the same things again and again, the habit becomes stronger and stronger day by day, and year by year, until at last Satan has the poor victim bound hand and foot, and he is absolutely helpless. No one is able to come and snap the cords, and set this poor helpless prisoner free, until God in His grace comes and liberates him from the evil habits with which he has bound himself, or with which he has permitted Satan to bind him.

It is very important that in the very beginning of life, we

should all form the habit of doing those things which are right. The doing of the right may at first afford us but very little pleasure, yet we are to continue to do right, and after a while it will become pleasant for us to do right.

At first it may not be very pleasant for a boy to go to school. He prefers not to exert himself; not to put forth any mental effort. But after he be-comes accustomed to going to school, and to putting forth mental effort, it be-comes more and more natural to him, and finally he comes to love study. After he has completed his studies in the pri-mary school, he goes to the intermediate, and to the grammar school, and high school, and possibly to college, and con-tinues to be a student all his life.

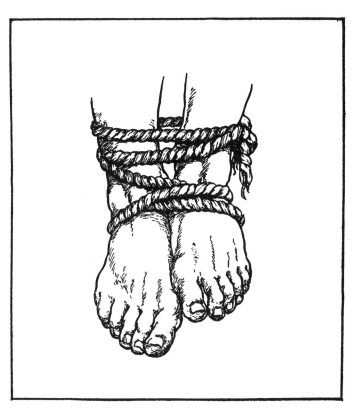

Feet Bound.

So it is with going to church; those who begin when they are young and go regularly, Sunday after Sunday, become regular church attendants all their lives.

Habits are formed very much like the channel of a river. Gradually, year after year, the river wears its course deeper and deeper, until finally through the soft soil and the hard rock, through the pleasant meadow and the beautiful woodlands, it has worn out for itself a very deep channel in which it continues to flow to the ocean.

So the mind, by repeated action, marks out its course. Whether the mental effort or manual work be pleasant or difficult, we become so accustomed to it, that we go on day by day, and year by year doing the same thing.

The Bible gives very wise instruction to parents when it says, "Train up a child in the way he should go: and when he is old, he will not depart from it." (Prov. xxii: 6.) It has also been wisely said, "Sow an act and you reap a habit; sow a habit and you reap a character; sow a character and you reap a destiny."

Be careful, boys and girls, what you do, for by doing anything you are forming a habit. If you do wrong things you will form bad habits, but if you do right things you will form good habits, which are always the best.

QUESTIONS.—Are small ropes or strings used to make big ropes? Can you tie a boy's hands and feet with thread so that he cannot make himself free? How are strong habits made? Is it a good thing that habits are formed in this way? Does this make it easy to form good habits? Does it also make it easy to break away at first from a bad habit? Which is easier, to form a bad habit or to break away from it? Who tries to bind us with bad habits? Who alone can break the ropes of habit with which Satan binds us? What does the Bible say about training up a child in the way he should go?

WATCH AND CASE.

THE SOUL AND THE BODY.

SUGGESTION:—A watch and case (preferably a double case) from which the works can be easily removed will answer the purpose. Jewelers often have such old watches that they would be glad to sell for a trifle, or even to give away. A small old clock from which the works can be removed would also answer the same purpose.

Keep up the play idea with the children. Older persons may weary of repetition, but to children their play is always new and interesting. After "driving to church", being shown to seats, and after some opening services, let one of the children preach in his or her own language the truth which most impressed them in last Sunday's object sermon, or the truth which they remember from the morning sermon in church, or from any passage of Scripture which they may prefer. No better school of oratory was ever formed, even though the primary purpose is devotional and religious.

NOW, boys and girls, what is this that I hold in my hand? (Many voices, "A watch.") I expected that you would say it was a watch. Every boy knows a watch when he sees it, and every boy desires to have a watch of his own —one which he can carry in his pocket, and one which will tell him the time of day whenever he looks at it.

But you cannot be sure, even from appearances, that this is absolutely a watch. It might be only a watch-case. In order to tell whether it is a watch, let us open it. After all, it is not a watch. It is only a watch-case. You would not wish to spend your money when you expect to get a watch, and on reaching home find that you have been deceived, and that you had nothing but a watch-case?

Now, boys and girls, what is this? (holding up the works of the watch). "A watch." This time you are right, this is a watch.

Watch-case.

It is a watch without a case around it. Now we will put the works into the case, and then we will have a complete watch. The works and the case together more properly constitute a watch.

You have, I suppose, been at a funeral, and have seen the body of the dead man or woman or child lying in the coffin. Unless somebody has told you differently, you may possibly have thought the person whom you had known was lying there in the coffin. But this was not the fact. Every man, woman and child consists of a soul and a body, and when a person dies the soul returns to God, who gave it. God made our body out of the dust of the ground, and when the spirit leaves the body, it is a dead body, and it begins to decay, and soon becomes offensive, and so we bury the body out of our sight, putting it again in the ground, and finally it moulders back again to dust.

A Watch-case and Works.

It is not so, however, with the soul. That is a spirit. When God had made Adam out of the dust of the ground, He breathed into his nostrils the breath of life, and man became a living soul. Now, this soul never dies. God has created it to live forever and ever, throughout all eternity. Those who are good and trust in the Lord Jesus Christ will be received at death to dwell forever with the Lord. And those who are wicked and do not repent of their sins, God will banish forever from His presence; for sin is hateful in the sight of God, who cannot look upon it with any degree of allowance.

The moment you look upon a body, without being able to tell how, you can nevertheless quickly distinguish between one who is asleep and one who is really dead. Even animals can tell a

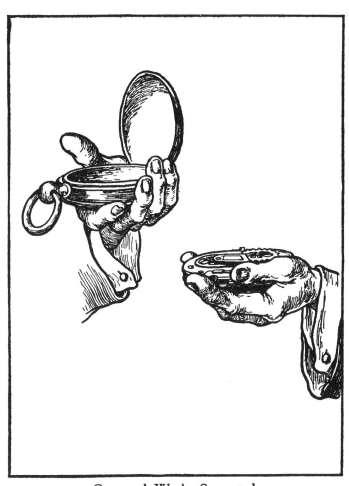

Case and Works Separated.

dead body. When a dead horse lies along the road, it is very difficult to drive a live horse near to the dead one. The living horse knows at once that the other is dead, although we do not know how he knows it.

Now, I want to show you that death does not affect the existence of the soul. I will now lift these works out of the watch case.

I now hold the case in my left hand, and the works in my right hand. As these works constitute the real watch, so the soul constitutes the real person, and as these wheels and hands continue to move, and to keep time regularly even after they have been removed from the case; so the soul, when God removes it from the body, continues to exist and to be possessed of all that makes the reasoning, thinking, immortal and indestructible being of man.

I might take this case, which I hold in my left hand, and bury it in the ground, but the works would not be affected by this fact, but would continue to run on just the same. Suppose I were to leave this case buried in the ground until it had all rusted away. Then suppose that, as a chemist I could gather up all these particles again and make them anew into a watch case, and then put the works back into the case which had been restored or made anew; that would represent the resurrection of the body, and the reuniting of the soul with the body, which will take place at the resurrection day.

Some years ago there was a great chemist, whose name was Faraday. It happened one time in his laboratory that one of the students, by accident, knocked from the table a silver cup, which fell into a vessel of acid. The acid immediately destroyed or dissolved it, and the silver all disappeared, the same as sugar dissolves or melts in a tumbler of water. When Professor Faraday came in and was told what had happened, he took some chemicals and poured them into the acid in which the silver had disappeared. As soon as these two chemicals came together, the acid began to release the silver, and particle by particle the silver settled at the bottom of the vessel. The acid was then poured off and the silver was all carefully gathered up and sent to a silversmith, who melted the silver and made it anew into a silver cup of the same form, design and beauty. It was the same cup made anew. So, my young friends, our bodies may dissolve in the grave and entirely disappear, but God is able to raise them up again. He tells us in the Bible that these bodies which are buried in corruption shall be raised in incorruption, and that these mortal bodies shall put on immortality.

I trust that I have illustrated to you how the soul and the body are separated when we die, and God's Word assures us that they shall be reunited again in the morning of the resurrection, for all these dead bodies "shall hear the voice of the Son of God and shall come forth." It matters not whether they were buried in the ground, or in the water, they shall arise from every sea and from every cemetery, and every grave in all the world, and shall live anew and forever, either in happiness with God in heaven, or in misery with Satan in eternal banishment from God's presence.

QUESTIONS.—What are the principal parts of a watch? Which part is like the body? Which part is like the soul? Which is the real watch? Could the works alone run and keep time without the case? When does the soul become separated from the body? Does death affect the existence and life of the soul? If a watch case were buried and rusted away, could it be made new again? Does the Bible say our bodies are also to be raised again from the grave? What is that raising up of the body called? Will it make any difference whether a body was buried in the sea or in the earth? ("The sea shall give up its dead"). Whose voice shall call the body to immortality? Will the immortal body ever die?

PEARLS.

ONE OF GREAT PRICE.

SUGGESTION :—A single pearl, or a string of pearls will serve well for illustration.

MY YOUNG FRIENDS: Here is a whole string of pearls. One time I found a large pearl in an oyster. I thought it might be valuable, and I took it to a jeweler, but he soon told me that it was not worth much, because it was not perfect. It was unusually large, but to be valuable it must be perfectly round and have no defects. When Jesus was upon the earth He told of a merchant w h o went in search of a very valuable pearl, and when he had found it, he sold all that he had and bought that pearl, in order that he might have the largest and most valuable jewel in all the world.

String of Pearls.

Cleopatra, Queen of Egypt, had a pearl that was worth three hundred and seventy-five thousand dollars, and one day she dissolved this costly pearl, and drank it in a glass of wine to the honor of Mark Antony, one of the Roman rulers.

130

Diving for Pearls.

There are pearls to-day worth two and three hundred thousand dollars, and possibly more.

The pearl in this parable is the symbol of salvation. Now, salvation has cost more, and is worth more than all the farms, and houses, and stores, and wealth of all this nation, and all the nations of all the globe, and all the created universe about us. It cost the life of the Son of God, and it is desirable, therefore, that you and I should obtain it, because of the many blessings it secures to us, both in this world and in the world to come.

For two thousand years men from all the largest nations of the earth have gone to the island of Ceylon, seeking pearls. It is a barren and deserted island, but during the months of February, March and April, every night at ten o'clock, many boats sail out about ten miles, to the place where men, with large leaden weights at their feet, dive down through the water until they come to the banks where the large pearl oyster has his home. They quickly pick up several of these oysters and drop them into a basket of net-work, and in about sixty or seventy seconds are again drawn up by their companions into the boat.

Men and women could not have pearls if it were not that these men are willing to risk their lives by diving way down under the water to obtain them. No one could secure salvation had not Jesus left His throne in heaven and come down to this wicked world to suffer and die, that He might make atonement for our sins upon the cross, so that you and I might not perish but have ever-lasting life—so that you and I might have salvation, both here and in heaven.

When I went to the jeweler, he told me that the defects on the pearl which I had found could not be removed and the rough places polished. Diamonds have to be cut and polished. Many precious and costly jewels when found look only like rough stones in the field, but the pearl is perfect when found; nothing can be done to make it more perfect or more valuable. Just so is the salvation of Jesus perfect; no human wisdom can improve upon it. The best book that any man ever wrote has been equaled by what some other man has thought and written. The religion of the heathen can be greatly improved, but the Bible and the salvation which it reveals, man has never been able to equal, much less to improve upon.

To-day, as thousands of years ago, pearls are worn as ornaments to the body, but the salvation which Jesus Christ came to bring is an ornament to the soul that possesses it.

The pearl is valuable and desirable, because it cannot easily be stolen away from its owner. When Jesus was upon the earth they did not have banks, with large iron safes where people could deposit their money and jewels for safe keeping. There were many robbers then, and people buried their money and valuables. Often the places where these were concealed were discovered, and then all that they had was stolen. A pearl is small, and could therefore easily be hidden in a place of safety. If war occurred, or for any reason a man and his family had to flee from their home or their country, they could easily carry even the most valuable pearls. The owner could hide it in his mouth, or even swallow it if necessary. If a man had much gold, it was too heavy to carry, and it could readily be discovered and stolen. But a pearl was not so difficult to hide and keep.

The Bible tells us that salvation is something that the world cannot give, and which the world cannot take away. Daniel had this pearl of great price, and even though the king cast him into the den of lions, he could not get it away from him. His three companions with those hard names, Shadrach, Meshach and Abednego, had this pearl of salvation, and even in the furnace of fire it was not destroyed or taken from them. If you have this pearl of salvation, you can keep it in spite of all the wicked people in the world; you can hide it away in your heart, and all the armies of the world cannot take it away from you. In sickness or in health it will be yours, and even death itself can not rob you of it. It will stay with you in this world, and it will be your joy and gladness in the world to come.

As the merchantman went out seeking the most valuable pearl, so all the world is to-day seeking for something which will satisfy and render their owners happy. There are many good things in this world, but none of them can make any one contented and happy, like the salvation which Jesus gives when we repent of our sins and in faith accept Him as our Saviour. Before you get, or even desire any other pearl, I want each of you to accept of this "Pearl of great price," which is Jesus Christ.

QUESTIONS.—Of what is a pearl the symbol in the Bible? Are pearls valuable? Is salvation valuable? Where are pearls principally found? How are they obtained? Are pearls polished like the diamond? Why do people wear pearls? Can we lose pearls by having them stolen? Can we lose salvation? Who would steal it away? Who can give us the "Pearl of great price"?

It is well to have the children learn the answers to many of the leading Bible questions. Try them in the following:—Who was the first man? Who was the first woman? Of what did God make Adam and Eve? Who was the first murderer? Who was the oldest man? Who built the ark? Who had the coat of many colors? Who was the strongest man? Who slew Goliath the giant? With what did David slay Goliath? Who was the wisest man? Who was cast into the den of lions? Who went to Heaven in the chariot of fire without dying? Upon whom did Elijah's mantle fall? and similar questions.

COAL AND WOOD.

JESUS THE SOURCE OF SPIRITUAL LIGHT AND WARMTH.

SUGGESTION:—The objects used to-day can be a piece of wood, a piece of coal, a candle and a piece of electric light carbon, such as are daily thrown away in towns where the arc lighting is used.

DEAR BOYS AND GIRLS: When Jesus was upon the earth, He said of Himself, "I am the light of the world." Now, I desire to-day to illustrate to you something of the truth which Jesus had in mind when He uttered these words.

The Sun and Moon.

We are told in the Bible, that when God created the world, on the fourth day He created the sun and the moon to give light upon the earth, the sun to rule over the day, and the moon to rule over the night.

I suppose you all know that the earth is round, and that while the sun is shining on our side of the earth, and making it day here, on the other side of the earth it is night and is all dark. Now, I want to tell you that the sun is the source of all light upon the earth. The sun shines and dispels the darkness, and makes it light. And do you know that the moon does not shine by its own light, but it simply throws back again, as we say, reflects, the light of the sun, just the same .as when a boy takes a small piece of looking-glass and throws the light across the street? There is no light in the looking-glass itself, but it simply takes the rays of light which fall upon it from the sun and bends them, or turns them, so that the boy can throw the rays of light across the street, or upon anything that he desires that is in range of him. So the light of the sun falls upon the moon, and is turned again or reflected back upon the earth. God has so placed the moon in the heavens that it reflects the light of the sun upon those portions of the earth which are in darkness. Or, in other words, as He says in the Bible, the moon has been "made to rule the night." So you see that even the moon does not shine by its own light.

Jesus Christ is the Sun of Righteousness. All the good there is in the world, all the righteousness, all that is holy and pure, come from Jesus Christ. The Church is also a source of purity, of holiness, of religion, and of Christianity. But the church does not shine of itself. It does not have these influences within itself. All its light is derived from the Sun of Righteousness. All influences which tend for goodness and holiness and purity are derived from the Lord Jesus Christ. He is the source of all that is good, and only in so far as the Church reflects the life of Jesus, and the truth which is revealed in His Word, and in the teachings of

Jesus, does it become the source of saving power in the world.

Now, here I have a piece of coal, and a piece of wood, and a candle, and a piece of carbon from an electric light. You might ask me whether the light that comes from the coal when it burns, or the wood when it burns, and the candle when it is lighted, and the electric light when it illuminates the street so brightly, whether they are not shining by their own light? No; they are not shining by their own light. All the light that there is in the wood, or in the coal, or in the candle, or in anything else that makes a light at all, derives its source and origin from the sun. The light that comes from the burning of this wood is simply the releasing of the light that has been accumulated from the rays of light shining from the sun upon the tree while it was growing, year after year, in the field or forest. And now, when it is burning, it simply releases or throws out that light which it received from the sun, and which was stored up in the wood of the tree while it was growing.

Candle, Coal and Wood.

This coal is simply a portion of a tree which grew many, many hundreds or thousands of years ago, and which, in some great convulsion of nature, was buried deep under the surface of the earth in what we now call coal mines. The coal has undergone some chemical changes, but, nevertheless, all the light there is in the coal is simply that buried sunshine, which was stored up centuries and centuries ago, in the form of vegetables and trees. Now, when it burns in the grate or in the furnace it simply releases that heat and warmth and light, which was stored up in these trees many, many centuries ago. It is simply buried sunshine which God has stored up for our use. The same is true of the light of the candle; if it were not for the light of the sun there would be no light giving power in any oil or tallow, or in this carbon, which is used in the electric light; they all derive their light from the sun itself.

Just so it is with all the truth and righteousness there is in the world. When you see a man who is good and Christlike, it is not because that man has the power in himself to be good, but it is because he has received that power from the Lord Jesus Christ. The light of the Sun of Righteousness has shone into that man's heart, and the light that goes out through his daily conduct and character, is only the light of the Son of God shining out through that man.

All objects which live in the sunlight drink in this light-giving power, and all people who live daily in the light of the Sun of Righteousness will partake of His nature and of His character, and then live that nature and character in their own daily lives. In this way they do as Jesus commanded, let their lights so shine, that others seeing their good work, glorify their Father which is in heaven.

You should be careful to note that Jesus does not say that we ourselves are to shine so that others may glorify us. No, not at all. Many people try to shine or to attract the attention of others to themselves, but that is not what Jesus said or meant, but rather the reverse. Neither are we to attempt to shine, or to attempt to attract the glory or honor to ourselves. Let not yourself so shine, but let your *light* so shine that others seeing your good works may glorify —not you, but your Father which is in heaven. We must let Jesus Christ shine in and through us.

Whenever you see men or women, or girls or boys who are living beautiful Christian lives, it is not they that light up the moral darkness that is in the world, it is Jesus Christ who lives in them and shines through them, that makes them good and holy, and consequently a source of light and blessing to all about them.

QUESTIONS.—What does Christ call Himself? What is the source of the light of the natural world? Does the sun shine by its own light? Does the moon shine by its own light, or does it reflect the light of the sun? What is the source of light displayed when coal and wood and other substances are burned? Does all natural light come from the sun? Who is the source of our spiritual light and knowledge? Are the Church and Christian people lights in the world? Do they shine of their own goodness like the sun, or are they like the moon in that they reflect the divine light? Does any person have the power in himself to be good? Where does this power to be good come from? Does Christ want us to shine as lights in the world? Are we to let our lights shine to glorify ourselves, or to glorify Christ?

LANTERNS.

THE BEST LIGHT FOR OUR PATH.

SUGGESTIONS—A lantern of any kind may be used. If one of the old-fashioned tin lanterns, perforated with holes through which the light was to shine, is available it would add greatly to the curiosity and interest of the children, although these are now very rare, as they were in use a half century ago.

After "driving to church", and after preaching by the children and the reading of the following sermon on lanterns, a few Japanese lanterns—one for each of the children—would enable the parents to form a little torch-light procession (although no lighted candles need be in the lanterns). After marching through the different rooms, give the children a talk upon the conditions existing in heathen lands like China and Japan, and the changes which are being wrought through the introduction of Christianity and the work of the missionaries.

I DO not believe that there is a boy or girl here to-day who could tell me what this thing is, that I hold in my hand. It is a lantern, a very different lantern possibly, from those which any of you have ever seen. This is the kind of lantern that your grandfather and my grandfather used many years ago, in the days when they did not have lamps, and gas, and electric lights, and such things as we enjoy to-day. When I was a small boy in the country we used to have only candles.

Old Lantern.

Later on in life, I

140

remember when they first had fluid lamps, and then kerosene oil, and then gas, and then, as we have it now, electric lights.

In the second congregation to which I ministered, there was an old gentleman who had one of these lanterns. He lived some distance from the church, and very dark nights you could always see him coming across the hill, carrying this strange lantern. After the candle was lighted and placed inside, the light shone out through these small holes, and if the wind blew very hard, the light was liable to be blown out.

Now, here is a better lantern. David says of God's Word, "Thy word is a lamp unto my feet, and a light unto my path." On a dark night in the country, you could not go out of doors and move about without running up against a tree, or the fence, or falling into the ditch, or soon finding yourself involved in serious difficulties; and on this account people in the country carry a lantern at night. In the Eastern countries where Jesus lived, where they did not have gas and electric lamps to light the streets, when people went out at night they always carried a lantern. And so David said, "Thy word is a lamp unto my feet, and a light unto my path." (Ps. cxix: 105.)

When people go out of doors into the darkness with a lantern they do not hold it way up high, but hold it down near their feet, so that they can see the path, and it enables them to walk with security and safety. Sometimes there are men who have gone to college, and have learned Latin and Greek, have studied the sciences and philosophy, and they think they have learned a very great deal. Perhaps afterwards they have studied medicine and become physicians, or have read law and become lawyers, and they think that they are able with all they know to find the true path of blessing through life. They think they have light enough of themselves. They do not seem to know that all about them there is a darkness of great mystery; that sin and death and destruction lurk all along

142   "Coming Across the Hill Carrying this Strange Lantern."

their way through life, and that their pathway is full of snares, and pitfalls, and dangers, but they try to walk with the little light that there is in the human understanding.

There is another class of men who go through college and who may, perchance, study much, and the more they study the more they come to realize how little they know, and how much there is beyond them that they do not understand at all. With the little light of human understanding they comprehend how very dense and dark are the mysteries all about them, and so in order that they may walk safely through life, and come at last to the city of eternal safety, they take God's Word "as a lamp to their feet." Just the same as a person in the country carries a lamp in order that he may find his path, so these good people take the Word of God and they make it the lamp unto their feet, and the light unto their path.

Boys and girls often look at learned men and women and think that when they get to be as old and to know as much as these people, that then they will know everything. But that is a great mistake. The more we know and the more learned we are, the more we discover that there is still further beyond us that which we do not understand. No one has ever been able to tell how the bread and the meat and potatoes and other food which we eat is made to sustain our life, how it is converted into and made a part of ourselves. How on our heads these things become, or are changed into hair, on the ends of our fingers to nails, and how other parts become flesh, and bone and eyes and ears and teeth. Nobody can understand how the ground in the garden can be changed by some life principle into fruit and vegetables and flowers and hundreds of different things, and yet all this wonderful variety, all growing out of the very same soil, or ground as we call it.

And so as you grow older and become more and more learned you will come more and more to appreciate how much there is that you can never understand.   There is mystery all about us, and we all need the light of divine truth, the light of God's Word, the Bible as a light to guide us through the darkness and the mysteries that are all about us.

If you have ever been in the country upon a dark night and have seen the railway engine come dashing along, with the great headlight that throws the rays of light far down along the track enabling the engineer to see very far ahead of him, you would understand what the Bible purposes to do for us, when God says that He will make it a lamp unto our feet, and a light unto our path.

As you grow older, and sorrow and sickness and trials come to you, you will need God's Word to be a lamp unto your feet.   And when at last the messenger of death shall come and summon you into God's presence, and you go through "the valley of the shadow of death," you will then need this lamp for your feet, and you will need the Lord Jesus Christ with you, that you may lean upon Him, and that you may say as David did: "Yea though I walk through the valley of the shadow of death, I will fear no evil, for thou art with me, thy rod and thy staff they comfort me."   May God give you this light through the journey of this life, and bring you to that city of light and life on high.

QUESTIONS.—Why did the people of the East carry lanterns at night? What did David call the Bible? Should the lantern be held above the head, or down near the feet? Which is the best light to our spiritual pathway, human wisdom or Divine revelation? Which is the safer light for us to follow, books which men write, or the book which God has given us? Can we understand all that we find in the book of nature? Can we understand all that we find in the book of revelation? Do they both have the same author? Is God infinitely greater than man? Does this explain to you why we cannot understand all that God has done or said? Can we put a bushel basket into a quart measure?—the smaller can not contain the larger.

CANDLES.

HOW TO REFLECT, OBSCURE, OR EXTINGUISH THE LIGHT.

SUGGESTIONS—A candle, a silver dollar, a large-necked bottle and a flask-shaped bottle are the objects used. It will add to the interest of the children if the parent will show the simple experiments of placing the bottle over the candle to illustrate how quickly the light is extinguished as the oxygen is exhausted. The same is the result when a light is hid under a bushel. The flame may also be concealed by the dollar; and in a darkened room a polished piece of metal or a small looking-glass will show how the light can be reflected by money properly used in Christ's cause.

MY LITTLE MEN AND WOMEN: To-day I have brought some candles in order to illustrate the text, "Ye are the light of the world." In a previous sermon I have shown you how all the light in the world is derived from the sun, and how all the light in the spiritual world is derived from Jesus Christ. Now, to-day I want to show you that we can extinguish this light. While we cannot prevent the sun from shining, or put out the light there is in the sun, yet we can extinguish, or put out the light of a candle. We can blow out the light, we can turn off the gas, we can cut off the electrical current, and thus prevent the carbon from burning and giving light. Just the same as the firemen can extinguish a large fire that is making a great blaze in the midst of a dark night, so we can put out these several lights.

Before this candle, which I hold in my hand, can be of any service to me in giving light, it must first itself be lighted. So it is with every person who is born into this world. He has no light in himself. Before ever he can exert any influence for good upon

145

others, or let any Christian light shine, he must come to the Lord Jesus Christ and receive this light. He must be lighted from above. But now after the candle has been lighted, suppose that I take this silver dollar which I hold in my hand, and place it in front of the light, you will see immediately how it makes it impossible for the light to shine out in front of the dollar. Those who are sitting down there in front of me cannot see this light. The light is entirely concealed by the dollar. So some people allow the love of money to gather around their hearts, until at last their money is placed between them and the peo-

ple whom God intends that they should benefit and bless in this world. Instead of being a help, their money is only a hindrance to their Christian life. They love their money so much that they permit the poor to go hungry, the destitute to be unblessed, and the Church to be without the money nec-

Light Obscured by Money.

essary to carry on its work. They allow the heathen to die in their ignorance. Selfishly grasping their money, they neglect to do that for which God has given them the means and the money.

I believe that money is a good thing. The Bible says that it is the *love* of money, the undue love of it, that is the root of all evil. Money itself is a blessing and not a curse; therefore I want to show you how this dollar can be made to help in making this light shine even more brightly. You will see that if I have this side of the dollar ground off and polished, so that it is very smooth and bright like a little looking-glass, and then place it back of the candle, instead of acting as it did when I placed the dollar between you and the candle, it will then reflect the light and throw the rays of light out further than they could otherwise shine. It helps to accomplish for the candle the same important service which the great reflector does when placed behind the lamp in the headlight of the railway engine, throwing the light way down the track in advance of the coming of the train.

In the same way, when a Christian has money, you see how he can readily use it in such a way as to enable him to accomplish a very great and grand work in the world. The man who has lots of money and has a conse- crated heart, and who is willing to use his money to help him in his work for Christ, will be able to accomplish very much more than the man who has no money. He can use his money in such a way that it will enable him to cast a light in many a dark corner of the earth, to

Money as a Reflector.

bring light in many a desolate home, and to cast the rays of his Christian influence even across the ocean into benighted heathen lands. In this way his money can be used as I could use this dollar if it were polished, and thus carry his influence to the ends of the earth and to the end of time, and become a great blessing to himself and to others for all eternity.

Jesus said, "Men do not light a candle and put it under a bushel, but on a candle-stick that it may give light to all that are in the house." There are some people who do not like to let their light shine for Christ. They do not want others to know that they are Christians. They do not want others to know that they are trying to be good. And so they seek to conceal their light, to hide it, as Jesus says, "under a bushel." If you were to light a candle and put it under a bushel, or under a box, the box would prevent it from shining, and therefore you would not know that there was any light at all in the room.

But I want to show you, by the aid of this large necked bottle,

Light Under a Bushel.

what is the effect of our trying to hide our light. I have chosen this bottle because you can see through it, and observe what is going on inside of this glass bushel or bottle. The neck being very large, you can readily see that the light is not absolutely smothered. Now, when I place this bottle over the light, you will see how very quickly it begins to grow dim, and then more dim until it dies out altogether. There, you see, it has gone out already! Just as quickly as it burns out from the air in the bottle the oxygen which it contains, the light dies, because it has nothing to feed upon. If I had not placed this bottle over it, it would have continued to burn.

Just so it is with those who try to hide their light under a bushel. After the light has been placed there, it gradually grows more faint, and more faint, and then goes out in darkness. You can never be a Christian if you are ashamed of Christ. You must be willing to let your light shine; you must be willing to confess Christ before men; you must be willing to have other boys and girls know that you are a Christian, and that you are trying to do right. Then with God's help you will succeed. But if you try to hide your light under a bushel, you will never succeed in being a Christian.

Here is another bottle. I am sure that the shape of this bottle will suggest to you the kind of stuff which is oftentimes sold in this kind of a flask. Sometimes when young men have given their hearts to Christ, and young women too for that matter, they go out in company and are invited to take a drink of wine or a drink of beer, or something else, and without any purpose or thought of ever becoming a drunkard, often they soon form the habit of drinking. Soon they have formed a love for the taste of liquor, and before ever they know it, like hundreds of thousands of others who have preceded them, they have become fond of liquor, and are on a fair road to become drunkards. As soon as a young man starts out in this direction he takes the road that leads down to death and destruction, and the love of God which he had in his

A Dangerous Bottle.

heart soon dies out. Let me place this bottle over the candle. You will now see how the candle begins to grow dim, and the light shines more and more dim, after a very few seconds, you will find that it goes out in darkness, the same as it did under the other bottle.

Let me say to you, always carefully avoid the terrible and destructive influences of drink, of which this bottle is the symbol. If you want to keep the love of God in your heart you must never,

never take the first step which leads toward the love of liquor, toward intemperance and a drunkard's grave.

QUESTIONS.—Can an unlighted candle give light? Can a candle light itself? Who must first give us the light if we are to be a light to the world? Can the light of the candle shine through a silver dollar? If a silver dollar is polished like a little looking-glass and placed behind the light, what does it do? Does this suggest how we can use our money to send the light to the heathen? Under what kind of a measure does the Bible warn against hiding our light? When people light a candle, do they put it under a bushel or on a candlestick? If it is put under a bushel what is the result? Is that the result with people who are ashamed to be known as Christians? Does intoxicating drink often put out the light of Christian people? How can all persons avoid the use of liquor? (By never taking the first glass.)

Daniel in the Lion's Den.

A BROKEN CHAIN.

BREAKING THE WHOLE LAW.

SUGGESTION:—A chain of any kind, even a watch chain, will answer. Children could use paste-board and cut out ten links to represent the Ten Commandments. These links could be numbered and the older children could be asked to repeat the Ten Commandments in their order.

MY LITTLE MEN AND WOMEN: I have here a chain; it is very strong indeed. It has ten links in it. You will remember how that, more than three thousand years ago, God gave the Ten Commandments to Moses on Mt. Sinai. These Ten Commandments are often called the Decalogue, because there are ten of them; the Greek word *deka* means ten.

Now the Bible tells us that "whosoever will keep the whole law, and yet offend in one point, he is guilty of all." (James ii: 10.)

A Broken Chain.

When a boy, I often wondered how it was that when a person broke one of the Commandments he was guilty of breaking the whole law. I could not understand it. Now, I desire to illustrate this truth to you to-day. Suppose that I were suspended over the edge of a great rock by this chain. If the chain should break, I would be plunged headlong, hundreds of feet down a very great

"Suspended Over the Edge of a Great Rock."

embankment, upon rocks at the bottom of the chasm, and lose my life. You will readily see that it would not be necessary to break every link in this chain before I would begin to fall. In order to break this chain, it is only necessary to break a single link. The moment one link breaks, the entire continuity of the chain is broken.

I think you will see that it is just the same way with the law of God. If you break one of these Commandments, you have broken the law. If you fail to "remember the Sabbath day to keep it holy," or if you disobey your parents, and thus break the Commandment which says, "honor thy father and thy mother," or any other of the Commandments—if you break a single one, you have broken the entire chain of the Ten Commandments.

Now, there are a great many laws in this land of ours. There are laws against murder, and there are laws against stealing, and there are laws against getting drunk, and thousands of other laws. If a man simply steals and should be caught in the act and brought before the judge, he would be convicted of the crime and be sent to prison. It is not necessary that a man should be a murderer and a thief and a robber, and should be guilty of breaking all the laws of this land, before he is cast in prison. It is simply enough that he should have violated one law. By breaking only one law he becomes a criminal, and therefore he is cast into prison. The man who has committed but one murder has his entire liberty taken from him. The man who has been caught in the act of stealing but a single time is adjudged a thief, and all his liberty is taken from him.

So I think you will see that, in order to become a criminal, it is not necessary that we should break all the laws of the land, but if we break a single law we become criminals. So it is with the law of God; if we break only one of the Ten Commandments we are criminals before God, we are guilty of all.

Now the laws which men make in this and every other country are human laws. They are not absolutely perfect. They are changed and improved from time to time. But the Psalmist tells us, and we all know it to be true, that "The law of the Lord is perfect," and God requires us to keep His law. He says, "My son forget not my law, but let thine heart keep my commandments; for length of days and long life and peace, shall they add to thee." (Prov. iii: 1.) If you and I are faithful in the keeping of God's law, then we can say like David, "I shall not be ashamed when I have respect unto all of thy commandments." (Psalm cxix: 6.)

Now, if I take this chain, and attempt to break it, I find that God has not given me sufficient strength. Samson could have snapped it in a moment, but I am not strong enough. God has given to some men much more strength than to others.

If I were to pull very hard on this chain so as to break it, where do you suppose it would break first? Why the weakest link in the entire chain would be the first to break. No chain is stronger than its weakest link. So it is with you and with me, our greatest goodness is no greater than our greatest weakness. When men want to think how good they are, they think of the best things they have ever done. But the fact is that no man is better than the worst things he has ever done. A man who has committed murder is a murderer. He might have done hundreds of good things, but the law does not estimate him by the best things he has done. The law estimates that man by the worst thing he has done, and by that worst thing he is judged and condemned. And so it is with you and me before God. The worst things which we have ever done will be the things which will condemn us in the sight of the Judge of all the world.

While I am not able to break this metal chain, yet God has made it possible for every person to break the chain of the moral law. God has given human freedom to all men; He has told us what we should do, but He has left us free to obey or to disobey.

Now, when we examine into the requirements of the Ten Commandments, we find that everybody has violated some one or more of them at some time. There is not a man or woman or child any where who is not guilty of having broken God's law. And when I turn to the Scriptures, I find in Galatians the third chapter, 10th verse, that God says, "Cursed is every one that continueth not in all things which are written in the book of the law to do them." I see then by God's Word that we are all sinners, that we are all guilty before God, because we have violated His law, and next Sunday I will tell you what is to be done in view of the fact that we are all guilty before God.

QUESTIONS.—What are the different parts of a chain called? How many links must be broken in order to break the chain? What did God give to Moses on Mount Sinai? How many commandments are there? Who makes the laws for the nation, the state and the city? Are laws perfect which are made by men? Do human laws change? Is God's law perfect? Do moral laws ever change? Was there ever a time or a place where it was right to lie, or steal or murder? Will there ever be such a time or place? How many murders must a man commit before he is a murderer? How often must he steal before he is a thief? Are men put into prison for breaking a single law? Is the entirety of God's law violated if we break only one commandment?

LOOKING-GLASS.

SEEING OURSELVES IN GOD'S LAW.

SUGGESTION:—The object used is a looking-glass of any desired size.

MY DEAR BOYS AND GIRLS: In my sermon last Sunday, I showed you that God had made the law perfect, but that none of us has perfectly kept the law, that we have all broken the law, and God has said, "Cursed is every one that continueth not in all things which are written in the book of the law to do them." (Gal. iii: 10.)

If the law is perfect, and no one has ever kept it perfectly, but all have broken the law in some one way or another, and on that account all are guilty before God, you may ask, what is the purpose of the law? Why did God make the law? Now, I desire to explain that to you to-day.

I have here a looking-glass. Now the Bible compares the law to a looking-glass. In the epistle or letter of James, in the first chapter, we are told, "If any be a hearer of the word, and not a doer, he is like unto a man beholding his natural face in a glass; for he beholdeth himself, and goeth his way, and straightway forgetteth what manner of man he was. But whoso looketh into the perfect law of liberty, and continueth therein, he being not a forgetful hearer, but a doer of the work, this man shall be blessed in his deed." (James i: 23-25.)

In other words, the Bible means to say that the law of God is like a looking-glass. When we read the law of God, we see just what God requires that we should both be and do. He enables

156

Copyrighted, 1911, by Sylvanus Stall.

Seeing Ourselves in the Looking-Glass of God's Law

us to see what He requires of us. It shows us also how imperfect we are. It shows us our sins. It reveals to us the importance of doing something in order to get rid of our sins.

It is just like a man whose face is all dirty. When he goes to the looking-glass and looks into it he sees the dirt upon his face. If he did not look into the glass, other people might see that his face was dirty, but he would not see it himself. But when he looks into the glass, he sees for himself that his face is all black and dirty.

Now, when the man finds that his face is all dirty, he does not take the looking-glass with which to wash his face. The looking-glass was not made to wash our faces with. It was only made to show us that our faces needed to be washed. And then, instead of using the looking-glass to wash our faces, we go and use soap and water.

Now, the looking-glass did not make the man's face black, neither will it wash his face. It simply shows him that his face is dirty.

So it is with the law of God. The law of God does not make us sinful. We are sinful, whether there be any law or not. The law is simply designed to show us that we are sinners, and that we are wicked, and that we need a Saviour. And when this law reveals to us our sin, and shows us our need of a Saviour, it purposes, as we are told in the Scriptures, to lead us to Christ (Galatians iii: 24.) No man can cleanse or wash away his sins by the aid of the law. But the law plainly shows him his sins, and then leads him to Christ—to the fountain which has been opened for sin and uncleanness. It is all very beautifully expressed in that hymn which, I trust, you all know:

"There is a fountain filled with blood,
Drawn from Immanuel's veins;
And sinners plunged beneath that flood,
Lose all their guilty stains."

Now, I want to tell you the effect of coming to this fountain and washing. When we come to Christ our sins and guilt are washed away, and we become more like Christ. And then we grow up into His likeness and into His image. (Eph. iv: 13.) We become more and more like the Lord Jesus Christ from day to day. This change which takes place in our hearts and in our lives is very wonderful. We cannot understand it, but we cease to be intentionally wicked. More and more we become holy. It is this wonderful change which is referred to in Second Corinthians, third chapter and the 18th verse, where it says, "But we all, with open face beholding as in a glass the glory of the Lord, are changed into the same image from glory to glory, even as by the Spirit of the Lord."

I think now, you will understand why we have the law. It is not to make us wicked, for we are wicked already. But it is to show us our wickedness, it is to reveal to us the fact that we are sinners, and that we are lost and undone without a Saviour. And then it reveals the Lord Jesus Christ to us, and we come to Him, the same as men with blackened faces go to the fountain to wash. So we come with our sins and our guilt "to the fountain which has been opened for sin and uncleanness," and we wash all our sins and guilt away; and then we are changed into His image and into His likeness, from glory to glory, until at last, in the world on high, we awake in the likeness of Jesus.

QUESTIONS.—To what does the Bible compare the law of God? For what purpose do people use a looking-glass? What does a man whose face is dirty see in the glass? What does it show that his face needs? Does it suggest that he should wash his face with the looking-glass? What does he use with which to wash his face? What does God's law show us? Does the law make us sinful? Can the law remove the effects of sin? Who is the fountain for the cleansing of our sin? Are we saved by the law, or by the grace of God?

RAIN.

GOD'S WISDOM AND POWER.

SUGGESTION:—A bottle partly filled with dust from the roadway will help to illustrate the condition which would quite universally prevail if the earth were not refreshed with frequent rains.

MY DEAR YOUNG FRIENDS: In view of the fact that the weather is so very warm, the earth so dried and parched and we have had no rain for a period of weeks, I thought it might be useful to-day to consider what would be the result if God should withhold the rain altogether, and then to tell you how, or in what manner God brings us the rain and refreshes the earth and makes it fruitful.

In order that you might see something of the present condition of the earth, I have brought in this bottle some dust, taken from the centre of the road. As I turn the bottle around, you see how dry it is and how it floats in the air, leaving the inside of this bottle all powdered with dust. The dust in this bottle is only a sample of what all the earth would soon become, if God did not send rain at frequent intervals throughout the year. I suppose you could all tell me of a number of instances in the Old Testament where we have accounts of drouths that extended throughout a period of years, and of the hunger and famine and death which followed.

When you are out of doors and look about you, you cannot but be impressed with how dry and dusty the trees and grass and everything about you is. If this dry weather were to continue long you could understand that soon everything would wither and die,

161

and if it were to continue for a few years, men and beasts would not only die of thirst, but even the air itself would suck out from our bodies the moisture that is in our blood, and death would speedily follow. But if you were to remove all the moisture from the air, the earth would not only become barren, but it would become intensely cold. It is due to the moisture which is in the atmosphere that the warmth which comes to the earth from the sun is retained near the earth after the sun has gone down. If it were not so, even in a summer's night after the sun has gone down, the coldness which exists above the clouds would quickly come in contact with the earth, and the cold would become so intense that every person and every living thing would be in danger of being frozen to death in a single night.

You will remember that the great Sahara Desert is a vast tract of thousands of square miles where no rain falls, and where the heat is intense. There is, however, much moisture in the air that floats over the plains, but the reason that no rain falls is because there are no mountains in that portion of the globe for thousands of miles.

Now suppose that there were to be no rain at all, and people should undertake to water the earth by bringing the water from the rivers. On an average of about thirty-three inches of rain fall upon the surface of the entire earth each year, in some places more, in others less. The weight of this water in one single square mile would be nearly two and one-half millions of tons, and if this water which falls upon one single square mile had to be drawn in cars, it would require 100,000 carloads of water to keep this one single mile as wet as God usually keeps it throughout the year by the rain from heaven. I think you will see, from what I have said, that all the cars in the entire United States, and there are hundreds of thousands of them, would not be sufficient to haul water from the rivers for any considerable distance to keep more than ten miles square of earth watered. But you can also see that if all these cars were to be run on a piece of ground only ten miles square, that entire piece of ground would be almost completely covered with railroad tracks, and we would scarcely be able to raise anything on it in the way of grain or vegetables or food of any kind. But even if we could successfully water ten miles square of land, what would that be compared with the absolute necessity of watering the entire continent and all the continents of the globe in order to make life possible upon the earth. Now the question arises, how does God accomplish this great result?

Train of Cars.

I suppose you have all noticed the teakettle when it is upon the stove and the steam is coming out of the spout, and around the lid. You have there had a practical demonstration of how God can cause the water, which is 800 times heavier than the atmosphere or the air, to rise and float, for you know that any substance heavier than air will always fall to the earth. In the instance of the teakettle you will see how heat causes the water to become steam and thus to rise in the air and float away, rising to the height of the clouds which float two, three and four and sometimes more miles high above the earth.

Now, just in this same way God makes the heat from the rays of the sun to cause that from every river and lake and all the expanse of the ocean, as well as from the surface of the earth, there shall constantly arise a very fine vapor, which, although it is somewhat like steam, is still so much finer that you and I c a n n o t see it with our unaided eyes. It is by means of this vapor that God raises the moisture from the oceans and all bodies of water and from the earth, to fall again in gentle showers.

Steam Rising from Teakettle.

But when this vapor has been lifted up from the ocean, you will see readily that if it were to descend again in rain upon the very places from which it had been lifted it would accomplish no good. It is necessary that instead of falling back into the ocean and into the lakes and rivers, it must be carried over the land. So you see that we might aptly compare the vapor to a great pump, by means of which God lifts millions of gallons of water every hour from the sea into the atmosphere.

Now just the same as men load grain and fruit and other things into the cars to ship them to some distant place, so God loads these vapors into the atmosphere or into the clouds. When the clouds are all loaded with vapor, or that which is to descend upon the earth in the form of rain, God sends the winds, and these winds blow the clouds from over the ocean far inward over the land until they come to the place where God wants to pour them out in showers and rain, and in snow and blessing.

But now, you will see that there is another difficulty. When all this vast quantity of water is held in the clouds, a mile or two above the earth, if it were to be poured out, it would come with such

Clouds and Rain.

force upon the earth that it would destroy every living thing. Now, as God used the warmth from the sun as His agent to lift the water into the clouds, so also, when He desires to unload the clouds, to pour the rain upon the earth, He causes the warm air which carries the water to be blown upon by the colder air which floats above it, and as the heat lifted the water, so the cold causes it to descend; and immediately it begins to form as clouds, one particle or atom of moisture touches another, and the two form the larger atom, and these again unite with others, until finally a drop is formed, and it begins to descend and comes down in gentle showers upon the earth as though it were sifted through a very fine sieve. These small drops fall upon the earth so gently as not even to bruise the leaf of the tenderest flower or the tenderest insect that walks upon the earth.

Possibly some children may not fully understand, but the older ones will get some idea of the vast quantity of water which God pours upon the earth, when they are reminded that all the water that flows in the rivers has been let down from the clouds. God is daily pumping up from the ocean and other bodies of water rivers as vast as the combined waters of the Mississippi, Missouri, Susquehanna, the Hudson, and every creek and streamlet and river that flows, not only on this continent, but in all the world. And God is doing this constantly by His own infinite wisdom and infinite might. The machinery with which men pump the water from the river for the supply of a single city wears out; but these great engines with which God is constantly keeping the earth supplied with water for man and beast, for tree and flower, for garden and field, never wear out. Truly with the prophet we may exclaim: "He that calleth for the waters of the sea, and poureth them out on the face of the land: the Lord is His name." (Amos v: 8.)

From what I have said I think you will all see how constantly we are dependent upon God for everything which we enjoy. If God were to withhold the rain or the sunshine, famine and want and death would soon follow. Yet in the most wonderful way God is constantly providing that with which we are daily to be fed and always to be clothed. God is not unmindful of us. He never forgets, but in His own good time and in His own most wondrous way He sends us the rain and every needed blessing.

God never forgets us, but I fear that we often forget Him and forget when we drink the refreshing glass of clear, cool water, that it is God who gave it to us. When you sit down at the table, do you remember that it is God who gives you the food, and do you thank Him for the food which He gives you, or do you, like the unmannerly boy who receives a gift and never thanks the donor, sit down and eat and go away without ever thanking God the Giver? When He watches over and keeps you during the night, do you forget to kneel down and thank Him in the morning? When day after day He clothes you, do you thank him? When He feeds and clothes you, do you love and serve Him, or do you accept of these blessings and then run off and serve Satan, God's great enemy?

These are serious questions, and I trust you will think seriously of them, and daily, when you receive God's blessings, that you will turn to Him in grateful thanksgiving and faithful service.

QUESTIONS.—What would the entire earth become if there should be no rain? If all moisture were removed from the atmosphere, what would be the result? What is the average rainfall? What is the weight of rainfall in a single square mile? How many cars would it require to carry water for one square mile? How does God accomplish this? How is the water raised up from the sea and the rivers? Can you explain it by the teakettle? Where does God store this vapor? How do the clouds carry the moisture to the places which need it? How does the moisture in the clouds fall? Does God do all things wisely and well? Is God ever unmindful of our needs? Do you ever forget to thank Him? Do you always remember to serve Him?

SNOW.

THE LESSONS WHICH IT TEACHES.

M Y DEAR BOYS AND GIRLS: When God desired to set Job to thinking, among other questions He asked him: Canst thou enter into the treasures of the snow? (Job xxxviii: 22.) While coming to church to-day, when I saw you frolicking and glad in the midst of the snow, which was falling all about you, I wondered whether you had ever stopped to think much about the snow. So I thought to ask you the question which God asked of Job nearly thirty-five hundred years ago: "Hast thou entered into the treasures of the snow?"

When you were all so glad on account of this first snowstorm of the winter, did you stop to think that the snow comes from God? Now like everything else which comes from God, the snow is wonderful. No philosopher has ever yet been able fully to explain how the snow is formed and to tell us all about it, and I do not suppose that all the mysteries concerning it will ever be fully and perfectly solved. It is wonderful, however, because it comes down so lightly and noiselessly. It drops upon the earth almost like feathers, covering the ground, hanging upon the limbs of the trees and shaping them into things of strange beauty, piling up on the post by the side of your gate, until perhaps it looks more like the white man from the flour mill than like that to which people tie horses. Yet it comes down so noiselessly that we scarcely notice it.

When the snow falls upon the ground a foot deep it is said to be equal in weight to one inch of rain. Now one foot of snow, on

168

one square mile of street, would weigh, it is estimated, about sixty-four thousand tons. If this snow, which covers only one square mile, were placed in wagons loaded with one ton each, and allowing sufficient space for these teams to move one behind another, these wagons would make a string or procession reaching from Philadelphia to New York, and from New York up the Hudson River almost to the city of Albany. I am sure you will be astonished at this, but when you consider that some snowstorms cover thousands of square miles, and are sometimes more than one foot deep, you will see how increasingly wonderful it is that all this great weight falls so gently upon the earth as to produce no disturbance, no shock, and generally goes away as quietly and peaceably as it came.

Like everything else that God has made, the snow is very beautiful. Did you ever hear that poem which begins:

> "Beautiful snow! beautiful snow!
>   Falling so lightly,
>   Daily and nightly,
> Alike 'round the dwellings of the lofty and low;
>   Horses are prancing,
>   Cheerily dancing,
> Stirred with the spirit that comes from the snow."

We oftentimes think that God is seen in the fields and flowers in the spring and summer, but He is also seen in the beautiful snow of winter. If you will let some of the snow fall upon the sleeve of your coat and then examine it carefully, you will be surprised at its beauty. It is beautiful when examined without a microscope, but much more beautiful and wonderful when examined with a microscope. Each flake is fashioned into stellar shape. It is formed and fashioned by the same hand which made the stars of the heavens and gave them their sparkle and beauty. Each

11

flake is a beautiful crystal. Each somewhat like the others, and yet no two exactly alike. There are hundreds of varieties, each beautiful and all glorious. These beautiful little snow stars are all formed with perfect geometrical accuracy. Some have three sides and angles, some six, others eight, and some have more. One resembles a sparkling cross, while others seem almost like the leaves of an open flower. Some are like single stars, others like double stars and clusters of stars; and although the ground in winter is covered with myriads of them, yet each one is formed with as much

correctness and beauty as if God had made each one for special examination and as an exhibition of His infinite skill and divine perfection.

But like everything else that God has made, the snow is also useful. You may possibly have thought of it as affording excellent sport in

Snow-flakes Magnified.

sliding down hill, enabling you to enjoy a sleigh ride behind horses with jingling bells, affording opportunity for a snowball fight, or as furnishing the material for making snow men or snow houses. In all these ways the snow is a source of delight and pleasure to boys and girls, but after all, the snow has a special mission in the world during the severe cold of the winter.

The severity of the cold is often greatly modified by the presence of snow. The snow forms a warm mantle to protect the grass

A Winter Sleigh Ride.

and grain fields. It wraps its soft warm covering around the plants, and thus protects them from the frost. Many animals also take shelter in the banks of snow, and are thus kept from being frozen to death. The snow of winter is as important in securing our food and blessing as the rain of the summer. As intense heat and the absence of rain produce the great deserts of the earth, so intense cold and the absence of snow would produce barren tracts upon the earth.

Now, what are the lessons we may learn from what I have said? I think the first lesson that we may learn is that God does everything perfectly. God is not in a hurry, as boys and girls often are when they do not take time to learn their lessons thoroughly or to do their work carefully. Perfection is one of God's attributes. We are impatient and imperfect. But God wants us to be perfect. We should constantly strive after perfection. We are to seek after perfection here upon earth, and although we cannot hope to attain it fully in this world, yet we shall attain unto it in the world of blessedness beyond. Remember that whatever is worth doing at all is worth doing well.

I think the second lesson that we may learn from what I have said, is that God does everything with some good purpose in view. God not only has a purpose in all that He does, but He has a purpose for good. Some boys and girls do things with a bad purpose. Now, God does not do anything with a bad purpose, and He would not have us do anything with a bad purpose. He has given us life and being upon the earth in order that we may accomplish something grand and good. What is the purpose of your life? What have you resolved to make the object which you shall seek to attain in this life? Have some noble purpose, some high aim in life. Whatever it shall be, let it always have in view the blessing and good of others and the glory of God.

The last lesson from this study of the snow is that God has made it a symbol of purity. God is pure, and He wants us to be pure. Do you put tobacco in your mouth? Then your mouth is not pure. Do you use bad words? If so, your mouth is not pure. Do you use your eyes to read worthless story papers and books, or to look at evil pictures? Then your eyes and thoughts are not pure. Do you permit your ears to listen to improper talk? Then your ears and mind are not pure. Do you harbor bad thoughts in your heart? Then your heart is not pure. Do you defile your body by improper eating and drinking? If you do, then your body is not pure. If you and I desire to be pure, we must go to God and earnestly ask Him as David did when he cried unto God and said, "Purge me with hyssop, and I shall be clean: wash me and I shall be whiter than snow."

Now let us sing this beautiful hymn:

"Wash me and I shall be whiter than the snow."

QUESTIONS.—About what did God ask Job, to set him thinking? Where does the snow come from? Does anyone know fully how the snow is formed? Is the snow as wonderful as it is beautiful? What do the flakes look like? Are they all formed alike? Are any two exactly alike? How is the snow useful in winter? Is snow as important in the winter as rain in the summer? Is God ever in a hurry? Are you always patient? What is worth doing well? Does God always have a purpose in whatever He does? Does God expect us to have a noble purpose? Of what is snow the symbol? Does God expect us all to be pure?

PLASTIC FACE.

CHARACTER IN THE COUNTENANCE.

SUGGESTION:—The object used is a small plastic face such as are often sold in toy stores, and even on the streets in large cities. The head of a rubber doll would also answer the purpose.

A couple of pictures of faces placed in bottles would illustrate the fact that as the faces are seen through the bottles, so our thoughts are not wholly hidden but shine through our faces.

MY DEAR BOYS AND GIRLS: Here is a soft plastic face; by squeezing it on the side I can make the face very long, and it looks very sober. If I place the face between my thumb and fingers and press upon the chin and forehead it makes the face short, and makes it have a very pleasant appearance. I can make it look as though it were laughing, or make it seem to be angry and cross.

Just so is it with our faces. When we feel pleasant our faces are short and drawn up; when we feel sober, or cross, or angry, they are lengthened and the character of the expression is entirely changed. You would scarcely know the face were you to see it radiant with smiles and pleasantness, and afterwards see the same face when the person is cross or angered. When you look at a person you can tell whether they are in good humor, or whether they are displeased or angry.

Do you know, boys and girls, that our character and our disposition are seen in our faces? It is impossible for us to conceal our

174

real selves, even though we might try. I will tell you how it is. If I were again and again to press this face only in this way, so as to make it look very long, after a time it would retain this expression. If I were to press it in this other way, so as to make it very short and give it a very pleasant expression, and were to hold it in that position for a very long time, it would assume that expression, and

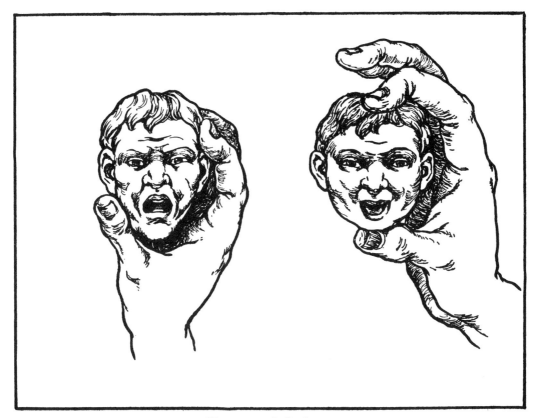

Frowns and Smiles.

retain it constantly. It is just so with our faces. When a boy is angered again and again the deep lines of his face become more and more permanent, until after a time he comes to have a face which expresses anger. If a boy is kind and good and generous, these feelings express themselves in his face, and if repeated over and over again, day after day and year after year, it becomes a permanent expression upon his face and the boy is known by all who meet him as a good-natured, pleasant and agreeable boy.

I suppose that most all the boys and girls here can tell a minister when they meet him on the street. And when you grow older I think you will not only be able to tell that it is a minister, but you may be able to tell, possibly to what denomination the man belongs —whether he is a Methodist, or a Presbyterian, or an Episcopalian or a Lutheran, or to what denomination he belongs. This cannot always be told, but in many instances this can be judged quite accurately. The study of the Bible and the contemplation of holy and good things inscribe themselves indelibly upon the face of those who give them thought and attention.

Beneath a good and generous face you will find a good and generous heart. Beneath a bad face you will find a bad heart. If we are Christians we shall become more and more like Christ. We shall grow up into His likeness, and into His image, and into His stature. We are told that not only will we become more and more like Him, but that at last, in the great Resurrection, we shall behold Him as He is, and we shall be like Him.

If I were to take some pictures and place them in a bottle they would shine out through the glass, and you could see them. So with the thoughts that are in your heart; they shine out through your face and give expressions to it. Even when the body is suffering pain the heart may be at rest. David, the Psalmist, said that God was "the health of his countenance." Even though his body was suffering pain his face might be pleasant, because God was with him, making him happy in his heart. There is an old adage that says, "handsome is, that handsome does." There are some young persons who may have a pretty face, and yet who may not be righteous and holy in their hearts; but as they grow older their character will shine out more and more, until at last their face shall be entirely changed, and all that is bad in their hearts will appear in their faces. If you want a good face you must have a good heart. Take Jesus into your heart, follow His teachings and imitate His example, and from year to year you will grow more and more like Him. Here is a very appropriate and beautiful poem, which was written by Miss Alice Carey.

TAKE CARE.

"Little children, you must seek
  Rather to be good than wise,
For the thoughts you do not speak
  Shine out in your cheeks and eyes.

"If you think that you can be
  Cross or cruel, and look fair,
Let me tell you how to see
  You are quite mistaken there.

"Go and stand before the glass,
  And some ugly thought contrive,
And my word will come to pass
  Just as sure as you're alive!

"What you have and what you lack,
  All the same as what you wear,
You will see reflected back;
  So, my little folks, take care!

"And not only in the glass
  Will your secrets come to view;
All beholders, as they pass,
  Will perceive and know them, too.

"Out of sight, my boys and girls,
  Every root of beauty starts;
So think less about your curls,
  More about your minds and hearts.

"Cherish what is good, and drive
    Evil thoughts and feelings far;
For, as sure as you're alive,
    You will show for what you are."

QUESTIONS.—How will a plastic face look when you squeeze it on the head and on the chin? When persons are serious or angry, are their faces lengthened? When people laugh what happens to their faces? Suppose one were to be cross and ugly constantly what would occur? If a person were to laugh constantly, what would be the effect upon their face? Can you tell a minister when you see him? If you put pictures in a bottle do they shine through? Do thoughts in the heart shine through the face? Can you repeat that couplet which begins: "Handsome is—"? If we think Christ's thoughts constantly do we become more like Christ? If we think bad thoughts do we become unlike Him? What book is it which says: "As a man thinketh in his heart, so is he"?

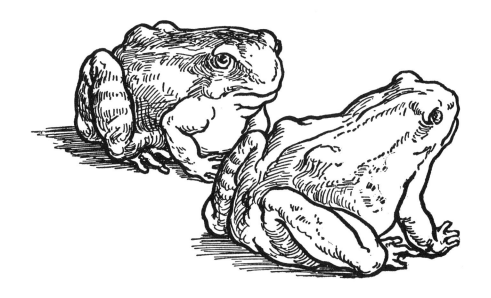

SEEDS.

THOUGHTS, WORDS, DEEDS—THEIR LIFE AND PERPETUITY.

SUGGESTION:—Seeds, or grain and fruit of any kind can be used for illustration.

MY YOUNG FRIENDS: I have here to-day quite a variety of seeds. Some of them are very small, and some, as you see, are quite large. The seeds of each class have in them a principle of life, which makes them differ from sand, or small stones of similar size, because if I plant these seeds in the ground they will grow.

Different Kinds of Seeds.

When you take different kinds of seeds, there is one thing that is very interesting a b o u t them. It is the different kinds of coverings in which they grow. For instance, if you take a chestnut, it grows in a burr with s h a r p thorny points; others are folded as though rolled up very tightly in leaves, as you will find in the hazel nut or filbert. Some seeds grow in rows, like beans and peas in a pod. Some grow in a very soft bed, like cotton seeds. Some grow imbedded in a downy substance which blows all around, carrying the seed with it, like the thistle, and the light fuzz of the dandelion. Sometimes the seed is buried in the inside of fruit, as in the case of apples, pears, peaches, plums, and various other kinds of fruit. Sometimes it is buried beneath the beautiful leaves of the flower. So you see there is great variety.

Now, these seeds may represent words. There are a great many varieties of words. All words have the principle of life in them, because they express thought; and these thoughts when received into our minds develop into action. Therefore we say that words have a principle of life in them, and it is important that we should be careful not to permit bad words to have a place in our minds. Very often you will see boys and girls reading worthless papers which they think will do them no injury. But the fact is, that these boys are influenced in all their living by that which they read in these papers. It might be very light and trifling, but it tends to corrupt the mind, to give the boy false ideas of life, and it gives him such opinions as are not real, and therefore very injurious to any one. It is much better that a boy's valuable time should be spent in reading good books and good papers, and securing such information as will be of value and assistance to him all through life. For the life of every boy and of every girl is a very great struggle, and no boy or girl can afford to waste time in the beginning. If they are ever to amount to anything in this world, it is important that they should begin very early in life.

I want to call your attention to another characteristic of these seeds. And that is when a single seed is planted, it grows up and produces a very great number of other seeds. If you plant a seed of wheat, it will produce 30, 60, or sometimes 100 other seeds. If you plant one sunflower seed it might produce as many as 4,000 seeds. If you plant one single thistle seed, it has been known to produce as high as 24,000 seeds in a single summer. If you were to plant only one grain of corn and let it grow until it is ripe, and then plant the seeds again which grew on these few ears of corn, and thus continue to re-plant again and again, we are told by those who have calculated it very carefully, that in only five short years the amount of corn that could be grown as the result of the planting of the one single seed would be sufficient to plant a hill of corn, with three grains in every square yard of all the dry land on all the earth. In ten years the product would be sufficient to plant not only this entire world, both land and sea, but all the planets, or worlds which circle around our sun, and some of them are even a thousand times larger than our own globe. So you see that there is wonderful multiplying power in the different kinds of grain which you plant.

So it is with the thoughts and the words which we have in our minds. Good thoughts enter into good acts, and these acts influence others just as though the same thought was sown into their minds, and then it springs up into their lives and influences them. Just so when we have read a book, whether the book is good or bad, its influence goes on reproducing itself, over and over again in our lives, every time in a multiplied form. Suppose with your money you send some Bibles to the heathen, and as a result a single person is converted. Immediately that person would influence other heathen people whom he would meet, and so, one after the other, these heathen would be influenced as the result of what you have done. This good influence would go on repeating itself over and over again, as long as the world shall stand, and only in eternity would the wonderful results of what you have done be fully known. So it is with all that we say and all that we do; it goes on repeating and multiplying itself over and over again.

Now, there is another interesting feature of these seeds to

which I want to call your attention.   And that is that the life in the seed may continue for a very long time, even hundreds of years.

Pyramids.

Over in Egypt, centuries ago, they built large pyramids, and when a king died, instead of burying his body in the ground, they

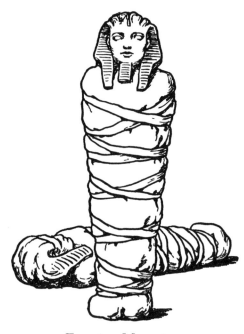

Egyptian Mummies.

embalmed it with spices and dried it, so that it would not decay. Then they wrapped it up in cloths, and with these cloths and bandages they sometimes wrapped wheat or some other kind of grain. Some of these mummies, for so they are called, which have been buried possibly twenty-five hundred years, have been found; and when the wheat has been taken out of the hands of these mummies and planted in the ground, under f a v o r a b l e conditions, it has grown just the same as the wheat which was harvested from the fields only last summer.   The life which was in the seed had not been destroyed by the many hundreds of years which have passed since it was placed in the hand of the mummy.

Some years ago there was a very interesting case of this kind in England. At Dorchester they were digging down some thirty feet below the surface, and at that depth they came upon the remains of the body of a man, with which there had been buried some coins. By the date upon the coins, they knew that this body had been buried at least seventeen hundred years. In the stomach was found quite a large quantity of raspberry seeds. The man had doubtless eaten a large number of raspberries, and then might have been accidentally killed very soon afterward, so that the seeds were not injured by the gastric juices of the stomach. These seeds were taken to the Horticultural Garden, and there they were planted. What do you think! After seventeen hundred years and more, these seeds grew, and in a short time there was an abundant fruitage of raspberries, just the same as though the seeds had been gathered from raspberries which grew only the year before. Although hidden and seemingly dead, yet these seeds retained their life for seventeen hundred years or more.

In this same way there is a deathless power in the words which we speak, even though they are spoken hastily and without thought upon our part. Our words have in them the element of a life which is well-nigh endless. You may yourself remember some unkind words which were spoken to you months and months ago. The boy or girl who spoke them may have forgotten all about them, but you still remember them, and they cause you pain every time you think of them. Or it may be that some kind person has spoken tenderly and affectionately to you. The person himself may have been so accustomed to speaking kindly that he forgot entirely what he had said, but his kind words still live in your memory. There is a beautiful hymn written some years ago, which begins: "Kind words can never die."

About fifty years ago there were some boys in a school yard

playing marbles. Two other boys were playing tag. One of the boys who were playing tag chanced to run across the ring in which the boys were playing marbles. One of these boys was accustomed to speaking ugly words and doing very hasty and cruel things. He sprang to his feet and kicked the boy who had run across the ring, wounding him in the right knee. The injury was of such a nature that the bones of that leg below the knee never grew any more, and as a result, for over forty years that boy has had to walk on crutches. You see how permanent the result of this injury has been; and the results of unkind words may be just as injurious and no less permanent than the unreasonable and wicked thing which this boy did in his anger.

You may sometimes be discouraged because the kind words which you speak and the kind deeds which you do seem to fail of a good result. But you can be assured that even though you grow to old age and your body were to be laid away in the grave, yet sometime, in the lives of those who come after you, the good you have done will surely bear its fruitage of blessing.

QUESTIONS.—Are there many different kinds of seeds? Do apple trees ever grow from peach seeds? Do good thoughts grow from bad words, or bad thoughts from good words? Do seeds have a principle of life in them? Do words and thoughts have a principle of life? How many centuries have seeds been known to retain their life? Have the teachings of the Bible retained their life for many hundreds of years? Into what do good thoughts turn? (Acts). Into what do good acts turn? (Character). Can any boy or girl afford to use their time in reading worthless books or papers? Do words and deeds have the element of unending life in them? Is it a dangerous thing to get angry? What did one of the boys who were playing marbles do to the boy who ran across the ring? As the result, how many years has the injured boy walked with crutches? Will the good that we do be as permanent as the evil that we might do?

SOWING.

THE SPRING TIME OF LIFE.

SUGGESTION:—The object used is a bag or sack, or a pillow slip would answer the same purpose, hung about the neck as a farmer uses it when sowing seed. While this is not essential, it can be used if desired.

M Y DEAR YOUNG FRIENDS: Spring is the most pleasant season of the year; the snow has melted, the cold weather has passed away, and now the warm, pleasant days have come. The trees are all in blossom, the fields look beautiful, and the air is full of sweetness. If you go into the country at this season of the year you will find the farmers plowing their fields, and some are sowing grain. The spring wheat has already been sown, the oat fields will soon begin to look green, and in the course of a few weeks the farmers will be planting their corn.

It must have been at a corresponding period of the year in the East, when Jesus spoke those beautiful words which are found in the 13th chapter of St. Matthew, contained in the parable of the sower who went out to sow. A great multitude of people had gathered to hear the words which fell from the lips of Jesus. They could no longer gain admission into the house, and so Jesus went down by the sea, or the large lake, and getting into a boat he pushed out just a little way from the shore, so all the people standing along the shore could see and hear Him, and then He began to preach to them. Just back of them on the plain was a farmer who was more intent upon sowing his field than upon listening to the words of the

Saviour. As Jesus saw him pacing to and fro across the field, scattering the grain in the furrows, Jesus very likely pointed to the man, calling the attention of the multitude to what he was doing, and said to the people, "Behold a sower went forth to sow," and then called the attention of the people to the character of the soil in the different places where the seed fell.

In the country the farmers use a sack or bag. After having tied the opposite ends together, they hang this over their neck and shoulder, and with the right hand left free, they march up and down the field, sowing the grain. This sowing is not so common any more, because farmers now often plant their grain fields with a machine called a drill.

With this sack suspended about the neck, in this way, the farmer reaches in and takes out a small handful of seed, and then swinging his hand, throws the seed over a considerable portion of the ground. Thus he walks from one end of the field to the other, sowing the seed, until he has the entire field sown and ready for the men who follow with the harrow to cover up the grain.

Well, boys and girls, this is the spring-time of life with you. These are the pleasant days and years of your life. You have very little care. Yet it is, nevertheless, the spring-time. You are now making preparations which will tell what is to be the harvest in the later years of your lives. As the farmer goes out and plows the field, so by discipline and by counsel, and by instruction are your parents preparing your minds and hearts that in after years you may enjoy a harvest of great blessing.

In the spring-time of life, when young persons are to do the sowing, they need much careful counsel and instruction. I suppose that there are many boys and girls who, if they were to go into the country, could not tell the difference between wheat and barley, or oats and rye. Some might not even be able to distinguish between

Copyrighted, 1911, by Sylvanus Stall.

Behold a Sower went Forth to Sow

oats and buckwheat. If the farmer were to send you out to sow, you would, most likely, sow the wrong kind of grain. In the same manner, it is important that you should be directed by your parents, because they can distinguish between right and wrong. They know what you should do, and what you should not do. There-fore it is important that they should direct you in the spring-time, lest you should sow the wrong kind of grain. And you know the Bible says: "What-soever a man soweth, that shall he also reap."

It is not only difficult for those who have never seen something of life in the country, to distinguish between the dif-ferent kinds of grain which the farmer sows, but even after the grain begins to grow, it is some-times difficult, even for those who are familiar with country life, to distinguish between the true and the false. In that same thirteenth chapter of the gospel by St. Matthew, to which I referred in the begin-

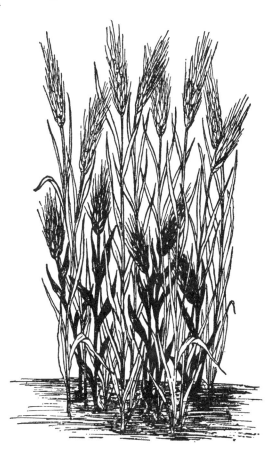

Wheat and Tares.

ning, Jesus tells of a farmer who sowed his field with wheat, and while he slept an enemy came and sowed tares. Of course he could not discover this until the grain began to grow. When it began to get ripe, then for the first could he distinguish between the stalks of the wheat and the stalks of the tares. By doing this wicked thing the enemy gave the farmer a great deal of trouble. Just so it is with you when you have tried to do right, Satan comes and puts evil thoughts and wicked purposes into your mind, and then if you permit these to grow up, you will find that they will give you a great deal of trouble. It is important that only the good seed should be sown in the field of your heart, and in the field of your mind, so that you may have a fruitage that shall be wholly good.

Sometimes you see boys and girls who are doing things which you would like to do, but your mother and father tell you that you should not. You may not be pleased because you are restrained from doing what you would like to do. I well remember how my father, when I was a boy, oftentimes used to restrain me from doing what I saw other boys doing. I used to think, at that time, that he was not considerate, and possibly not kind to me. But now that I have grown older, and have seen the results which have come to those boys, some of whom have gone astray, and others who have turned out badly in life, I see how wise my father was. Although I did not feel at the time that he was doing that which was for my good; now I see it all very plainly.

In closing, let me say to you, do as Isaiah suggested, "Sow by the side of all waters." That is, be very diligent, that day by day you may do some kind act, which will hereafter spring up into a fruitage of very great good. The Bible enjoins upon both young and old to be very diligent in this work, for it says, "In the morning sow thy seed, and in the evening withhold not thine hand; for thou knowest not whether shall prosper, either this or that, or whether they both shall be alike good." (Eccl. xi: 6.)

When you go to school during the week, and to Sunday-school and church service on Sunday, and when being instructed and taught at home, remember that all the instruction you are receiving is like the seed that falls upon the waiting soil in the early spring-time from the hand of an intelligent farmer. In the parable which Jesus spake, He tells how that some of the seed fell by the wayside, some among thorns and some upon stony ground, while others fell upon good ground. While the seed was the same kind in all instances, it was only that which fell upon the good ground which brought forth a fruitage of thirty, sixty and an hundred fold. If the fruitage of your life in the harvest of the after-years is to be abundant in good and blessing, it can only be because you receive the instruction of your parents, your teachers and your pastor into a good and honest heart. Others may sow faithfully, but after all the result must depend upon you.

QUESTIONS.—Which is the most pleasant season of the year? Why? What is the farmer's special work in the spring-time? Why is the farmer careful to sow good grain? What period of life is best represented by spring? If the farmer failed to sow in the spring, would he have a harvest in the autumn? How does he know what kind of grain he will reap at harvest time? Does wheat ever produce oats? Or clover seed produce wheat? What happened while the farmer slept? Who sowed the tares in his field? Who sows the tares in our minds? What do we call these tares? Should they be removed or permitted to grow? Should we be thankful to our parents for preventing tares from being sown? In what kind of soil did the grain grow to a fruitage of thirty, sixty and an hundred fold?

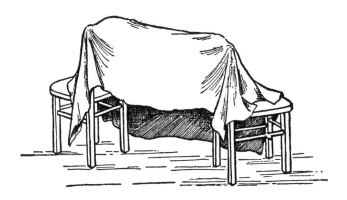

REAPING.

THE HARVEST TIME OF LIFE.

SUGGESTION:—The object used is a small sheaf of grain. For this might be substituted fruitage of any kind—apples, peaches, pears, grapes, etc., and after reading the sermon, the parent could apply in the manner suited to the objects used.

M Y DEAR LITTLE HARVESTERS: Last Sunday I talked to you of spring-time—the spring-time of the year, and the spring-time of life. To-day I have brought a small sheaf of grain to tell us of the harvest-time. The spring-time is very pleasant, the air is fragrant, the birds are singing, and all nature seems to be rejoicing in its freshness and beauty. The world looks just as new and beautiful as it did thousands and thousands of years ago. Each spring it puts on youth anew.

But when the summer-time comes, when it gets along to the harvest time, along in July and August, then the weather is very warm. The color of the fields has then greatly changed, the blossoms have disappeared from the trees, and we find that everywhere the fruit is beginning to appear. The harvest fields are ripe and are waiting for the husbandmen.

Sheaf of Grain.

192

There is just about that same difference in life. Youth is the spring-time. It is full of hope, and full of bright prospects. But, as we grow older, and the cares and responsibilities of life multiply, then we begin to bear the toil and labor which comes with the later years. Then we are like the farmer who enters into the harvest field where hard work has to be done under a very hot and scorching sun.

A man, called a naturalist, who has devoted a large amount of time to the study of plants, tells us that there are about one hundred thousand different kinds of plants. Each kind of plant bears its own seed, and when that particular seed is sown, it always bears its own kind of fruit. Wheat never yields barley, nor do oats ever yield buckwheat. When you plant potatoes, you expect to gather potatoes and not turnips. An apple tree has never grown from an acorn, or a peach tree from a chestnut. Each seed, always and everywhere, bears its own kind. It is on this account that the Bible says, "Be not deceived; God is not mocked: for whatsoever a man soweth that shall he also reap." (Gal. vi: 7.)

There are some grown persons, as well as children, who think that they can do very wrong things while they are young, and afterwards suffer no bad results. People sometimes say, "Oh, well! let us sow our wild oats while we are young." Now the Bible tells us that if we sow wild oats, we must reap wild oats. Four or five handfuls of wild oats will produce a whole bag full of wild oats when gathered in the harvest of after life. Be assured, my dear friend, that "those who sow to the flesh shall of the flesh reap corruption," and "those who sow the wind shall reap the whirlwind." "Sow an act, and you reap a habit. Sow a habit, and you reap a character. Sow a character, and you reap a destiny."

It may seem a long period between the spring and the harvest

194 "The Harvest Fields Are Ripe and Are Waiting for the Husbandmen."

time of life; but be assured, my dear young friends, that the early years will speedily pass. Before you are aware of it, you will be men and women with all the responsibilities of life upon you, and then you will be sure to reap the reward of what you do now while you are boys and girls. Lord Bacon said that "Nature owes us many a debt until we are old," but nature is always sure to pay its debts. The ancients had an adage that said, "Justice travels with a sore foot," but it usually overtakes a man.

A few Sundays ago I told you that as the result of planting a single grain of corn, a fruitage sufficient to plant the entire earth might be secured in only five years. It is told us by historians that, in olden times, the harvest in Egypt and Syria would return an hundred fold for one sowing, and in Babylonia oftentimes two hundred fold for one sowing. Now, if a single grain of wheat were planted in soil as fertile as that of Egypt, at the end of eight years of sowing and reaping, if we had a field large enough, the product would be sufficient to feed all the families of the earth for more than a year and a half. But if we were to undertake to plant one grain of wheat in this way, after a few years we would fill all the fields which would be suited for a wheat harvest. Down near the equator it would be too hot for the wheat to grow success-fully. In the north it would be altogether too cold. On the mountain side the soil is not fertile, and oftentimes is very rocky. For these, and various other reasons, it would be impossible to cover any large portion of the earth with wheat, for not every portion would be suited to produce a harvest. Were it not for this fact, in the course of seven or eight years, the entire earth might be made to wave as one vast field of wheat.

But there is one truth which God has planted in this world. That truth is God's love manifested in the gift of His Son Jesus Christ for the salvation of all mankind. This truth is suited to every age of the world, to every nation of the earth, to all classes and all conditions of people, and to every human heart. During the past centuries men have been planting and replanting this seed of divine truth, sowing and resowing the earth with it, gathering and reaping the harvest and sowing again. And the days are coming when all the earth shall wave as one vast harvest field, waiting for the reapers of God, who shall gather this blessed fruitage into the garner of the skies.

It is your privilege and my privilege, both one and all, to have some part in this glorious work of sowing and resowing, and the Scriptures assure us that "he that goeth forth and weepeth, bearing precious seeds, shall doubtless come again with rejoicing, bringing his sheaves with him."   (Psalms cxxvi: 6.)

AFTERWARD.

ANONYMOUS.

Now, the sowing and the reaping,
   Working hard and waiting long;
Afterward, the golden reaping,
   Harvest home and grateful song.

Now, the pruning, sharp, unsparing,
   Scattered blossom, bleeding shoot;
Afterward, the plenteous bearing
   Of the Master's pleasant fruit.

Now, the plunge, the briny burden,
   Blind, faint gropings in the sea;
Afterward, the pearly guerdon,
   That shall make the diver free.

Now, the long and toilsome duty,
   Stone by stone to carve and bring;
Afterward, the perfect beauty
   Of the palace of the king.

Now, the tuning and the tension,
  Wailing minors, discord strong;
Afterward, the grand ascension
  Of the Alleluia song.

Now, the spirit conflict-riven,
  Wounded heart, unequal strife;
Afterward, the triumph given
  And the victor's crown of life.

Now, the training strange and lowly,
  Unexplained and tedious now,
Afterward, the service holy,
  And the Master's "Enter thou!"

QUESTIONS.—Last Sunday our lesson was about the spring-time and sow-ing; what has it been about to-day? What are the only results which a farmer can reap at harvest? If he sowed wheat, what will he gather? About how many different kinds of plants are there in the world? Do peach trees grow from chestnuts? The Bible says, "Whatsoever a man soweth"—can you repeat the rest of that passage? Can boys or young men, girls or young women, sow "wild oats" and reap blessing later on? If we sow "wild oats" what must we reap? If you sow an act, what do you reap? If you sow a habit, what do you reap? If you sow a character, what do you reap? How did the old adage say that jus-tice travels? Could all portions of the globe be converted into a wheat field? Why not? Is the truth concerning God's love and salvation suited to all ages, all nations, and all people?

WHEAT AND CHAFF.

THE COMING SEPARATION.

SUGGESTION:—If the children can secure a few handfuls of some kind of grain and chaff, the idea of separation can be beautifully illustrated by pouring the grain and chaff from one hand to the other, and at the same time gently blowing the chaff, separating it from the grain. By turning it in this manner once or twice and blowing gently, the chaff may be entirely separated from the grain. If a larger quantity were used, it could be poured from one basket or pan to another while blowing the chaff from the grain with a palm leaf or some other fan. This would illustrate how the grain and chaff were separated at that period of the world in which Christ lived.

MY DEAR YOUNG FRIENDS: I want to read you a very beautiful little psalm, or hymn, or poem, written by David. It was originally written in metre or verse, but poetry when translated becomes prose. This first Psalm of David reads as follows:—

"Blessed is the man that walketh not in the counsel of the ungodly, nor standeth in the way of sinners, nor sitteth in the seat of the scornful; but his delight is in the law of the Lord; and in His law doth he meditate day and night; and he shall be like a tree planted by the rivers of water, that bringeth forth his fruit in his season; his leaf also shall not wither; and whatsoever he doeth shall prosper.

"The ungodly are not so; but are like the chaff which the wind driveth away; therefore the ungodly shall not stand in the judgment, nor sinners in the congregation of the righteous; for the

Lord knoweth the way of the righteous; but the way of the ungodly shall perish."

We find in this Psalm how the righteous are set forth, and how the ungodly are compared to chaff. John the Baptist said of Jesus, "Whose fan is in His hand, and He will thoroughly purge His floor and gather His wheat into the garner; but He will burn up the chaff with unquenchable fire."

Now, when you have been in the country, you have observed the wheat growing in the field. If you had been careful to examine it, you would have found that while the wheat is growing the grain is enclosed in a thin covering called chaff, just the same as Indian corn or sweet corn is enclosed by the husks which grow about it.

Threshing Grain with Flails.

So it is with us; while we are in this world, there are many things which are essential to our growth and well-being. They minister to our physical needs and supply our temporal wants. Although we cannot wholly dispense with these things while we are in this world, yet they are not the sole objects of our living. The wheat does not exist for the chaff, or the husk in which it is enclosed, but the husks or chaff exist for the wheat.

After a time, when the harvest comes, the farmer enters the field and cuts down the wheat, and it is then taken to the barn or threshing floor. Years ago, when I was a boy, farmers used to spend a large portion of the winter in threshing grain. They would spread it out upon the floor of the barn and beat it with a heavy stick, which was tied so as to swing easily at the end of a long handle. This was called a flail. Machines for threshing grain were not then common, as they are to-day. When the farmer threshes his grain, he does not do it to destroy the wheat, but simply to separate it from the chaff.

The Bible tells us that we must enter into the kingdom of God through much "tribulation." And do you know that the word "tribulation" comes from a Latin word, *tribulum,* which means a flail? So the teaching of this passage of Scripture is, that God places you and me under the flail, and smites again and again, in order that the noblest, best and most Christ-like in us may be separated by trials and tribulations from that which is worthless; and which needs to be cast off in order that just as the farmer gathers the wheat into his garner or granary here on earth, so God may gather us eventually into His garner above.

Boys and girls oftentimes have tribulations in this world, just the same as older people do. Disappointments come to them, and because of ambitions which are not lawful or right, purposes which are not in harmony with God's word and with God's will; because of needed discipline, or for some good reason God is tribulating them by sorrows, disappointments and trials, and making them better by means of the experiences through which they are called upon to pass.

If you have been with the farmer in his barn after he is through with the threshing, you have seen him take the fanning-mill, and perhaps you have turned the crank for him, while he has slowly shoveled the grain into the mill and the chaff was being blown away by the wind set in motion by the revolution of the large fanning wheel. In the olden times they did not have fanning-mills, but when the farmer desired to separate the chaff from the wheat, he did it with a fan. He poured the grain from one basket or box, or some other receptacle, into another while the wind was blowing, or else used a fan to create a draught of wind to blow the chaff, and thus separate it from the wheat. It is

Winnowing or Separating Wheat and Chaff.

this ancient custom to which John the Baptist refers. He says, concerning Christ, "Whose fan is in His hand, and He will thoroughly purge His floor, and gather His wheat into the garner; but He will burn up the chaff with unquenchable fire." (Matthew iii: 12.)

So God designs to separate from your character, and from mine, that which is worldly and temporal, and worthless so far as eternity is concerned. Take money as an illustration. Now money is essential, and it is well that we should be willing to work hard for it, and that we should be economical in its use, and seek to save our money so that we may use it for good purposes, and that it may be helpful to us in old age. Money serves a very excellent purpose while we are upon earth, but God does not mean that we should make it the chief aim of our life. Therefore, to divert our minds from money in one way or another, financial reverses and failures sometimes come, and thus God seeks to separate the man from the money. We all came into this world empty-handed, and we must go out of it empty-handed. Even though we were worth many millions of dollars we could take no money with us. You might place it in the coffin and bury it with a dead body, but it would not and could not go into eternity with the man's undying spirit.

Now, after the farmer has separated the chaff from the wheat, he gathers the wheat into his garner, or into his granary; and so, after God has separated from our nature and character all that is of no use, which is simply earthy, He will gather our souls into heaven, His garner above.

While we live upon the earth we should use the things of this world but not abuse them; remembering that finally we must go and leave everything behind us, and that we can take nothing with us into eternity except the characters which we formed here. Wealth and reputation, and all worldly things will have to be left behind us; but character, that which you and I really are, shall never pass away, but shall enter into an eternal state of being on high. All these earthly things are the mere chaff, while character is our real selves.

QUESTIONS.—Who wrote the book of the Bible called the Psalms? Can you tell what the first Psalm is about? What is the covering called which is about the grain while it is growing? How are the chaff and grain separated from the straw or stalk? After being threshed, how is the chaff separated from the grain? Are there many necessary things in life which, after all, do not constitute our character? What are tribulations like? Does God separate the essential from the non-essentials in our life? Is character injured or helped by tribulations? Where does the farmer put the grain after it has been separated from the chaff? What is spoken of in the Bible as God's garner?

The Children of Israel Camping in the Wilderness.

THE HEART.

THE MOST WONDERFUL PUMP IN THE WORLD.

SUGGESTION :—The objects used are a tumbler of water colored red, a small glass syringe such as can be purchased at any drug store for five or ten cents, also a six-ounce bottle of water colored red. This red coloring can be easily done with red ink. If that is not available, a drop or two of black ink will answer.

MY DEAR YOUNG FRIENDS: In the 139th Psalm, 14th verse, David says, "I will praise thee, for I am fearfully and wonderfully made." Now I want to talk to you to-day about our wonderful bodies, in the creation of which God has so marvelously displayed His infinite wisdom.

I suppose you have been either near or inside a factory. You have heard the noise of the shafts and the pulleys and machinery. You have seen the carding machines, and listened to the noise of the great spinning jacks which twisted the cotton and the wool into yarn or thread, and heard the deafening sound of a great many looms as the shuttles flew backward and forward, while the many threads were being woven into cloth. A factory is quite wonderful, but do you know that in your bodies are found the elements of almost all the kinds of machinery that are used in the world? God has so created us that we do not hear the noise of the machinery of our bodies, but if you will place your fingers gently in your ears you will hear a peculiar roaring sound. That sound which you hear is the noise of the machinery of your body, which is in constant motion.

204

Now, the heart, which pumps the blood into all portions of the body, makes the greater portion of this noise. Do you know where your heart is located? I supposed that most of you would point to your left side, because you have so frequently heard it spoken of as being located there. You have seen public speakers and others, when referring to their heart, place their hands upon their left side. But if you will bend your head forward so as to press your chin against your breast, as far down as possible, the heart will be under and a few inches below your chin. It is in the center of the body, and the lower portion of it comes near to the ribs on the left side, and when it beats we can feel it throb by placing our hand upon our left side; but the heart is more nearly in the center of the body, and not wholly at the side. If you were to close your hand as the boys do when they say they make a fist, the size of your closed hand will be somewhat smaller than the heart.

Water and Syringe.

In this tumbler I have some water which I have colored with red ink, so as to represent blood. Here is a small glass syringe, such as can be bought for a few cents in any drug store. Now, when I draw this little handle up, you will see how the syringe is filled with this red water, and when I press it down how the water is forced out of the syringe back into the glass. This very clearly illustrates the principle upon which all pumps and steam engines which pump water are made. Even the large fire engine, which

throws water such a great distance, is made largely upon this principle.

You may possibly have been in the engine room, where the
huge pumps force the water into the reservoirs which supply the
city with water for drinking and other purposes. From the pumps
and the reservoirs there are great pipes which lead the water under
the streets to many thousands of houses which compose the city.
After the water has been used it is turned into the sewers, runs
down into the river and back to the sea, where it is evaporated, rises
again in the clouds, and by the wind is carried hundreds of miles
over the country. Then it descends again in the form of snow and
rain, soaks down through the earth and finds its way again into the
springs and great veins of water under the earth, from which it is
carried back once more to the city. Thus it is made pure again
and again, to be used over and over by the people whom God has
created and whom He supplies with water in this way.

Now, in somewhat the same way, the heart, which is both an
engine and a pump, forces the blood out through the pipes or tubes
of our bodies called the arteries, distributing it to every portion of
the body, furnishing the materials for building and renewing the
muscles and the bones and every portion of our system.   Then
gathering up that which is worn out and no longer of service, the
impure blood returns through the veins back to the right side of the
heart, where it is pumped into the lungs and purified by being
brought into contact with the air we breathe. The blood is then
returned to the left side of the heart, pumped again into the arteries
and distributed through all parts of the body, and so it goes on cir-
culating. Thus the blood is pumped by the heart into the arteries
and is distributed to all portions of the body, and returned again to
the heart, from fourteen to twenty times each hour of our life.

In this bottle, which holds six ounces, I have placed some of this colored water, which represents about the quantity which is pumped out of the heart of an adult each time the pulse beats. As I have already intimated to you, the heart is double, and at each throb about one-half the quantity in this bottle is pumped out by the right side, and the other half by the left side of the heart. Now, if the heart were to pump different blood with each pulsation,

A Wagon Load of Barrels.

instead of pumping the same blood over and over again, in twenty-four hours the heart of a man of ordinary size would pump 150 barrels of blood.

The Bible says that the days of our years are three-score years and ten, or, in other words, that the allotted period of an ordinary life is 70 years. Now, in 70 years the heart would pump 164,-

389,786 gallons; or, to give it to you in barrels, it would make 4,566,382 barrels. If you were to place six barrels on a wagon, and this would make a good load for two horses, you would have 761,063 loads of these barrels. If you were to place these teams, with the wagons containing six barrels apiece, with 36 gallons each, at a distance of 25 feet apart, it would make a string of teams stretching away 1,778 miles, or as far as from New York City to Des Moines, in the state of Iowa, or from New York City down to the Gulf of Mexico.

I think you will now be able to understand what a wonderful little steam engine and pump each of us has within our own breast. And it may surprise you when I tell you that Dr. Buck says that the heart at each throb beats with a power equal to 100,000 pounds.

An ordinary engine or pump would soon wear out, but this little engine of the heart goes on beating day and night from the time we are born until we are 70 years of age, if we live to be that old, and even while we rest in sleep, the heart never stops for a moment. Is it any wonder that David said that "We are fearfully and wonderfully made"?

I might tell you many other wonderful things about the heart, but this will have to suffice.

If the natural heart in these bodies of ours is so wonderful, how much more wonderful still is that heart which is the seat of the moral life and character? As the natural heart is hidden away in these bodies of ours, so the spirit or the soul is spoken of in the Bible as the heart, because it is hidden away in the life which we have in these bodies of ours; and it is this moral character and spiritual life to which the Bible refers when it says, "Keep thine heart with all diligence, for out of it are the issues of life."

QUESTIONS.—How did David say we are made? Does the machinery in a great factory make much noise? Are our bodies like a factory in this respect?

How can we hear the noise inside of our body? Where is the heart located? What does the heart do? Can you tell how water is supplied for a great city? Is the blood carried to all portions of our body in a similar way? How much blood is pumped by the heart in twenty-four hours? What does the Bible say is the allotted years of a person's life? How long a string of teams would it require to carry all the blood which the heart ordinarily pumps in seventy years? Does the heart keep on pumping while we sleep? What is still more wonderful than the physical heart? Can we see either the physical heart or the spiritual heart? Does the fact that you cannot see them prove that you do not have them? Are both necessary to your complete being and existence?

THE EYE.

THE MOST VALUABLE AND MOST WONDERFUL TELESCOPE.

SUGGESTION:—The objects used are a field-glass or opera-glass, spy-glass and sun-glass.

MY DEAR LITTLE MILLIONAIRES: You know that when people are very wealthy, have hundreds of thousands of dollars, they are spoken of as millionaires. Oftentimes these rich people do not have any more actual money than poorer people, but they have property which is sup-

Field-glass, Spy-glass and Sun-glass.

posed to be worth a great deal of money. Now, I want to show you to-day that each one of you possesses that which is worth millions of dollars.

I want to talk to you about your eyes, and I hope that you will be able to understand that they are worth hundreds and thousands, yes millions of dollars to each of you. In order that I may better illustrate a few of the many wonderful things about the human eye, I have brought this field-glass, and here is a small spy-glass, and also a magnifying lens, or sun-glass, as boys sometimes call them. Inside of this spy-glass and these field-glasses are lenses or magnifying glasses, similar to this sun-glass. They are, however, more perfect, and are so adjusted or related to each other, that when I place this smaller lens of the spy-glass to my eye I also look through the larger lens which is at the further end of the instrument. When properly adjusted, it enables me to see objects which are at a great distance, and to so magnify them as to cause them to seem much nearer to me than they really are.

Now, if you take this spy-glass and look at the stars, it will not make them appear any larger than they appear to the eye without the spy-glass. It will assist the eye when I look at the moon or the planets, but not at the stars which are so much further removed from the earth than the moon and the planets. Astronomers have desired something larger and more satisfactory, and so have made the great telescopes, which are simply large spy-glasses. The telescope and the spy-glass, and the field-glasses, are all imitations of the human eye; the same as many of our greatest inventions are only copies of that which God has already created, and which we have but feebly imitated. The eye is a more wonderful instrument than even the largest telescopes which have ever been made.

If you desired to look through a telescope at one of the stars or a planet, or the moon, you would have considerable difficulty in directing it so as to be able to see the desired object. Even with this small spy-glass it is very difficult so to direct it as to find a particular star in the heavens at night. It is not easy, even to find a distant object upon the earth.   But with these wonderful eyes, with which God has endowed us, you and I can look almost instantly from one star to any other star, and find instantly upon the earth any object which is distinctly pointed out to us.   It takes a very experienced person successfully to operate a telescope, but the smallest child can direct and control and use his own eyes successfully.

The large telescopes have to be turned and adjusted by

machinery, and when, it is desired to direct them from one star to another star on the opposite side of the heavens, they even have to turn around the entire roof or dome of the observatory. But you and I do not need any ponderous machinery to adjust our eyes, or to turn them about in order to look in a different direction. We can easily turn our heads by bending our necks, or, if necessary, we can turn our entire body around and look in an opposite direction.   In looking from one object to another, our eyes change their direction so quickly that we are not conscious of any effort upon our own part.

Small Telescope.

If you were to look through a large telescope, or even one of these smaller spy-glasses, you would immediately discover that when you desire to look at objects at different distances, or in different degrees of light and shade, you would have to constantly adjust the telescope or spy-glass to these different conditions. If you would look at objects which are near, and then turn the spy-glass to look at those which are distant, you would not be able to see distinctly until you had adjusted the lenses to suit the distance. With our eyes the same adjustment has to be made, and yet it is done so quickly and without any conscious effort upon our part, that it seems as if it were not done at all. When we look at an object which is only a few inches from our face, and then turn and look at a distant object, instantly our eyes are adjusted to the difference of distance and varying degrees of light and shade.

But what makes this all still more wonderful is the fact that we have two telescopes, two eyes instead of one. Both of these little eye-telescopes instantly adjust themselves, and both adjust themselves to precisely the same necessity. If they adjusted themselves differently we would see two objects instead of one; the same as a drunken man who has lost the use of his muscles and faculties, whose eyes do not work in harmony, and therefore, instead of seeing only one object, he sees two objects and sees them in a confused way.

Did you ever think how wonderful it is that when you close your right eye, and look at something with your left eye, that you can see the object distinctly? Now, if you close the left eye, and look at the object with the right eye, you again see the same object distinctly. When you open both eyes and look at the same object, instead of seeing the object twice, or seeing two objects, you see only one object. That is because the eyes work in such perfect harmony, and that is what the Scripture means when it says that you and I should "see eye to eye" in everything that is good.

Now there is another thing to which I desire to call your attention, and that is the size of the eye. If you owned one of these very large telescopes which cost hundreds of thousands of dollars, you would be regarded as a very wealthy person, but you could not carry that telescope with you from one place to another. It would be of no service to you in looking upon the beautiful scenes which surround you from day to day. If you wanted to use the telescope you would have to stay where the telescope was, instead of taking the telescope with you where you desired to go. But God has made these little eye-telescopes so perfect, and yet so compact and small, that wherever we go, on land or sea, we can take them with us, and they can be in constant use and give us the most perfect delight and satisfaction.

I am sure there is not a single boy or girl who would trade off one of these perfect little telescopes—yes, I will call it a telescope and an observatory also—for God has beautifully encased our eyes, and shielded and housed them more beautifully and satisfactorily than the most perfect observatory which was ever built for any man-made telescope. We would not trade away one of our eyes for one of the finest telescopes in the world, and we would not be willing to give both of our eyes for all the telescopes which have ever been made.

But one of these large telescopes and observatories would cost a great deal—even hundreds of thousands of dollars; yet God has *given* you and me these telescopes, our wonderful eyes. But because God has given them to us they are none the less valuable on that account, and I think therefore that I was correct when I addressed you to-day as little millionaires.

Now, God has given you, not simply one eye, but He has given you two eyes, two wonderful telescopes and observatories. He has given you two, so that if by any accident one should be destroyed, you would still have the other to depend upon. God has given you two eyes, and two hands, and two feet; but He has given you only one soul, and if by sin you lose that one soul, then you have lost everything, for the Scripture says, "What shall a man give in exchange for his soul?"

In Palestine, the country in which Jesus lived when He was upon the earth, the sun shines with wonderful brightness and clearness; the land also is very light in color, and consequently the eyes are oppressed by the glare, just the same as those of you who have ever been at the seashore have experienced the glare while walking along the beach; or, to some extent, like the bright sunlight shining upon the snow in winter. This light color of the soil and brightness of the sun in Palestine are the cause of blindness to many of the inhabitants. When Jesus was upon the earth, one of His greatest acts of mercy to suffering humanity was to open and heal the eyes of those who were either born blind, or who had become blind afterward.

Now, in this country of ours, and in all countries of the earth, there are hundreds and thousands and millions of people who are spiritually blind. Jesus Christ is to-day passing by, just the same as when the blind man sat by the roadside near Jericho, when Jesus was then passing by. As that blind man called upon Jesus and said, "Thou Son of David, have mercy upon me," so you and I should call upon God and upon His Son, Jesus Christ, that He would have mercy upon us and open our spiritual eyes. We should make the language of the Scriptures the petition of our hearts, "Open Thou mine eyes, that I may behold wondrous things out of Thy law." I pray that God may give each of you to see and to understand spiritual things.

QUESTIONS.—Instead of money, in what does the wealth of millionaires often consist? Is the human eye worth more than money? Would you take a million of dollars for your two eyes? Are your eyes worth more than telescopes? Which is the more perfect, a telescope or the human eye? Are telescopes adjusted like the eye? Which can be adjusted more quickly? Where are telescopes kept? Are your eyes kept in a little observatory? Why has God given us two eyes instead of one? How many souls has He given us? If the soul is lost, what is the result? What causes so much blindness in the country in which Jesus lived? Did Jesus open the eyes of the blind and restore the sight of people in Palestine? Are many people spiritually blind? Does Jesus wish to give them spiritual sight or vision?

THE EYE

THE SMALLEST CAMERA, THE MOST VALUABLE PICTURES.

SUGGESTION :—The object used is a small camera of any kind.

I AM going to address you again to-day as LITTLE MILLION-AIRES. Last week I showed you how your eyes were more valuable than the most costly telescopes, and to-day I want to show you how, in another way, you are little millionaires.

Very wealthy people sometimes travel in different countries, and gather very rare and beautiful paintings and pictures, often-times paying a thousand dollars, ten thousand dollars, and sometimes very much more for a single painting. Then they bring these paintings all together in their own homes and hang them on the walls, and as the result of the expenditure of many thousands, and sometimes of hundreds of thousands of dollars, they have a very

Camera.

beautiful and rare collection. But God has made you and me the possessors of a vast number of pictures, more beautiful, of greater variety, and infinitely more valuable, than all the paintings that were ever hung upon the walls of any art gallery in the world.

217

To illustrate my thought, I have to-day brought a camera. Sometimes such a camera as this is called a Kodak or Snap-shot. As the finest telescopes have been modeled after the human eye, so the camera is only a very imperfect imitation of the human eye. As the spy-glass and telescope have lenses, so does this camera have a lens, which you see here in the front. Just back of this lens is the dark chamber in the camera, and back of it is a ground glass, as you will see here. Now whatever is directly in front of the camera is shown on the ground glass, as you will observe, but in an inverted or up-side-down position. So the eye has its various parts, and as

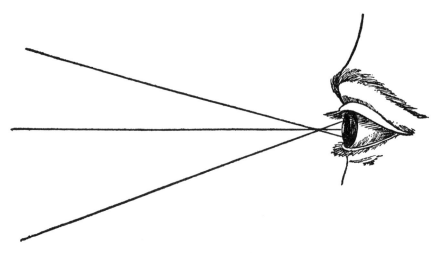

The Human Eye.

the rays of light pass through this lens and reflect the picture on this ground glass, so rays of light coming from any object pass first through the small opening of the eye, to the retina, where the picture is inverted just the same as upon the ground glass. When this picture is thrown upon the rear wall of the eye, which is called the retina, the seeing nerve, which is called the optic nerve and is connected with the eye, conveys the impression to the brain, and the result is what we call seeing.

What I have told you is correct, and can easily be proven by a simple experiment with the eye of some animal. If you take the eye of a dead rabbit, and cleanse the back portion of it from the fat and muscles and then hold a candle in front of it, you can see the image of the candle formed upon the retina. If you take the eye of an ox and carefully pare off from the back portion, so as to leave it very thin, and place the eye in front of (or against) a small hole made in a box; then cover your head to shut out the light you will see through the box the picture of any object which is directly in front of this eye of the ox. In both instances they will be in the inverted form. This experiment would fully demonstrate to you that the camera is only an imitation, and a very poor one too, of the human eye.

Now when pictures are taken by means of the camera, the negative can not be exposed to the light, but must be taken into a dark room, and be carefully developed by the use of necessary chemicals or liquids. Then specially prepared paper must be used for printing the photographs. This paper must also be kept in the dark until it has been thoroughly washed and cleansed. But, with the pictures which are taken upon the retina of the eye, no such delay and labor is necessary before you can look at them. The moment the eye is turned in any direction, instantly the picture is photographed upon the retina of the eye, and then stamped indelibly upon the memory and becomes a part of ourselves.

There is no cost for chemicals, no delay in adjusting the instrument with which the picture is taken, no necessity for carrying around a large camera.

The camera has many disadvantages which are not found in the human eye. The camera must be adjusted to objects near or far, and different cameras have to be used for pictures of different sizes and for different classes of pictures. These cameras are costly to purchase, a great deal of time is consumed in securing a few pic-

14

tures, they are always attended with expense; and when pictures are to be removed from one place to another, the owner is subjected to much trouble and annoyance. Then, the camera also does not give us the colors of the different objects which are before it. That is the reason why, in the beginning, I spoke of these millionaires purchasing such costly paintings, because in the paintings different colors are represented.

Now, in the hundreds of pictures which are constantly being taken by your eyes, there are no delays, no expenses, no inconvenience when the pictures have once been taken. Different shades and colors are all clearly represented. And even though you were to stand on a high mountain, where you could look off over one or two hundred square miles of beautiful landscape, all that beautiful scenery would be pictured on the retina of your eye; and the picture, complete and perfect, would not be larger than one-half inch square. What would real wealthy people be willing to give for a perfect picture only one-half inch square, in which the artist had clearly defined every field and tree, the rivers, houses, roads, railways and all the beautiful landscape contained in a vast area of many square miles?

Our eyes are wonderful cameras, which God has given us so that we can be constantly taking these beautiful pictures as we pass through life, and look at them not only for the instant, but that we may treasure the pictures up in our memories and make them the rich treasures and joyous heritage of coming years.

The older we grow, the more we appreciate these memory pictures of the past—memories of our childhood days, beautiful landscapes, foreign travel, lovely sunsets, the glorious sunrise, green fields and orchards of golden fruit. As you grow old, I suppose the richest treasures in your picture gallery of the past will be the memories of your childhood home, of mother and father, brother and sister. Possibly when you have grown old, you will remember how one day your heart was almost broken, when for the first time you were leaving home; how mother's eyes filled with tears when she kissed you good-bye, and, following you to the gate, how she stood and waved her handkerchief, while home faded from your view as you rounded the turn in the road and realized for the first time that you were launching out into real life for long years of struggle.

Just as the hearts of the parents go out in great tenderness toward their son, who is leaving the Christian influences of his home to begin service in a distant city, surrounded by evil influences, and oftentimes by wicked people; so the heart of our Heavenly Father goes out in great tenderness towards you and me, while we are separated from the great eternal mansion of the skies. God's heart yearns over us in great tenderness, and while we live in the midst of the evil of this world we are constantly to remember that God has made us millionaires; not only in the possession of the eyes, and other faculties with which He has endowed us for use here upon the earth, but we are to remember that we are children of the King of Heaven, and that we are heirs of everlasting life and of everlasting glory. We are heirs of God and joint heirs with Jesus Christ, to an inheritance which is incorruptible, undefiled and that "fadeth not away." We are not simply millionaires, but we are heirs of everlasting glory.

QUESTIONS.—What instrument for taking pictures is like the human eye? Which can take pictures quicker, the eye or the camera? What is lacking in pictures taken by the camera? Do our eyes show the colors of the objects? Of what is the camera an imitation? Is it expensive to take many pictures with the camera? Why do people pay large sums for oil paintings? Was there ever a picture painted by an artist or photographed with a camera so beautiful as the small pictures taken by the eye? For size, color, variety and convenience, which are the finest pictures in the world? Which pictures are most treasured in old age?

FROGS.

THE PLAGUES IN EGYPT.

SUGGESTION:—Objects: Some paper frogs, which can be purchased at any Japanese store for about five cents each. They are often found also in toy stores.

MY DEAR YOUNG FRIENDS: I am sure you will all be able to tell me what this object is which I hold in my hand (voices: "Frogs, bullfrogs"). Well, it looks exactly like a bullfrog, and was made to imitate a bullfrog. The bullfrogs I have here are made of paper, and were made

in Japan. I bought them that I might show them to you and preach you an object sermon on the subject of the "Ten Plagues in Egypt."

You all remember how Joseph was sold by his brethren into

bondage in Egypt, how he was cast into prison and afterward taken out and made prime minister over all that land; how during the seven years of plenty he laid up corn for the seven years of famine which followed, and afterward his father and his brethren—in all the seventy persons who constituted Jacob's family— came down into Egypt to be fed. After two hundred and fifty years this family had increased until it numbered nearly two millions of people. Pharaoh had made slaves of them, and compelled them to work in the brickyards of Egypt. The task-masters were very cruel. They beat them with whips, and demanded excessive labor from them. These people were the chosen people of God, and their voice was lifted to God their Father for deliverance from all the wrongs which they suffered. God heard their prayer, and raised up Moses to deliver them out of Egyptian bondage.

When Moses and Aaron went to Pharaoh to request him to let the Children of Israel go from Egypt to the land of Canaan, which God had promised to Abraham and to his seed after him, Pharaoh would not consent to let them go. He was a proud, wicked king, and God sent ten great plagues upon him and his country, to humble him and cause him to do as God desired that he should do.

In the first plague the rivers were turned into blood. This plague lasted seven days, and at the end of that time Moses stretched forth his rod, and all the rivers and ponds and lakes of water brought forth great frogs throughout all the land. They came, not by hundreds, but by thousands and millions, until the frogs covered all that land. They were in the houses of all the people. The king's servants were busy sweeping and carrying them out of the palace, and yet they stole into the rooms, and at night when the king would go to lie down he would find these frogs in his bed-chamber and upon his bed. When his bakers went to make bread for the king, they would find them in the bread-troughs in which they kneaded or mixed the bread, and in the ovens where they baked the bread. The frogs were everywhere in the palace and in the huts of the common people; upon the streets and in the roads; wherever the people walked they stepped upon them, and the king's carriage could not be driven through the streets without crushing thousands of them. The plague was so great that Pharaoh sent for Moses and Aaron, and entreated them to call upon their God that He would remove the frogs; and when God heard the prayer of Moses and Aaron He caused the frogs to die. The people gathered them up in great heaps and these dead and putrefying frogs in the streets and the water of the river caused the air to be loaded with a great stench that filled the nostrils of all the people.

After this plague of frogs came the plague of lice, when all the dust of the country was turned into lice, and after that the plague of the flies; and so on through to the last plague, which was the slaying of the first-born, of which I will tell you in another sermon.

I wish you would at your earliest opportunity turn to the second book in the Old Testament, the Book of Exodus, and in the early chapters read about these various plagues of Egypt. When you read the account of the various plagues, you will see how after each affliction Pharaoh's heart seemed to relent. He would consent for a time that the Children of Israel might be liberated from their bondage, and depart from Egypt and start on their journey to the land of Canaan. When he was in affliction he would make good promises, but as soon as God had removed the plague, and the sorrow of his people seemed to be ended for a time he again hardened his heart against God, and refused to do what he had promised. Again and again the king refused to do that which he had agreed, and caused the unhappy Children of Israel to continue in their bondage.

We may think that we are not wicked like Pharaoh was. We may not be wicked in the same degree, but we are wicked after the same nature and kind; and so God brings upon us various providences, some of which are not very pleasant. God is seeking to educate us by the trials and sorrows and disappointments and afflictions which He permits to come upon us, so that we will be more obedient, and more faithful, and more Christlike. But I suppose you have seen people who were just like Pharaoh. When they were sick they would promise to become Christians, and live good and right lives, and join the Church and be faithful followers of Christ all the rest of their lives. And yet when God would raise them up from their beds of sickness they would forget all their promises, and generally, as it always was in the case of Pharaoh, their hearts became harder and harder. Instead of being better after God had raised them up and made them strong and well, or removed some trial or affliction, they became worse than before.

Have you not found something of this also in your own experience? When you have desired something which you have asked your father or mother to secure for you, you have promised that you would run all the errands they asked, or that you would go to school and study your lessons very faithfully, or that you would go to bed cheerfully at night without complaining, or you have made your parents some other promises; and yet, after you have received the object you asked for, you have failed to keep your promise.

Or, to go a step further, has it not been so with what you have promised God that you would do? You may have entered into covenant with Him, made certain promises, and then afterward forgot to fulfill those promises. Let us always remember when we

226   Moses Leading the Children of Israel Through the Red Sea.

make promises to God, or to our parents, that we are not to be like Pharaoh. After God has answered our prayers we should not forget to be obedient to Him and to keep our promises.

Pharaoh was a great covenant-breaker, but when at last he gave the Children of Israel permission to leave Egypt, and then broke his promise and followed them with his army that he might destroy them, God opened up the waters of the Red Sea and the Children of Israel fled from before Pharaoh. When this wicked king and covenant-breaker saw them, he pursued after them with his horses, his chariots and his army; and when they were all in the midst of the sea, God took away His restraining power from the water which stood piled up on both sides of the way along which the Children of Israel had marched safely, and the water came down in great torrents and buried this wicked king and all his horses and his chariots and his men. So God destroyed this great covenant-breaking king, because after all of the judgments and wonderful miracles which He had wrought before Pharaoh, in order to teach him that Jehovah was God, Pharaoh's repentances were all mere shams.

This was a great object sermon which God did before the eyes of all these thousands of the Children of Israel, and it should teach you and me that we are to be honest in all our covenants with God, and be obedient to the will of God in all that we do and say.

QUESTIONS.—Upon what king of Egypt did God send the plague of frogs? How many plagues were there? What effect did each plague have upon Pharaoh? Was he honest when he repented? What did he do each time after the plague was removed? What was the last plague? After the death of the first-born, did he allow the Children of Israel to go? After they started, what did he do? How did God enable the Children of Israel to cross the Red Sea? When Pharaoh followed into the sea after them, what occurred? Should we always keep our covenants, both with God and men? If we do not keep our covenants, whom are we like? Will we also be punished?

BLOOD.

THE FEAST OF THE PASSOVER.

SUGGESTION :—The object used is a bottle of red ink to represent blood.

CHILDREN OF THE COVENANT-KEEPING KING: Last Sunday I talked to you about Pharaoh, as the great covenant-breaking king. I showed you some paper frogs, and told you how after all of God's long-suffering with Pharaoh, He eventually destroyed him and his army in the midst of the Red Sea.

Now, to-day I have this bottle, which has this deep red colored fluid in it. This is red ink. But I have brought it not to talk to you about ink, but to talk about something else which is of the same color; namely, of blood.

You remember that there were ten plagues in Egypt; the first was the turning of the rivers into blood, then the bringing up of the frogs from all the rivers and lakes; and then the turning of the dust into lice; and then the plague of the flies; and then of the murrain which destroyed the cattle; and of the boils which came upon all the people; and of the lightning, and rain, and hail which destroyed man and beast. Then the locusts came which ate up everything that remained; afterward the three days of continuous darkness; and after these nine plagues God had yet in store one great plague which He purposed to bring upon Pharaoh and his people. After each of these plagues which I have named, Pharaoh promised that he would let the Children of Israel go, but instead he hardened his heart and refused to keep his promise. At last God was going

228

Copyrighted, 1911, by Sylvanus Stall.

Preparing for the Passing Over of the Angel of Death

to bring upon him and his people the greatest plague of all. (Ex. xii: 1-28.)

God told Moses and Aaron to command the Children of Israel that on the tenth day of the month, each family should select either a lamb or a kid and shut it up until the fourteenth day, and in the evening of that day they should kill it. This was to be a male lamb, one year old, and without spot or blemish. The blood, as it flowed from the neck of the lamb, was to be caught in a dish, and with a bunch of hyssop the blood was to be sprinkled upon the door-posts or the door frame, both above and around the door, so that when the Angel of Death whom God purposed to send upon that eventful night, when he should pass throughout all the land of Egypt and see the blood upon the door posts and upon the lintel over the door he would pass by or "pass-over" these houses of the Israelites and would not smite their first-born with death; as would be the case in every other home of the Egyptians throughout all the land.

After the Children of Israel had sprinkled the blood upon the door-posts, they were to roast the entire lamb, and they were to eat it with unleavened bread, which was bread baked without yeast, and eat it also with bitter herbs, while at the same time their long, loose garments were to be tucked up under their belts which went around their waists, or as the people in those days would have said, with their loins girded. They were to have their shoes on their feet, and a cane or staff in their hand, so as to be all ready to start out upon their journey at any moment.

At midnight, after these Israelites had eaten this "Passover" meal, and had also destroyed, by burning, any portions of the lamb which might remain, the Angel of Death passed through all the land of Egypt and slew the first-born, the oldest in every house, where there was no blood sprinkled upon the door-posts.

As soon as the angel had passed by, the people rushed out into the streets in terror and alarm, for in every home there was one or two or more persons lying dead. The Egyptians brought out their jewels and gold and valuables, and offered, not only to let the Israelites retain the jewels which they had already borrowed, but to give them more if they would only depart immediately, so that God should bring no further afflictions upon them. Pharaoh consented to their going, and immediately the Children of Israel started on their long journey to the Promised Land.

This eventful night was called, and is to this day called, "the night of the Passover," and to this day the Jewish people still celebrate the Feast of the Passover. It occurs in the spring of the year, and corresponds very closely to our Church festival day, known as Good Friday, at which time we commemorate the crucifixion and death of Jesus Christ upon Calvary.

You will see from what I have said, how the lamb which was chosen was a figure of Jesus Christ, the Lamb of God, slain from the foundation of the world to take away your sins, and my sins, and the sins of all who would believe on Him. As this passover lamb was a year old, without spot and without blemish, so Jesus Christ was perfect, without blemish, He never committed a sin of any kind; He was but thirty years old when He was crucified, and consequently was young in years.

As the blood sprinkled upon the door-posts and the lintels of the doors was the sign by which the Angel of the Lord was to know the homes of the Israelites, and deliver their first-born from death, so the blood of the Lord Jesus Christ cleanses us from all sin and delivers us from eternal death.

You and I and all mankind must die, but after this death of the body there comes either everlasting life or spiritual death. Now, when the spirit leaves the body, or is separated from these bodies, we speak of the body as being dead. The death of a person is just the same as when wheat is sown into the ground and is said to die; the life that formerly was in the seed only springs up into the stalk and grows into a new life and into a multiplied fruitfulness.

The life of each grain of wheat does not cease to exist, but is simply separated from the seed or grain which was sown in the ground, and lives in the new plant and new grain which springs up. So also when the life or the soul leaves the body, the body is dead, because it is separated from the soul. In like manner also, if the soul is separated from God, the Bible speaks of the individual as being spiritually dead, even while yet living in this world. Now, if because of sin any soul that is banished forever from God's presence, and is eternally separated from God in the next world, that eternal separation of the soul from God is spoken of in the Bible as eternal death.

From this eternal death you and I can only be delivered by the blood of the Son of God. Jesus Christ is our Passover Lamb. Neither is He a dead, but a living Savior.

> "He ever lives above,
>   For me to intercede;
> His all-redeeming love,
>   His precious blood to plead;
> His blood atoned for all our race,
> And sprinkles now the throne of grace."

QUESTIONS.—What was the tenth plague? How were the homes of the Israelites to be marked, so that the angel of death would pass over them? How old was the lamb to be that was to be slain? What was to be done with the body of the lamb? When they ate it, how were they to be clothed? (So as to be ready to start immediately upon their journey.) What did the angel of death do where the door posts were sprinkled with the blood? What was the event called? (The Passover.) What people continue to celebrate the Feast of the Passover to-day? Of whom was the slain lamb the symbol? What is Christ frequently called? From what does the blood of the Lamb of God save us?

PINE BRANCH.

THE FEAST OF TABERNACLES.

SUGGESTION:—The objects used are a green branch of a tree and a glass of clear water.

DEAR YOUNG FRIENDS: Last Sunday I told you about the Feast of the Passover, how it came to be instituted, and what it signified. To-day I want to talk to you about the Feast of Tabernacles. The Feast of the Passover occurred in the spring, nearly corresponding to our Easter; and at such times when the Israelites from every quarter of the land came up to Jerusalem, as was the custom at the three annual feasts, some provision had to be made for their entertainment.

At the Feast of the Passover all the Jews living in Jerusalem had to throw open their homes, and entertain under the cover of their own roofs, all who came to them. They could not decline to receive the thousands of worshipers who came up to the Feast, but were required to afford them a place of shelter in their homes. Therefore it was that before the Feast of the Passover Jesus sent two of His disciples, and told them to go into the city, and they would find a man bearing a pitcher of water; they should follow him and ask him to direct them to a room in his house, where Jesus might eat the Passover with His disciples. (Matt. xxvi: 17; Mark xiv: 13.)

At the Feast of Tabernacles, which occurred in the fall of the year, after the harvest and the fruit of the vines and the trees had all been gathered in, it was very different. At this Feast, when the

234

Building Booths at Feast of Tabernacles.

235

Israelites came up to Jerusalem, not only those who came from a distance, but even those who lived regularly in the city, were required to tent or live in booths made by simply placing some poles in the ground, with other poles reaching across the top, so as to form a roof or covering. This roof was not shingled, but was formed by laying branches of trees upon the sticks which had been laid across from one pole to the other. (Neh. viii: 14, 15.)

You now see why to-day I have chosen this branch of a tree to show you in connection with this sermon. I have chosen this to impress upon your mind the character of the arbors used at the Feast of Tabernacles; the tops or roofs of which were formed or made of olive, and willow and pine, myrtle and palm branches. These booths or arbors were to remind the Children of Israel of the journey of their forefathers through the desert, when for forty long years they did not live within the walls or under the roof of any house, but dwelt only in booths.

I am sure that you and I would like to have looked in upon Jerusalem at the time when one of these Harvest Home festivals was being celebrated. We would like to have seen the booths on the tops of the houses and along the side of the hills, outside of the walls of the city, and sloping down through the valleys and crowding far out into the country upon the Mount of Olives and beyond. We would like to have seen the bright faces of the happy throngs of people as they moved in procession through the streets, waving their palm branches; and to have listened to the music of the trumpeters of the Temple, as they sounded their trumpets twice every hour throughout the entire day. I am sure we would have been delighted to look down upon the festive crowd at night, when, instead of waving palm branches as they did during the day, they carried bright flaming torches, amid the clashing of cymbals and the blast of trumpets.

"He Bore it Aloft as He Ascended the Stairs."

This Feast lasted for eight days. The first day and the last were especially sacred. And now I want to call your attention to this second object which I have; namely, this water, and I want to tell you how it was related to and used at this Feast of Tabernacles. On the morning of each day, while the smoke of the morning sacrifice was ascending in beautiful wreaths in the still air, a priest bearing a large golden bowl, and followed by a long procession of boys and girls waving palm branches, descended the side of the hill to the pool of Siloam, which was in a quiet recess at the foot of Mount Moriah, on the summit of which the Temple was built. When the priest had filled the golden bowl with water from this clear pool, he held it above his head and bore it aloft as he ascended the stairs. As the procession entered the Court of the Temple, the trumpets sounded, and all the throngs of people gathered within its walls took up the words of the prophet and sang, "With joy shall ye draw water out of the wells of salvation" (Isaiah xii: 3), and as the priest came to the base of the altar he poured the water from the golden bowl into a silver basin amid shouts and gladness. Upon the eighth day, "the last day, that great day of the feast" (John vii: 37), the joy was greater than upon any of the other days. The priests in glad procession moved around the altar seven times, singing the Psalms.

It was at the last Feast of Tabernacles which Jesus attended, that He stood in the midst of this glad assembly, and beheld their joy as they remembered how God had supplied their fathers with water in the wilderness; and how God had given them a land of streams, and rivers, and wells of water, and it was then when Jesus heard them crying "Hosanna, blessed is He that cometh in the name of the Lord," that Jesus stood up in the midst of the Temple and of the people and said, "If any man thirst, let him come unto me and drink." (John vii: 37.) To those of us who have always lived in the midst of a bountiful supply of fresh, clear, crystal water, these words are not as impressive as they were to the people to whom they were then spoken. For their land was surrounded by deserts, and they lived in the midst of nations whose people often famished and died, because there was not a sufficient supply of water to drink.

While we live in a country where there is always an abundant supply of water to satisfy the thirst of the body, yet spiritually, like these people at the Feast of Tabernacles we have the same spiritual needs that they had, and if you and I thirst for the water of life, if we desire everlasting salvation, if we thirst for the knowledge of sacred things and desire to do that which is right, Jesus invites you and me to come to Him, and says to us: "Ho, every one that thirsteth, come ye to the waters." (Isa. lv: 1.) "If any man thirst let him come unto me and drink," (John vii: 37.) "Whosoever drinketh of the water that I shall give him shall never thirst; but the water that I shall give him shall be in him a well of water springing up into everlasting life." (John iv: 14.)

QUESTIONS.—At what season of the year was the Feast of Tabernacles held? How long did it last? In what did the people live or dwell during the Feast? Of what were the booths built? Why did they dwell in booths instead of in their houses at this time? Of what was all this to remind them? Which was the great day of the Feast? On this last day of the Feast what did the high priest bring from the well? By whom was the priest accompanied? Into what did he pour the water from the golden bowl? Of what was this water the symbol? Does every human being thirst for or desire righteousness? Did Jesus invite such to come to Him and drink? Should we always go to Him to satisfy our spiritual hunger and thirst?

LEAVES.

THE LESSONS WHICH THEY TEACH.

SUGGESTION:—Objects: Some autumn leaves or green leaves of different varieties.

MY DEAR BOYS AND GIRLS: To-day I picked up these few beautiful leaves, which during the summer were lifted aloft on the trees and cast their grateful shadows upon the weary traveler as he journeyed under the scorching rays of the sun. But with the coming of autumn these leaves have faded, and the first frost of winter has tinged them with crimson and glory. I am sure we cannot look upon them without thinking of the words of the Prophet Isaiah, in the sixty-fourth chapter and sixth verse, where he says: "We all do fade as a leaf."

Autumn Leaves.

I desire, however, to use these leaves to teach you not only this lesson, but also several others which they suggest.

If, during the summer, you go out into a forest and study the leaves, one of the first things which you will notice will be that the leaves which grow upon one kind of trees differ from the leaves

240

which grow upon every other kind of trees. Indeed, if you pick up a leaf from the ground and examine it carefully you will find that the leaf is largely a picture of the tree upon which it grew. The shape of the leaf will correspond very largely with the shape of the tree from which it has fallen. If you study the leaf more carefully you will discover that the veins in the leaf will quite closely resemble the shape of the limbs of the tree. You would not be able to study the different leaves which you pick up without being impressed with the resemblance in many instances between the leaf and the tree upon which it grew.

Now, I think that we may learn a very profitable lesson from the leaves in this respect. I think that you will find, when you are able to study with a little closeness of observation, that the scholars of different Sunday-schools are different from each other, at least in some respects. Those who come from the school where good order is maintained, where there are consecrated, devoted teachers who give themselves carefully to the preparation of the lesson, secure the attention of their scholars, impress the truth deeply upon the minds, and hearts and consciences—you will find that the scholars of this school become attentive and orderly, and well behaved, and all the scholars in the school partake of the influences which are exerted over them from Sunday to Sunday. The scholars who attend a school where the superintendent does not keep good order, where the teachers are irregular and disinterested, and where everything is permitted to go along as by mere chance, these scholars will partake of the influence of the school, and will individually become like the school. So you see how important it is that each and every scholar should be attentive and thoughtful, and give the very largest amount of help possible to the superintendent and teachers to render the school orderly, and to encourage the teachers who desire to devote themselves to the teaching of Bible truth and the impressing of the spiritual lessons, so that those who are under their influence may be brought to a saving acquaintance with Christ.

What I have said with reference to the Sunday-school is also true with reference to the Church. There is an old saying, that "like priest, like people." When a pastor continues for a long period of years in the same pulpit, ministering to the same people, if he has their sympathy, co-operation and assistance the people will become very much like each other in their spiritual character, and all will become more and more like the pastor and his teachings. If he is godly, and consecrated, and upright, his people will become increasingly so. And you will find not only that each scholar becomes a miniature of the Sunday-school which he attends, but each Christian becomes a miniature of the congregation of which he is a member.

But the leaves teach us another lesson. The great trees which you see in the forest are the result of the united efforts and labors of the leaves. Each leaf is gifted with individual power, and together they all drink in the influence of the sunlight and the showers, and unitedly they build up the great oaks and elms and poplars, and all the trees of the fields and forest. The coal, which is now dug from the mines, was once a great tropical growth of forest trees which were afterwards buried by some great convulsion in nature, and now when we dig up the coal and burn it in our stoves we are simply releasing the buried sunshine which was accumulated and stored up by the individual leaves of the great forests of centuries ago.

As we look upon the leaves of the trees I think we must be impressed with the fact, that each one labors in his own appointed place. There is no conflict, there is no crowding of one, thinking to exalt himself above the others. There are no little parties of leaves joining together and trying to crowd themselves to the top of the tree, but each and all work faithfully and zealously in the place which God has appointed them.

They are not only faithful workers, but they are unselfish workers. No leaf can have the joy which belongs to another, or the glory of all the leaves. Each leaf has the reward of doing a little, and when its work is done it must drop to the ground and perish in the dust. The work which it has done and the tree which it has helped to build will be its monument and reward. If each

The Budding of the New Leaf.

leaf gives its life faithfully for the building up of the tree, no leaf can fall to the ground or be shaken from its place by the autumn wind and perish in despair.

If you will go into the forest at the autumn period of the year, or go into the orchard and examine where the leaves are about to drop off, you will find that at the base of the stem of each leaf, already there appears the budding of the leaf which is to be unfolded next spring, and even though the leaf withers and falls to the ground, leaving the barren limb alone to battle with the winter storms, yet there is the promise and the evidence that when the gentle breath of spring shall come and break open the icy sepulchres of the winter, these little buds will feel the genial warmth and unfold their green beauty in a radiant springtime of beautiful foliage. So one generation of men may die and pass away, to have their work continued and completed by those who are to come after them.

But these leaves also teach us of our mortality. For, as Isaiah says, "We all do fade as a leaf." We are all very apt to forget that we must die. And so each year, when the summer is over and the fruit is gathered, the leaves begin to wither, and the early frost tinges the forests of the closing year, like the sun oftentimes makes the clouds all crimson and glory at the close of the day. These things should teach us that as advancing years come, we also must fade and die. God spreads out before us this great panorama along the valleys and on the hillsides each autumn to teach us that as the leaves perish, so we must also fade and droop and die.

But there is one great encouragement, and that is, that although the leaves fall, the tree stands. The leaf perishes, but the tree abides, and year after year, sometimes for centuries, it goes on increasing in stature and in strength, abiding as the giant of the forest. So also, when at last each of us must die, that which we have built shall abide, and what we have received from others and to which we have added our efforts and our labors, others shall receive from us, and they also shall carry on the work in which we have been engaged. So each generation receives and carries on the work of those who have gone before. As the poet has well said,

> "Like leaves on trees, the race of man is found,
> Now green in youth, now withered on the ground;
> Another race the following age supplies;
> They fall successive, and successive rise;
> So generations in their course decay
> So perish these when those have passed away."

The tree stands a monument of strength and beauty at the grave of all the dead leaves which lie buried at its feet. So what each boy and girl, each man and woman, shall have accomplished of good or evil, will remain after they have perished and passed away, to tell of their lives, and God will note the result. He who says that not even a sparrow can fall to the ground without His notice, and who tells us that the very hairs of our heads are all numbered, He will note our deeds, and He will be our reward.

If I were speaking now to older people I might call attention to the fact that the autumn leaves are more beautiful than the summer leaves. And so boys and girls, it seems to me, and it has always thus seemed to me, that there is something more beautiful in manhood and womanhood, during the later years of life, than during the earlier years. Always honor and respect the aged whose heads are gray, whose features are venerable and whose characters are Christ-like.

QUESTIONS.—Are the leaves alike on all trees? In what ways are the leaves like the tree on which they grew? Are Sunday-school scholars much like the school that they attend? Are grown people greatly influenced by the pastor who preaches to them, and the people with whom they are associated? Of what are great trees the result? How do leaves accomplish this? When a leaf drops from the tree, what has already started? What do fading and dropping leaves represent? Does the tree abide when the leaves fall? When we die do the great influences which we have helped forward remain to bless the world? Who still notes our deeds when we pass away? Which are more beautiful, summer or autumn leaves? What periods of life are they like?

THE TURTLE.

MEN LIKE AND YET UNLIKE THE ANIMALS.

SUGGESTION :—While it is not at all necessary to present any special objects, it will add to the interest if the parent has a turtle shell or even the shells of oysters, clams or abalone, which are somewhat the same in principle, the outside cover of the animal constituting both its home and defence, although differing from the turtle in other respects.

M Y DEAR BOYS AND GIRLS: I want to show you to-day how in some respect we are like the animals, and how in other respects we are very unlike them. To illustrate what I desire to say I have brought this small turtle shell. From the way that some boys treat flies and bugs, and birds, cats and dogs and all kinds of animals you would suppose that many boys and some girls think that animals have no feeling. Boys who have never suffered any bodily pain themselves, oftentimes act as though they thought that animals could not suffer pain, but in this they are greatly mistaken. Animals can and do suffer pain, the same as people suffer pain, and in order to defend them against their enemies God has provided these creatures of His hand with some means of protecting themselves. The birds can fly away. Some animals, like foxes, have holes in the ground where they can hide. Others, like the squirrel, hide in the hollow trees. Bees can sting. Some cattle have horns for defence, and some others, which are not as capable of defending themselves against the stronger animals, God has marvellously provided with two stomachs. The cow goes out in the field and crops off the grass rapidly and can then go to a

246

place of shelter and lie down, and there, protected from the attack of wild beasts, chew what she has gathered. This is known in the country as chewing the cud. The same is true with sheep; they also bite off the grass and swallow it quickly. It passes into a first stomach and then they can lie down in some quiet place and chew the cud; or in other words chew that which they have hastily bitten off in the fields.

Now the turtle cannot escape from his enemies because he cannot run very rapidly, and so God has covered him with a coat of mail and given him a helmet, a hard, bony covering for the head

and this large bony covering for his body, which we can very properly call his house. When danger approaches, the turtle quickly draws his head and his feet into this large shell, and is quite safe from the attack of his enemies. Whatever a n i m a l might desire to eat the turtle is

The Turtle.

prevented on account of this hard outer shell. On this lower part you will notice how the turtle can draw the front portion up more closely, and thus the more securely shut himself within his house. So you see how God has provided all the animals with a means of protection and defense, first, to protect their lives, and secondly, to save them from pain and suffering.

While God has thus successfully protected them against other animals, they are not protected against the superior intelligence and ingenuity of man. The birds can fly faster than the man can run, but man can shoot the bird with an arrow or with a rifle. So with all the other animals. Now God has made it right for us to kill animals for food, but it is very wrong for us to destroy animals for the simple pleasure of taking life, and it is also very wicked to inflict pain unnecessarily upon any of the animals.

I want to tell you about a boy who was once strolling through the fields with his sister. They found a nest of rabbits. The sister was charmed with the beautiful nest itself and with its living occupants, but the boy teased them, mimicking their squeaks and their struggles. In vain his sister plead with him not to hurt these pretty little creatures, but the wicked boy flung them up into the air one by one and shouted when each fell dead upon the stones. Ten years after the sister sat weeping again by that boy's side. He was in chains, sentenced to be hanged for shooting a farmer who was hunting in a neighbor's field. They were waiting for the awful procession to knock at the cell door. "Sister," he said, "do you remember the nest of rabbits ten years ago; how you begged and prayed, and how I ridiculed? I verily believe that from that day God forsook me, and left me to follow my own inclinations. If I had yielded to your tears then, you and I would not be weeping these bitter tears now."

You see how it is that boys who have no regard for the suffering, or the preservation of the life of animals are likely to inflict pain and even to take the lives of people.

But I want to call your attention to another respect in which we are like the animals, or perhaps, more correctly, in which the animals are like us. The forms of most all animals have some resemblance to each other, and all are somewhat in form like man. If you take the bird, his wings correspond to our arms, his legs and feet are somewhat like ours, only his toes are longer, and the nails are slightly different in form. If you will take the horse you will see that his neck is longer than ours, that his front legs correspond to our arms, and if you take your fingers and press them together you will see how, if you were to study the anatomy of the horse's foot carefully, it resembles the bones in our hands, and the bony foot of the horse corresponds to the nails on the ends of our fingers, only that in the case of the horse the nails are all in one, forming the hoof, to which the blacksmith nails the shoe. The horse's hoof, however, is not solid as you might think, but only a shell, the same as the nails on the ends of our fingers.

Now if you were to take the turtle that lives in this shell or house you would find that he also has four legs, the front legs corresponding to our arms, and his hind legs corresponding to our legs and feet. On the end of each of his feet he has nails, the same as you and I have at the extremities of our hands and feet. But I am sure

Birds.

you would say that the turtle was very much unlike us, in that he has such a hard shell of a house which he carries about with him. But if you will feel of your hands you will discover that you have bones inside of your hands. So you have bones in your arms and all through your body. These bones of your body are covered with flesh, so our bones are *inside* of us. But with this turtle almost all of his bones are made into one bone, and that is on the *outside* of his body.

Our muscles, with which we move our hands and feet and different portions of our body, are attached to the bones which are inside of us. His muscles are attached to the bone which is on the outside of him. So you see that we are like him, in that both of us have bones, only his are on the outside while ours are on the inside.

His bone or shell is a covering and a defense. Our bones, on the inside of us, are so constructed as to enable us to defend ourselves also. God has given the turtle a house, but He has given us the knowledge and the skill, so that we can construct our own house. We are created with capacity to till the earth and to subdue the wild beasts of the forest, and with our superior intelligence to be king over all the other creatures which God has created.

Now, there are several lessons which we may learn from what I have said. God has protected all animals against their foes. He has not fully protected the animals against us, but He expects us to use our intelligence and our better nature, to be thoughtful and careful not to inflict pain even upon the worm or insect which crawls upon the ground beneath our feet.

While our bodies are somewhat like the bodies of birds and beasts, in our moral nature we are not like the animals, but like God. We were made in the moral likeness and image of God. We have intelligence and God has made us to know right from wrong. The animals have no conscience. Cattle do not recognize any wrong when they break out of their owner's pasture and break into a neighbor's cornfield. We do not say that cattle have sinned, because they know nothing of ownership. They do not know what is right and what is wrong, and, therefore, are not accountable beings. In our intellectual, moral and spiritual nature we are superior to everything else that God has created. We have a moral nature. We know what is right and what is wrong, and, therefore, we are accountable beings. God has made us free to follow our own purpose and, therefore, we are to be held accountable. God has created us not for a few days of life upon the earth, but He has made us immortal, and if we have faith in the Lord Jesus Christ, and accept Him as our Saviour and love and serve Him upon the earth, our condition in the next world will be one of great blessing and happiness.

God has given the turtle a house. He has given us intelligence and all the materials and left us to construct the house in which we are to live upon this earth. But in heaven He has built our house for us. Jesus said: "In My Father's house are many mansions." The German translation has it, "In My Father's house are many homes." "I go to prepare a place for you. And if I go and prepare a place for you, I will come again, and receive you unto myself; that where I am, there ye may be also."

Death may be a misfortune to a poor turtle, but not to a Christian man or woman, or a Christian boy or girl. Death is only the blessed Saviour coming to take us unto Himself.

QUESTIONS.—Do animals feel pain? Has God provided for their protection? Does the turtle have bones? Are your bones on the outside or the inside of your body? Where are the turtle's bones principally? How does the turtle protect himself? Tell the story of the bad boy and the little rabbits. Are the forms of animals similar to the form of our bodies? To what part of our body do the wings of the bird and the front legs of a horse or cow correspond? Do animals have a moral nature and a conscience? Are they accountable to God for their conduct? Are we?

GRASSHOPPER AND ANT.

NEGLIGENCE AND INDUSTRY.

THE largest city of the world is across the ocean, in England. In the busiest part of London is a very large building, called the Royal Exchange. On the top of the pinnacle, or tower, of this large stone building is a large grasshopper, and the English people have this legend in reference to it: It is related that some three hundred and seventy-five years ago, a woman, whose purposes we cannot know, might have been seen hurrying along a country lane, some distance outside of the city. Hastening along she came to a gate leading into a field, and looking in every direction to be sure that no one was near, she took off her shawl and wrapped it carefully around a little baby which she had concealed under her arm, and laid it gently by the side of a hedge. And then turning back to the lane, she soon disappeared in the distance. An hour or two later a little girl and a rollicking, frolicking boy, possibly returning from school, were crossing the field. It was in the later days of summer, when butterflies and grasshoppers abounded. As this light-hearted boy was whistling along his way, a large grasshopper bounded across his path, and, true to the instincts of childhood, the boy started in pursuit of the grasshopper. The chase was only begun when the grasshopper crossed the fence and landed in a grain field, which in England is called a corn field. Stooping to catch his prize, the boy discovered near by what proved to be a bright little baby, fast asleep in its mother's shawl. Joyful with the prize which they had found, the

252

The Royal Exchange, London.

boy took it up in his arms, and hastened to his mother, who, although a farmer's wife, with many cares and several children, resolved to adopt the little stranger as her own.

Years passed on, and the infant boy grew to be a man of industry and economy, and finally became one of the richest and most influential men in the city of London. Queen Elizabeth, who was then upon the throne, often consulted him, and in after years, as an expression of gratitude to the great city in which he had accumulated his wealth, and for the royal favor which had been shown him, he built the Bourse, or what is called the Royal Exchange, and in recognition of the kind Providence which had

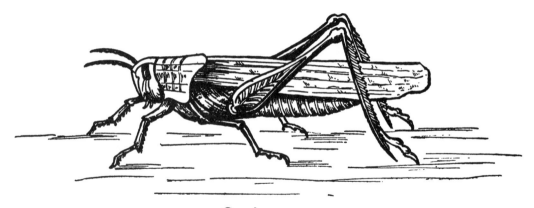

Grasshopper.

used the grasshopper to lead the steps of the boy to where the baby was lying in the fields, Sir Thomas Gresham, for that was his name, placed this large grasshopper in stone, upon the topmost pinnacle of this Royal Exchange. While I cannot vouch for the historical accuracy of this legend, yet it beautifully illustrates the truth that God often uses an humble insect for the accomplishment of His great providences.

Now, I want to tell you something about the grasshopper, and also about the ant.

The grasshopper is very much like that class of boys who

want to have a good time, play and frolic from day to day, but
never go to school or work, but live for the play and pleasure to be
enjoyed each day as it passes.   The grasshopper jumps from place
to place across the field, eating his food wherever he can find it,
and then spends his days and weeks in idleness.   He never stops
to think that the summer will soon pass away, the fields will then
be barren, the cold autumn will come, when the fields will be left
desolate and covered with snow.   So finally when the autumn
comes, he has no food laid up for the winter, but dies of poverty
and hunger.   This little poem which I read in the schoolbooks,
when I was a boy, will tell the whole story:

SONG OF THE GRASSHOPPER.

I saw a brown old grasshopper,
   And he sat upon a stone,
While ever and anon he chirped
   In a sad and mournful tone:
And many an anxious, troubled look
   He cast around the naked plain;
Where now was but a stubble field,
   Once waved the golden grain.
What ails thee, old brown grasshopper?
   His voice was low and faint,
As in the language of his race
   He made this dire complaint:
"O! in the long bright summer time
   I treasured up no store,
Now the last full sheaf is garnered,
   And the harvest days are o'er."

What didst thou, brown old grasshopper,
   When the summer days were long?
"I danced on the fragrant clover tops,
   With many a merry song;
O! we were a blithesome company,
   And a joyous life we led;
But with the flowers and summer hours,

My gay companions fled:
Old age and poverty are come,
    The autumn wind is chill,
It whistles through my tattered coat,
    And my voice is cracked and shrill.
In a damp and gloomy cavern
    Beneath this cold, gray stone,
I must lay me down and perish—
    I must perish all alone.
Alas! that in life's golden time
    I treasured up no store,
For now the sheaves are gathered in,
    And the harvest days are o'er."

He ceased his melancholy wail,
    And a tear was in his eye,
As he slowly slid from the cold gray stone,
    And laid him down to die.
And then I thought, t'were well if all
    In pleasure's idle throng,
Had seen that old brown grasshopper
    And heard his dying song:
For life's bright, glowing summer
    Is hasting to its close,
And winter's night is coming—
    The night of long repose.
O! garner then in reaping time,
    A rich, unfailing store,
Ere the summer hours are past and gone,
    And the harvest days are o'er!

The little ant is not so foolish. For thousands of years the ant has always been wise and industrious. In the Book of Proverbs, written over twenty-five hundred years ago, Solomon tells us in the thirtieth chapter and twenty-fifth verse: "The ants are a people not strong, yet they prepare their meat in the summer." And in the sixth chapter, sixth, seventh and eighth verses he says, "Go to the ant, thou sluggard; consider her ways, and be wise;

which having no guide, overseer, or ruler, provideth her meat in the summer, and gathereth her food in the harvest." You have probably noticed the industry, activity and perseverance of these little ants. They attempt great things. Sometimes you will see one of these little insects carrying a burden which is several times larger than its own body. If they come to a stone, or a log, or some obstacle, over which they must carry their burden, if they do not succeed the first time, they will try again; and even though they should fall, or fail as much as a hundred times, they will persevere until they have accomplished their undertaking. If you watch them, you will see how rapidly they move. They are not lazy, they do not loiter along the way, but are always in a hurry.

Ants.

They work with energy and gather food during the summer, which they lay up for their supply during the winter. Whatever the little ant can gather, it carries home and lays up in store, not for itself alone, but all work together, each laboring for the good and well-being of all the others.

This grasshopper very fittingly represents the feeling and thought which come into the mind of every boy when he is at first required to work, to go to school and study, when he is being taught to be industrious and useful. When the days are pleasant, boys do not like to go to school. When a pleasant Sunday morning comes in the springtime, they often wish to stay at home, to go out to the park, or to roam about the fields, and if most of the boys and girls had their own way about it, in the beginning, they would live pretty much like the grasshopper. They would get what pleasure they could out of the days as they pass, grow up in ignorance and idleness, and in manhood and womanhood find themselves in poverty and want. I think that pretty much all boys and girls are naturally lazy, and that feeling can only be cured by being required to work, being compelled to go to school and study, and being kept persistently at it from week to week and year to year, until at last they learn to love to work. If the parents of the grasshopper had not themselves been lazy and grown up in idleness, they would have taught the young grasshopper that in the spring and summer he was to look forward to the wants and needs of the winter. The older ants always teach the young ants to work, and in that they are very wise.

Perhaps you have seen boys and girls who have learned to work, who are always very active, who seem always to be busy, but after all accomplish nothing of any moment in life. If we want to live to some purpose in this world, we must remember that we should have a purpose worthy of ourselves, and of the great Father in Heaven who has created us. After a few months and years the grasshoppers and the ants and all the insects die, but you and I shall live on forever and ever. These bodies will be laid away in the grave, but our immortal spirits shall still continue to live. The stars in heaven which have been shining for thousands and thousands of years shall eventually grow pale. The sun itself shall cease to shine, and all the heavens and the universe about us shall be rolled together as a scroll. But these immortal spirits of yours and mine shall live on with God throughout all eternity. It is important, therefore, that our industry and our thought and our labor should not be for those things which perish with the using; that we should not simply lay up treasures which we must after a time go away and leave behind us in this world, but that we should lay up treasures in heaven, where moth and rust do not corrupt, and where thieves do not break through nor steal; that where our treasure is, there our hearts may be also; and that we may possess and enjoy our treasure throughout all eternity.

I hope that every time you see a grasshopper or an ant, you will remember the lesson which I have sought to teach you to-day.

QUESTIONS.—What is on the top of the Royal Exchange in London? Who built the Exchange? Why did he put the grasshopper there? Tell all you can about the little boy and girl going through the field. What kind of boys and girls is like the grasshopper? What does the grasshopper do in summer? What happens to him when winter comes? Is the ant like the grasshopper, or is he industrious? What does the Bible say about the ant? How does he spend the the summer? Does he have food for winter use? Does each ant work for itself alone? Who teach the young ants to work? Do boys and girls all have to be taught to work? Do all people who are busy accomplish something worthy of their effort? What should we live for?

BALANCES.

HOW GOD WEIGHS PEOPLE.

SUGGESTION :—Objects: A pair of ordinary balances. A very good pair for illustration can easily be made from a piece of wood, a few strings and a couple of little paper boxes.

DEAR BOYS AND GIRLS: I suppose you have all stood on the scales and been weighed. I have here a pair of balances. This was doubtless one of the earliest kind of instruments with which people weighed different things, and it is the kind of scales which are still used when the

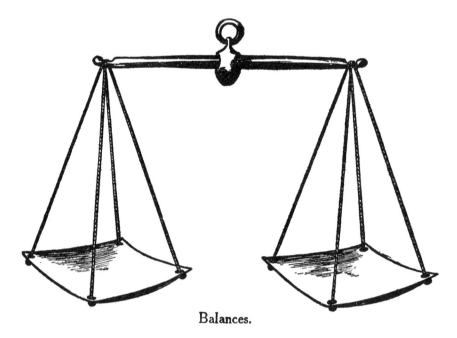

Balances.

greatest accuracy is desired. These are called a balance, because when I hold them by this string you will see that this end of the

arm and that end of the arm are equal in length and equal in weight
and they exactly balance each other. Now when I place anything
in the pan on this end of the arm, and place a small weight in the
pan on the opposite arm, and then lift the balance up, you will see
how I can readily tell how much the piece of metal, or piece of
wood, or whatever I have placed in the balances, weighs. In the
drug stores they use this kind of scales to weigh medicines, and they
can tell accurately the weight of a very small quantity. In the laboratory, or the place where medicines are made, they have this
kind of scales that will weigh the smallest particle of dust; even a
small piece of a hair laid on the scales can be weighed accurately.

In the fifth chapter of the Book of Daniel we read about a
king whose name was Belshazzar, who lived in the great city of
Babylon, surrounded by a great wall three hundred feet high and
eighty feet broad, and with a hundred gates of brass, twenty-five
gates on each side of the city, and a street running from each of the
gates upon the one side, straight across the city to each of the corresponding gates upon the opposite side, a distance of some twelve
or fifteen miles; and then other streets crossing these first twenty-
five streets, running between the gates which were upon the other
two sides of the city. God had blessed this king of Babylon and
given him great wealth and great power; but he became proud and
defied God. One night he made a great feast and invited a thousand of his lords and the generals of his army, and sent for the
golden vessels of the Temple, which Nebuchadnezzar had brought
down from Jerusalem, and Belshazzar drank wine out of these
sacred vessels of the Temple. And, like men and women when
they drink liquor, they lost their reason, and they praised the gods
of gold, and of silver, and brass, and iron, and wood, and of stone,
and thus dishonored God; and there appeared in the banqueting
hall the fingers of a man's hand and wrote on the wall so that all

might see and read it, and these were the words which were written before that wicked king: "Thou art weighed in the balances, and art found wanting."   (Daniel v: 27.)

Now you see that God weighs men and women, not for the purpose of telling how many pounds their bodies weigh, but He weighs their character, He weighs their conduct, He weighs their purposes, and He weighs their principles, and so He weighed Belshazzar, and He said of him and to him, "Thou art weighed in the balances, and art found wanting."   God weighed Belshazzar as though he were placed in this side of the balance, and on the other side of the balance were placed all his opportunities, privileges and his blessings, and all that God had done for him. When God thus weighed him against all these things Belshazzar was found so light that he did not weigh as much as the privileges and blessings which God had given him, and therefore, God said that he was weighed in the balances and was found wanting.

In just this same way God weighs you and me, in order that we may see whether or not we weigh enough. Suppose we turn to the twentieth chapter of Exodus and there find what God requires of us. You will find that God says, "Thou shalt have no other gods before me. Thou shalt not make unto thee any graven image, or any likeness of anything that is in heaven above, or that is in the earth beneath, or that is in the water under the earth: thou shalt not bow down thyself to them, nor serve them: for I the Lord thy God am a jealous God, visiting the iniquity of the fathers upon the children unto the third and fourth generation of them that hate me; and showing mercy unto thousands of them that love me, and keep my commandments."

Now suppose I place this requirement in one side of the balance, and then ask you to place your obedience to this requirement in the other side of the balance. I am sure there are a great many

מְנֵא מְנֵא
תְּקֵל וּפַרְסִין

"Thou Art Weighed in the Balances, and Art Found Wanting."   263 grown men and women who could not be weighed against this requirement. If a man loves money, so that he sacrifices his obedience to God, or sacrifices his character, or gives too large an amount of time to money-making, and money-getting; if his love of money is very great, you see how he makes money a sort of a god—that is, that he exalts his love of money above his love of God. In the same way a person can worship pleasure, and ease, and fame in such a way as to exalt these above God. Now any one who has done this, cannot be weighed against this requirement of God's law without being found wanting.

If we take the next Commandment, it reads, "Thou shalt not take the name of the Lord thy God in vain; for the Lord will not hold him guiltless that taketh his name in vain." Now anybody who has ever sworn cannot be weighed against this Commandment. A man who curses and swears is a very wicked man. I hope that none of you, boys or girls, will ever profane God's name and disgrace yourself by swearing.

I want to caution you, also, against the use of by-words. Sometimes boys swear without knowing it; they say "By Jiminy." Now, the word "Gemini" means "Twins," and refers to two heathen gods whose names were "Castor" and "Pollux," and when boys use the expression, "By Jiminy," they are swearing by those two heathen gods. Jesus said, "Swear not at all." (Matt. v: 34.) Then not only those who literally swear, but all those who use God's name without reverence and who make light of sacred things break this Commandment. So you see that many are not able to be weighed against this Commandment.

Then take the next: "Remember the Sabbath Day, to keep it holy." There are many people who remember the Sabbath Day simply to make it the occasion of visiting, letter writing, and to enjoy a trip into the country, or in the park. They remember the

Sabbath Day, but they do not remember it to keep it holy. So you see that you would not be able to be weighed against that requirement.

Now take the next: "Honor thy father and thy mother: that thy days may be long upon the land which the Lord thy God giveth thee." If God were to come into this community and weigh the boys and girls against this Commandment, how many do you think would be found to whom God would turn and say, as He did to Belshazzar: "Thou art weighed and art found wanting"? Any boy or girl who speaks of his father as "The old man," and of his mother as "The old woman"; any boy or girl who is disobedient; any girl who yesterday when mother asked her to dust the furniture, or any boy who when mother asked him yesterday to run upon an errand, grew petulant, and scowled and scolded, perhaps went out of the room and slammed the door behind them, all such boys and girls would be found wanting. You see how, with one after another of these Commandments, if God were to weigh us we would be found wanting.

If we take the other Commandments, "Thou shalt not kill," anybody who has hated his brother in his heart; "Thou shalt not commit adultery," any one who has harbored lust in his heart; "Thou shalt not steal"; "Thou shalt not bear false witness"; "Thou shalt not covet"; think of each of these and see how many times in your life you have broken them, if not in letter, yet in spirit.

Now, if you cannot be weighed against these different requirements and you have come short of them in the past, how can you expect to stand in the great Day of Judgment, when God shall take into account every idle word that we have ever uttered, every wicked thought; when we shall be weighed in the just balances of an infinite God? When God shall place these requirements upon one side of the balance, and you and I shall step in upon the other side of the balance, there is only one possible way in which we could then be heavy enough, and that is if we could have our Elder Brother, Jesus Christ, to step into the balance with us, as He is willing to do, and God should accept the obedience and holiness of His own Beloved Son, Jesus Christ in our stead. Unless you and I have Jesus Christ with us when we step into that balance, it will be said, "Thou art found wanting." Have you accepted Jesus Christ as your friend, and are you trying to serve Him? If you have not now made Him your friend, how can you hope to have His friendship then? May God help you to have Jesus as your friend in life, as well as in death; in this life as well as in the life to come, now while being tempted and tried in this world, as well as when being weighed in the next.

QUESTIONS.—What was the handwriting on the wall at Belshazzar's feast? Does God weigh our bodies? What does He weigh? Against what was Belshazzar weighed? What are we weighed against? Are we weighed against each commandment separately? Can a person who has sworn be weighed against the third commandment? Is the use of by-words swearing? Are we honoring our parents by speaking disrespectfully of them? Can we break a commandment in thought as well as in deed? Tell how. Will all these requirements over-balance us? What must we do to make a proper balance? Is Christ willing to step into the scales with us?

WHITE AND CHARRED STICKS.

GOOD AND BAD COMPANY.

SUGGESTION:—Objects: A few pine sticks, some charred; ink and water.

ALL boys and girls like to have companions, some one to play with, and therefore it is very wise that I should talk to you to-day about good and bad company.

First of all let me read some passages from the Bible. "Blessed is the man that walketh not in the counsel of the ungodly, nor standeth in the way of sinners, nor sitteth in the seat of the scornful." (Psalms i: 1.) "Forsake the foolish and live; and go in the way of understanding." (Proverbs ix: 6.) But here is a passage of Scripture which is exactly suited to my purpose to-day: "He that walketh with wise men shall be wise; but a companion of fools shall be destroyed." (Proverbs xiii: 20.)

When you go into a large library to select books you will always find that they are classified. Some of the shelves have books of history, others have books of poetry, and so on throughout the entire library. In this way God has classified different people in this text. One class is called wise, and the others are called foolish. A companion of wise men shall be wise, but a companion of fools shall be destroyed. In the same way there are good boys and bad boys, good girls and bad girls; and when you choose your companions it is important that you should choose them among the good, and not among the bad.

I think you will better understand the teaching of the text, when I show you this one stick that has been burned black, or charred, as we say. Now here are several clean sticks which have not been burned, which are white and not tarnished. Let this black stick represent the boys who smoke, or chew, or swear, or lie, or deceive their parents; boys or girls who do not go to Sunday-school, who do not obey their parents, and who do not love God. These clean sticks will represent good boys and girls. Now suppose the good boys and girls choose the bad boys and girls as their companions and playmates; what do you think would be the result? I will mix these sticks together. I am sure that nobody would expect

White and Charred Sticks.

that the white sticks would transfer their purity and cleanness to this black stick. When I mix them, or rub them together, the black sticks get no whiter, but all the white sticks get blacker.

That is the way it always is with the boys who keep bad company. Instead of exerting a good influence, so as to reform and purify, and make good boys of the bad boys, the bad boys make bad boys of the good boys. At first the good boys are horrified at what they hear and see the bad boys say and do. After a while it ceases to be unpleasant to them. A little later they may possibly laugh at the bad boys, but after a while they will come to like the bad boys, and finally they will do as the bad boys do and become like them in conduct and in character.

Perhaps you have seen boys who like to take cork and burn it in the candle or fire, and then blacken their faces with it, so as to make them look like colored people. Now, it is not the best thing for a white boy to try to look like a colored boy, but if he does rub this black on his face, he can wash it off with soap and water. But when a good boy goes with bad boys and his character becomes tarnished and blackened, he cannot cleanse and purify it so easily. He not only gets a bad character but a bad reputation as well, both of which are very difficult to cleanse or to get rid of.

Now, here I have a glass of water and a bottle of ink. If I take and pour a half a teaspoonful of this water into the ink, it makes no particular difference in its color. But if I

Glass of Water and Bottle of Ink.

take only two or three drops of ink and mix them with the water, it discolors the entire glass of water at once. One or two good boys in the midst of many bad ones are likely to be influenced in a bad direction. This is especially true if the good boys have sought the bad boys as companions. Even one or two bad boys, placed in the midst of several good boys, may exert a very bad influence over them. I suppose you have all seen this illustrated in the school room. You may have had a set of good boys, or a set of good girls in your class, but some day a bad boy came to the school, or a bad

17

girl joined the class and they were frivolous, laughed and talked and were disorderly, disobeyed the teacher, played truant and did all kinds of naughtiness when in school, and it had its bad effect upon the entire class, and sometimes even upon the entire school.

The text teaches us that we should avoid such foolish boys and foolish girls; boys and girls who do not obey God or revere the Bible, who do not listen to their consciences, nor do that which is right. Such should be avoided at all times, and in choosing our companions, we should always prefer those who will have an influence for good upon us socially, intellectually and morally.

The influence of bad companions will tend to destroy all our best interests physically, by leading to every kind of vice and evil; destroy us financially, by causing us to be inattentive to our work, causing us to prefer idleness and pleasure to labor and usefulness; destroy us morally, by making light of the teachings of the Bible, the importance of the Sunday-school and of the Church, the authority of father and mother and the wisdom of what they teach and require of us.

But in addition to all this, we should remember that those who are our companions upon earth, will be our companions in the world to come. If we go with the wicked and the profane here, we shall dwell with them forever in the world to come. If we desire to go to heaven and to be forever with those who are good and righteous, pure and holy; if we desire to be happy for ever and ever in the world to come, we must choose as our companions here, those who are living not for this present fleeting life, but who are living for the glory of God and who are trusting sincerely in Jesus Christ for everlasting salvation.

May God help us all to be wise and to walk with the wise, and not to be foolish and choose fools as our companions, both for time and eternity.

QUESTIONS.—Into what two classes has God divided people? What does the Bible tell us will happen to a companion of fools?—of wise men? Whom do the charred sticks represent? Who are like the white sticks? If the sticks are rubbed together, what is the result? What happens to good boys who keep bad company? Do the good boys become bad immediately? What do bad companions do to one's character? Can a boy wash "burnt cork" from his face? Can he wash the stains from his character? What else besides a bad character is given? Will a few drops of water change the color of a bottle of ink? Will a few drops of ink change the color of a glass of water? Who are like the ink-drops? Who are like the water-drops? Why? Whom shall we choose for companions? Who will be our companions in eternity?

The Children of Israel Camping in the Wilderness.

DOGS.

THE DOGS OF ST. BERNARD.

SUGGESTION:—If a real live dog is too diverting, an earthen or bisque dog, or the accompanying picture of the dogs of St. Bernard, may be sufficient.

MY DEAR BOYS AND GIRLS: I want to talk to you to-day about dogs. The dog is what is called a domestic animal, and wherever you find civilized men and women, you will find dogs of some kind. Dogs are not only loved because they are companionable, but because they are also, oftentimes, very serviceable.

In Switzerland there are some very high mountains, and some years ago, when there were no tunnels yet dug under the mountains, as there are to-day, travelers during the winter, when going from Germany to Italy, or returning from Italy to Germany, had to cross over the tops of these mountains. The snow was always deep and the journey was always dangerous, particularly in the winter.

There are several places where the mountains can be crossed, and these places are called "passes," such as the Simplon, St. Bernard and St. Gothard passes. Some years ago, in company with a friend, I crossed the St. Gothard pass on the 20th of June. That year the season was very late, and after we got well up the mountain, we found the snow from five to ten feet deep on the level, and when we arrived on the top of the mountain, the snow was even with the roof of a two-story building which stood there, and the

272

Copyrighted, 1911, by Sylvanus Stall.

The Dogs of St. Bernard

people living in it had tunneled under the snow, around the outside of the building. If this was the way it was on the 20th of June, you can easily imagine what an awfully cold and stormy place it must be to live during the entire winter. It took our horses a long time to take us up the mountain, but when we went down on the Italian side they went quite rapidly, and in one hour and forty minutes from the time we left the Hotel de la Prosa, where the snow was so very deep, we were down in the village of Airolo, where little girls were selling ripe cherries. It seemed as though we had jumped right out of the heart of winter, into the pleasant and fruitful days of summer.

On the top of each of these mountain passes, there is built what is called a hospice, which means hospitality, the same word from which we get our word hospital. These buildings are erected for the entertainment of poor travelers, who are compelled to cross the mountains in the winter. There are a number of monks, who live in each of these places of entertainment. On each of these mountain passes the monks have some large dogs, which are known as the dogs of St. Bernard. In the winter when it is snowing, and travelers are likely to be exhausted by their efforts to ascend the mountain, and are liable to be lost in the snow-storms which prevail almost every day, these dogs are sent out by the monks with a supply of food and wine suspended from their necks, and they go all over the mountain, barking and making a great noise. When they discover a poor traveler who is perishing in the snow, they allow him to take the food and the wine in order that he may be stimulated and revived, and then these faithful and intelligent dogs lead the way to the place of safety and security.

Oftentimes they find men who have become nearly frozen, who have fallen down in the snow in an unconscious state and are ready to die. If left for a time these men would soon freeze to death beneath the snow that falls very rapidly upon them. These dogs are very intelligent, and immediately they will begin to scrape the snow off the traveler, lick his hands, and if he does not give any indications of life they will then lie down upon his body, that the warmth from their own body may quicken him again into consciousness, that he may drink the wine and eat the food and be stimulated enough to do something toward getting himself on to the place of safety. If the man is not too heavy, the dog might even be able to carry him.

At the hospice on the St. Bernard pass they once had a faithful dog which had been successful in thus rescuing sixty-eight persons from freezing to

Dogs Rescuing Traveler.

death upon the mountains. The dog was very sagacious, and seemed to know exactly what to do when he found a poor traveler dying in the snow. One day he found a man who had evidently been lying for some time in the snow, which had already quite buried him. The man was entirely unconscious, and when the dog found him he began immediately to scrape away the snow and then lay down upon this dying man, that the warmth of his own body might quicken him again into consciousness. When the man began to revive, and discovered that there was something warm lying upon him, he thought it was a wolf or some wild animal which possibly designed to take his life. He reached into his belt and drew a dagger, which he thrust into the body of the faithful dog that had come to rescue him from freezing to death. The poor dog was fatally wounded. He started back home, but in a short time after reaching it bled to death. The monks had this dog's skin stuffed and placed in the hospice, and now he seems constantly to teach an object lesson to all travelers who cross the Alps and stop at the hospice.

The story of this faithful dog and his sad death reminds us of that loving Saviour, who came from heaven to this world, to seek and to save those who were lost. And although He came to redeem and rescue us from death, yet wicked men in this world crucified Him by nailing Him to a cross upon Calvary, and this is what every person is doing to-day who rejects the Lord Jesus Christ. He comes to you and to me, desiring to save us from our sins and from everlasting death; to save not only our bodies, but our souls for all eternity. If we reject Him we are told in the Bible that "we crucify Him afresh, and put Him to an open shame." I am sure no thoughtful boy or girl would be guilty of wilfully stabbing any kind dog that would come to their rescue if they were perishing in the snow, and I trust that none of you will ever reject Jesus and thrust Him away from you, and thus crucify Him for yourself and put Him to an open shame before the world.

This faithful dog should also teach you and me another lesson. If a dog can make himself so useful as to save the lives of sixty-eight people, you and I should ask ourselves the question whether we are doing as much for the blessing and the salvation of men as this faithful dog did on the mountains of Switzerland? But you can do a great deal more than this dog. He could only save the lives of people, but God can use you to save their souls as well, by the influence of a noble Christian life, by what you say and do, by your contributions to missions, and in various other ways you may help to save the souls of many who must otherwise perish.

But this faithful dog teaches us a lesson of constant, daily duty. It was no easy thing for this dog to go out in the fierce cold through the deep snow and run about all day to hunt for lost travelers, but it was by keeping constantly at it and working faithfully day after day that he accomplished this grand result. He did not save sixty-eight people all at one time, but saved one at a time, and sometimes worked for days and weeks without finding a single traveler whom he could help. In the same way, if you desire to be useful in this world, you must use every little opportunity which comes to you daily. You must be willing to work hard and keep at it, and even though you cannot succeed in doing any great thing at any one time, remember that you must keep doing little things all the while. I trust that God may inspire each of you to desire to accomplish grand results in your lives by the constant doing of both little and great things for God and man.

QUESTIONS.—Are dogs serviceable? What kinds are the most useful? Where do they live? For what and by whom are they used? What do the dogs do to revive a traveler? Tell the story of the dog of the St. Bernard Pass. Of what does this story remind us? Does Christ try to rescue us? What are we doing when we reject Him? What lesson does this dog teach us? Can we do as much as this dog did? Why? What can we do which the dog could not do? What other lesson does this dog teach us? Did the dog save all the sixty-eight people at one time? Are we able to accomplish God's work all at one time? How must we do it?

THE CAMERA.

GOD'S PICTURE BOOK.

SUGGESTION:—Objects: A small camera and a small looking glass.

WHILE talking to you to-day about pictures, it will not seem strange that I should have a camera as the object with which to illustrate the sermon. But my purpose may not be so plain to you when you hear my text, which is taken from the book of Revelation, twentieth chapter, twelfth verse: "And I saw the dead, small and great, stand before God; and the books were opened: and another book was opened,

A Camera.

which is the book of life: and the dead were judged out of those things which were written in the books, according to their works."

These words refer to the great Judgment Day. I suppose that you know that we must all die, but possibly you did not know, or

280   "Throwing a Black Cloth Over His Head He Moved About the Camera."

have forgotten, that after a time God will raise up all the dead and will separate the good people from the bad people, the righteous from the wicked. The time when God will do this is called the great Judgment Day. It is then that the words which I have read as my text tell us that "the books shall be opened," and then all that we have ever done or said in this life shall be found written in these books.

Now, if God is keeping a record of all our deeds and words, and even our inmost thoughts, which He also knows; and not only keeping a record of your words and thoughts and mine, but also of those of every man, woman and child—a record of all the fourteen hundred millions now living upon our earth—you might think that millions of angels would be kept very busy writing all these things down in these books. I do not know just *how* God is doing this, but I do know two ways in which He could easily accomplish what to us may seem a difficult or impossible task.

I will now try to show you how God might keep the record of everything we do; and next Sunday I will try to tell you how, with equal ease, God might secure and keep the record of all we say, of each and every word we speak.

I suppose you have all gone to a photograph gallery and had your pictures taken. When you stood before an instrument, something like this, only perhaps much larger, the artist went behind the big instrument, which was pointed right toward you, and throwing a black cloth over his head, he moved about the camera, told you just how to hold your head, and finally when everything was arranged and he was ready, he pressed a small rubber ball which opened the little slide, just as you would open your eye to look at any object, and in an instant your picture was taken.

That large camera, with which the artist took your picture, was in principle just like the smaller and more simple one which I have shown you, and both are made to imitate, or in a rude way to be like the human eye.

Now, if I point this camera toward you, make it dark back of the camera, either by placing a black cloth over my head or in any other way, your picture will at once appear upon this glass which is at the back of the camera. Now the reason why I can see your photograph on this ground glass is because the rays of light which are reflected or come from your face, into this opening in the camera, have your likeness upon them, and when the light falls against this glass I can see your picture which is photographed upon the rays of light, just the same as your picture is photographed on paper. So every object about us is photographed on the rays of light and the picture becomes visible when we turn our eye, which is a small but perfect camera, so that the rays of light can go straight into our eye and the picture fall upon the back of the eye, which is called the retina, and with which this glass in the camera corresponds.

An ordinary looking-glass will demonstrate or show the same thing. This covering on the back of the glass corresponds to the black cloth with which the photographer shuts out the rays of light which come from the back of the camera. In the same way the ground at the bottom of the pond cuts off the rays from beneath, and on this account you can see the hills, or stars, or clouds reflected in the water; so also in the looking-glass, as you turn it in different directions you can see the photographs of persons or objects which are pictured upon the rays of light.

You may have thought that you saw the person or objects themselves, but this is not the case. With your eyes you can see nothing in the dark; even the cat and the owl must have some light, although they do not need as much as we, before they can see. The rays of light carry the pictures of the objects, and where there are no rays of light we can see nothing.

Now, while your photograph is being taken from the few rays of light which pass into a camera, you see that we might place hundreds of cameras one above another, and if they were all pointed at you they might each take a photograph of you at the same instant—the same as one thousand different persons in an audience with their two thousand eyes all look toward the speaker and see him at one and the same instant.

Now, if I have succeeded in making my thought plain, you will readily understand that as we have great books with pictures upon every page, so God might use these rays of light as the pages of the great book upon which each act of our life instantly records itself, it matters not how rapidly it is done or how many persons and objects there may be in motion or action at the same instant. The fact that the different rays of light carry the pictures of the objects from which they are reflected, is illustrated in the wonderful cameras with which "moving pictures" are taken.

To older persons I might add that if you recall the scientific fact that these rays of light, bearing the images or photographs of persons and objects from which they are reflected, dash out into space at the rate of 192,000 miles in one second, and that they continue to move on indefinitely, you see how the rays of light which were reflected and are now carrying the image of Adam and Eve in the garden of Eden, of Noah coming out of the ark, of the battle of Bunker Hill, and those carrying the pictures of all other objects and actions since the Creation until now, are still sweeping on through space, and if you and I could be present where these rays of light are now sweeping onward, we could see these things as actually and really as if they were even now taking place in our presence upon the earth. And you will also understand how, as God is everywhere present, He is also present in space where these rays of light are at this moment, and so every scene in the entire history of the world is perpetually visible to Him. And so, even with our feeble understanding, you see how the past may always be present to the Infinite and everywhere-present God.

Now, my dear young friends, remember as we see the acts of each other, so God sees all that we do, even when no one else is present to see us. Do not think that God sees and then forgets. All we do is being constantly photographed, not in a camera like this, but upon the rays of light as upon the pages of a great book, and in the great Judgment Day, God will judge us out of the things recorded against us in these books. Our acts record themselves, and in that great day we shall no more be able to deny the correctness of the record than we would be able to deny the personality or identity of our own photograph.

QUESTIONS.—What is meant by the great Judgment Day? What will God do on that day? Of what does God keep a record? Do we know exactly how He does it? What two ways are there in which He might do it? What brings the person's image upon the ground glass of the camera? What have we that is like the camera? Which part of the eye is like the ground glass of the camera? Why can we not see in the dark? Could God use the rays of light instead of the pages of a book? Is the image of Adam and Eve in the Garden of Eden still existing? Where? Are the images of all other events also passing through space? Can God see them all at once? Does God see all of our acts?

THE PHONOGRAPH.

BOOKS THAT TALK.

SUGGESTION:—Object: A small tin box, with a cover and bottom removed. Over one end draw and tie a piece of parchment, or even of strong manilla paper, in the center of the miniature drum-head thus formed fasten a thin string, and you will then have a rude but real telephone and a good representation also of the phonograph.

LAST Sunday I talked to you about the great Judgment Day and tried to illustrate to your minds what is said in Revelation, twentieth chapter, twelfth verse, where it says, "The dead were judged out of those things which were written in the books, according to their works." I tried then to make plain how God pictures or photographs all our acts upon the rays of light, and how we see the objects about us when the rays of light fall upon the retina of the eye. I tried to show you how every ray of light carries a photograph or picture, and that these rays of light are sweeping out into space at the rate of 192,000 miles per second, and that if you and I could be present where these rays, carrying the picture of the battle of Bunker Hill are now hurrying through space, you could see the battle, as if it were taking place at present. If you had a camera with you, you could actually take a photograph of it, the same as you could have done had you been on the hills out-side of Boston on the day when this great battle was being fought.

But that is only one book; God has other books also. But you know you can not photograph what a person says. So I want to try and show you how our words and all we say also go into a great book and write themselves down, so as to become permanent for all time.

Now, I have here a baking-powder box, from which I have removed the ends, and in place of the tin have covered it with a stout piece of paper which I have tried to draw very smoothly. With two such boxes, connected by a string, we could make a tele-phone so that we could talk together a short distance. Or with only one box we could construct a very rude but yet very suggestive phonograph.

Let me tell you how it is that you can hear over the telephone, whether made of a simple box and string like this, or with a wire and electric battery, for in one respect they are both alike.

If you will place your finger gently on your throat, against what is sometimes called "Adam's Apple," but what is really the delicate little instrument with which we speak, and then utter some words in a strong, clear voice, you will doubtless feel a vibration or trembling in your throat, just the same as I now feel in my throat while I am talking. My effort to speak causes these little chords in my throat to vibrate, just the same as when you pass your fingers over the chords of a harp or violin, or when you strike the keys of a piano you make the wires tremble and thus produce sound, so these chords in my throat tremble and cause the air to tremble, producing what we call sound-waves. Just the same as when you take a stone and drop it into the lake, you see the little waves or ripples, as we call them, go out in small circles, wider and wider, further and further, until they strike the distant shore. So the air is made to vibrate by my effort to speak, and these little sound-waves in the air strike against the drum of your ear, back of which there are nerves,

"The Little Waves or Ripples."

ever ready to convey to the brain the sensation which we call sound.

"Like clear circles widening round
Upon a clear blue river,
Orb after orb, the wondrous sound
Is echoed on forever."

Now, this small baking-powder box represents the ear, and the paper at this end represents the drum of the ear, and this string represents the nerves. This string may be prolonged for a considerable distance, and if you were to connect the end of the string with another box of the same sort you would then have a telephone with

18

which you would be able to hear quite plainly the words which are spoken by some other person at the opposite end of the string. When I speak into this box it makes the paper tremble, and that makes the string tremble, and if there were another box at the far end of the line it would cause the paper on the end of that box to tremble just the same, and that would cause the air to tremble where that box is, and if you were to hold your ear to that box you would be able to hear the words.

If I take this box, and instead of a string I should place the point of a needle back of it, and a cylinder to revolve, so that the needle would scratch the vibrations upon the cylinder, I would then have a phonograph. I would then be able to record the words, and with another smooth needle to go into the scratches which had been made by the sharp needle, I would be able to reproduce the sound; or, in other words, to make the cylinder talk back again to me the words which I had spoken into the tin box and recorded upon the cylinder.

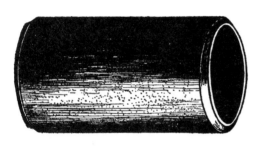

Phonograph Cylinder.

Just as light carries the photograph or picture, so the air carries the sound of our words and other vibrations of the atmosphere which we call sound. Thus you see the light is one book and the air is another, and God doubtless has many other forms of making and keeping the record of our actions and words—yes, even of our thoughts, and in the great Judgment Day these words which we utter will say themselves over again in our ears. If you uttered any bad or wicked words yesterday or to-day, or shall do so to-morrow, remember you will have to give an account of them in the great Day of Judgment.

But there is another thing connected with our uttering of bad words, as well as the fact that we must give an account of them. Bad words are connected with bad thoughts, and so every bad word which we utter indicates the character of our thoughts and has a bad influence upon our minds and hearts.

Not only do these words record themselves upon the atmosphere, but they also record themselves in a lasting—yes, in an eternal influence upon the hearts and the minds and the lives of those who hear them. Just the same as the words which are spoken into a phonograph are recorded and can be repeated over and over many times, so the bad words and the wicked thoughts which are expressed into the ears of others make an indelible record upon their thoughts and hearts, and are oftentimes repeated to others, thus multiplying the record, and at last all these records will appear against us in the great Day of Judgment. How careful you and I should be to speak only good words and to think only good thoughts.

QUESTIONS.—Has God other record books beside the one of deeds? What does one of the other books record? What is a telephone? What is a phonograph? What happens to the air when our words strike it? What are these air-vibrations called? What does the air do with sound? What two things may be used as God's recording books? Must all bad words be accounted for? What do bad words indicate? Upon what instrument can words also be recorded? Are all words like those which are recorded by a phonograph? Why? (Permanent). Will God hold these records against us on the Judgment Day?

MAGNET AND NEEDLE.

GOD'S GUIDING HAND.

SUGGESTION:—Objects used: A magnet, a piece of paper and an ordinary sewing needle. In the illustration lay the needle flat against the paper directly under the magnet. The ordinary magnet, purchased for a few cents in a toy store, will answer the purpose.

MY DEAR LITTLE MEN AND WOMEN: The Bible everywhere teaches us that God is the Supreme Ruler of the universe. Not only has He created the vast system of worlds about us, but He directs each in its orbit. He rules over the destinies of nations, and although wicked men plot and plan, yet over and above them all God is ruling, and He makes even the wrath of men to praise Him.

When you are older and can make a careful study of the Book of Daniel, which is in the Old Testament, and then read the history of the world in the light of the teachings of that Book, you will see how God used the five great empires of the earth to prepare the world for the coming of the Messiah, and how since the time of Christ He has used the other nations to prepare the world for the full acceptance of the truth and the final triumph of righteousness.

But God not only governs in the affairs of nations, He also governs and directs in the life of each individual. He not only gives us being and preserves our lives and health, but He has redeemed us from sin and death by the gift of His Son, Jesus Christ; and if we are willing, He will guide us in all the affairs of

290

life. Nothing is too minute nor too insignificant to receive His thought and attention, and not even the sorrow of a child over a broken toy escapes His notice or fails to touch His loving heart.

But many people are not able to understand, and seem also unwilling to accept anything that they cannot see, or comprehend with one of their five senses. I have therefore brought this magnet, this piece of paper, and this needle, such as women use when they sew, in order to show you how God can guide us by His unseen hand.

When I lift this needle with my fingers and then let go of it you will notice how it drops immediately to the floor. Now, when I lift this magnet in the same way, and then let go of it, it will also drop in the same manner. But now I am going to hold this magnet up, and bring the needle close to the magnet. Now when I let loose of the needle with my fingers you see how it is held by the magnet. The gravity, or, as we would say, the weight of the needle, which would cause it to fall to the floor, is overcome by some greater or stronger power which is in the magnet. Now, you

Magnet and Needle.

cannot perceive that power with any of your senses; you can neither hear it, smell it, taste it nor feel it. You can see the effect of that power, but the power itself you cannot see. In like manner, also, there are powers and influences all about us which we cannot perceive with any of our senses, but which are constantly exercising their influence upon us and upon things about us.

But now, by the use of this paper, I desire to show you something additional. I am going to place the magnet above the paper, and the needle below the paper, and show you that even through the paper this influence or power which holds the needle exerts itself.

You will see now that when I lay the needle lengthwise against the paper, with the magnet upon the opposite side, that the needle is held up against this paper and does not fall, as it would if the magnet were removed. You will notice also that, as I move this magnet from place to place, the needle on the lower side of the paper follows the magnet. In this simple little experiment you are able to see the magnet, but suppose for a moment that this paper were increased in size until it was as large as the ceiling of this entire room. You will understand that then the magnet and any person moving the magnet might be entirely out of sight, and as the magnet would be moved from place to place on the upper side of the paper, entirely out of view, the needle on the lower side, which could be easily seen, would move from place to place, following the magnet.

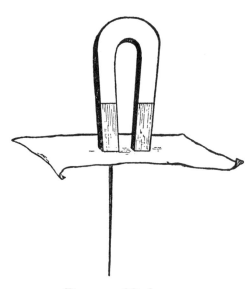

Paper no Hindrance.

This little experiment illustrates to us *not how* God guides us, but it will show us that there are powers unknown and unseen by us which can hold and guide even insensible metal. How much more easily, then, can God sustain and guide our thoughts, our purposes, our steps and our lives.

We are free moral agents. God has left us free to resist His power and His grace, and to live in defiance of all that He has commanded us, and of all that He desires us to do. But if we are willing to be led by His Spirit, and to walk in His way, God is willing to guide us, if we will come to Him and ask Him for the

Holy Spirit to lead us in the way in which He would have us to walk.

There are many who do resist God's will and purpose, and live in open defiance of all His teachings, and of all that God would have them to do. I take it for granted, however, that there are no such people here, but that you all desire to live in such a way as to secure your greatest happiness and your greatest good upon this earth, and your eternal happiness and blessedness in the world to come.

In closing this little sermon, I therefore desire to impress upon your minds the fact that you and I are without experience in many of the most trying and most important events which come to us in life. We are constantly liable to be mistaken. We cannot see ahead of us, and do not always know what is for our own good. God knows all things, the future as well as the past. He cannot be mistaken and must therefore know beyond the possibility of error what will be for our good. God not only knows what will be for our good but He desires our good, therefore we should let Him guide us.

Now, the question might arise in your minds, how does God guide us? He guides us by the teachings of His Word. He has told us in the Bible how we ought to live, what is for our present and eternal good. If we desire financial prosperity, or physical blessings, or mental quickness, or spiritual peace, we will find in the teachings of God's Word how to obtain them.

God also guides us by the exercise of our consciences, and therefore it is always important that you and I should do what conscience tells us to be right. First of all we should study God's Word, in order that we may have an enlightened conscience, and then we should always follow conscience.

God also guides us by the Holy Spirit, and it is our duty to come to Him daily and ask Him for the presence and power of the Holy Ghost to guide us through each day, and to bring us at last to Heaven above.

Now, I trust you will all be able to enter heartily into the prayer which we are going to sing, for when we sing thoughtfully we will find that many hymns contain petitions as well as praise, and this is one of the kind which partakes largely of the nature of petition. Let us all sing the hymn,

"Guide me, O, Thou great Jehovah."

QUESTIONS.—Who is the Supreme Ruler of the Universe? Who governs the life of every person? Does any little thing escape His notice? Are some people unwilling to believe what they cannot see? Can we see, hear, smell, or feel the power in the magnet? Why do we believe it is there? Are there influences around us like the power in the magnet? Can they all be seen? Will the paper between the magnet and the needle destroy the attracting power of the magnet? Who are like the needle? Like whom is the magnet? Does He guide us? Can we see Him? Are we free to do as we choose? When will God lead us? Do some people defy God? Do we always know what is best for us, or what to do when in trouble? Who does know? By what three means does God guide us?

FISH IN AQUARIUM.

THE ALL-SEEING EYE OF GOD.

SUGGESTION:—Object: A small aquarium with a few small fishes.

MY DEAR YOUNG FRIENDS: I have here an aquarium with a few very pretty goldfishes in it. As they swim from side to side they look very beautiful. When they see me coming nearer to the aquarium, or moving my hand upon this side or the other, they dart very quickly to the opposite side of the aquarium. They try to get out of sight, but it makes no difference whether they are upon this side or upon the other side of the aquarium, I can see them just as well. I can look right through the aquarium; I can see through the glass, and I can see through the water. And wherever the fishes are in this aquarium, I can see them. It is impossible for them to hide away, or to get out of my sight.

Fishes in Aquarium.

Now, the Bible tells us that "the eyes of the Lord are in every place, beholding the evil and the good." (Prov. xv: 3.) We are very clearly taught in the Bible, that it makes no difference where we are, God can see us just as well in one place as in another. He can see us in the night just as well as in the daytime, for "the darkness and the light are alike unto Him." David said, "He

295

that keepeth Israel shall neither slumber nor sleep." (Psalm cxxi: 4.) So it makes no difference whether you are in the house or out of doors, whether it is day or whether it is night, God can see right through the house, just as you and I can look through this aquarium and through the water, so God can see right through the thick walls of a house, or even through a great mountain. If you were in the valley beyond the mountain, God could see right through the mountain; that would make no difference. He can even see way through the earth, from this side through to China. It makes no difference to God, for He can see just as well through material substances, through which you and I cannot look, as we can see through the air; indeed much better, for distance limits the possibility of our seeing distinctly and clearly, while God's power to see is not limited or circumscribed.

Once there was a very excellent, good woman, who had a very nice and conscientious little boy, but the mother was poor and had to go out from day to day to earn her living. Each night when she returned home the little boy was very lonely, and would watch very patiently for his mother, and when he saw her coming, he would always run to the door to meet her, and throw his arms about her neck. But one evening when she returned, she noticed that little Willie was not at the door to meet her. She could not understand why, when she came into the house he seemed to be afraid of her. He tried to avoid her. After a time the mother called Willie to her and threw her arms around his neck and kissed him very tenderly. This was too much for the little boy's heart. He looked up into his mother's face, and said, "Mamma, can God see through a crack in the door?" His mother said, "Yes, God can see everywhere." He said, "Mamma, can God see in the cupboard if it is dark in the cupboard?" "Yes, Willie, God can see in the dark as well as in the light."

"There is One Direction That You Have not Looked."   297

Willie looked up into his mother's face and said, "Then I might as well tell you. To-day I was very hungry, and although you told me that I should not take the cake which you had put in the closet, yet I went to the closet, and when I had closed the door, and it was all dark, I felt around till I got a piece of the cake, and I ate it. I did not know that God could see in the dark. I am very sorry that I have been so wicked and so naughty." And so little Willie threw his arms around his mamma's neck and laid his head upon her shoulder and wept very bitterly.

Eye in the Pulpit.

Once a man went to steal corn out of his neighbor's field. He took his little boy with him to hold the bag open, while he should pull the corn and put it in the bag. After they had reached the cornfield the father looked this way and that way, and looked about him in every direction, and when he had given the little boy the bag to hold open, the little boy looked at his father and said, "Father, there is one direction that you have not looked yet." The father was quite frightened and supposed that his son had seen some one coming in some direction. But the son said, "You have not looked up. There is some one in that direction I am sure who sees us." The father was so much impressed that he turned away from his sinful purpose, and returned home, never again to steal from anyone.

Many years ago, among some of the denominations when they built a church, they used to build the pulpit very high. It was built almost as high as the gallery. And when the people sat in the pews and desired to see the minister, they had to bend their heads back, and look up very high toward the pulpit. At Reading, Pennsylvania, there is still one of these old pulpits which was formerly in use. On the under side of the shelf upon which the Bible rested in that pulpit, there was painted a large eye. And when the people would look up from the pews to see the minister, or towards the Bible, underneath this lid upon which the Bible rested they would always see this large eye. This eye would seem to look right down upon each one individually, and thus they would constantly be reminded of the text, "Thou God seest me," and the text which I repeated at the opening of this sermon, "The eyes of the Lord are in every place, beholding the evil and the good." And so Sunday after Sunday, and year after year, from childhood to manhood, this object sermon was constantly being preached to them.

Whenever Satan tempts you to do wrong, remember that you cannot escape from the eyes of One who sees you constantly, and although no human being might know of your wickedness, yet God sees you, and God knows it all, for "His eyes behold, His eyelids try the children of men." (Psalm xi: 4.)

QUESTIONS.—Can the fish in the aquarium hide from our sight? How are we like the fish in the aquarium? What does the Bible say about the eyes of the Lord? Can darkness hide us from God's sight? Can He see through the earth? Tell about the little boy who ate the cake in the dark. Tell about the little boy whose father wanted to steal corn. Why was a large eye painted on the pulpit in the church? When we are tempted by Satan, what should we remember?

THE CLOCK.

MEASURING TIME.

SUGGESTION:—Object: An ordinary clock or watch.

I HAVE here a clock, with which I desire to illustrate and emphasize the truth taught us in the twelfth verse of the ninetieth Psalm, where it says, "So teach us to number our days, that we may apply our hearts unto wisdom."

Whatever is valuable we measure. Some things are measured by the yard, some things by the quart or gallon, other things by the pound or by the ton. Land is measured by the acre. One of the most valuable things that God gives to us is time. Queen Elizabeth, when she was dying, was willing to give her entire kingdom if she could only have one hour more in which to prepare for death.

As time is very valuable we measure it in seconds, minutes, hours, days, weeks, months, years, centuries. In the earliest time men had no means of measuring time, except as they saw it measured with the great clock which God has set in the heavens; for He tells us in the first chapter of Genesis that He made "the sun to rule the day, and the moon to rule the night." The most accurate clocks in the world are those which most nearly keep time with the sun. All the effort to regulate clocks and watches is simply to adjust their movements so as to have them keep time with the movement of the sun. God has given us a conscience which is designed to regulate our lives until they shall be in harmony with the life of Christ, who is the Sun of Righteousness. Hundreds of

300

years before Christ came, people may have had some very rude way of dividing the time during the day and night, but their principal division of time was simply day and night, summer and winter. These changes of day and night, summer and winter, helped to mark the progress of time, and they still do. If it were all daytime, or all night, and we had no clocks, we would have no means of measuring time. When Baron de Trench was liberated from his dungeon in Magdeburg, where the King of Persia had confined him in darkness for a period of ten years, where he had no means of measuring how the time passed and had even very few thoughts—when he was liberated, and was told that he had been in prison for ten years, his astonishment was almost beyond expression, for it had not seemed to him to be so long. It had passed away like a painful dream.

In the early period of the world's history, human life was much longer than at present. Men lived to be several hundred years old. I suppose you can all tell how old Methuselah was. He was the oldest man who ever lived. When human life became shorter, time consequently became more valuable and men were more anxious to measure it.

I want to show you how to measure time, and what makes it valuable; for David asked to be taught properly to number his days; and the purpose was so that he might apply his heart unto wisdom.

Now, this watch and this clock are instruments with which we measure time. Once there was a king who desired not to forget that, like other men, he must die, and he had a man whose duty it was to come before him each hour and repeat the words: "Remember thou art mortal!" That is, every hour he had this man remind him that sometime he would have to die. Each time the man came in before the king, he was reminded that he had one hour less to live; so, each and every time that you hear the clock strike, you should be reminded of the fact that another hour has passed, and that you have one less to live. In this sense every clock has a tongue, and when it strikes it tells us that we will now have one hour less to live upon the earth.

The earliest device for measuring time was doubtless the sun-dial. Perhaps you have never seen one. It is simply a round plate or disc of metal, with a small piece of metal standing upright in such a position that when the sun shines, the shadow will be thrown upon the round cylinder or disc, around which are figures like those

Hour-glass.

on the face of a watch or clock. Such methods of measuring time we know were used at least seven hundred and thirteen years before Christ, for in the book of Isaiah, thirty-eighth chapter and eighth verse, we find a very direct allusion to it. King Alfred of England used to use candles that were of uniform length; each candle would burn three hours, and by burning four candles, one after another, he could measure the hours of the day. In order to prevent the air from blowing against the candle and thus making it burn more rapidly or interfering with its accuracy in measuring time, he placed a horn or shield around it, and in the old cathedrals this was the way they measured time. Later on they had hour glasses, such as you sometimes see placed on the piano when girls are practicing their music lesson. Sometimes you see small ones in the kitchen, which are used for timing the eggs while they are boiling, and it is to these forms of glasses that various poetical allusions are made when death is spoken of as the "sands of life" running out.

Later came the clocks. They were first made about 2,000 years ago, but were very rude and awkward. The first watches were made about 475 years ago, but they were very large, and you would almost need to have a man to carry your watch for you, it was so heavy. Smaller watches were first made about 200 years ago, and now they have some that are so very small that you could carry six or seven of them in your vest pocket without inconvenience. How else could we tell about the time of the departure of trains and steamboats, the hours to go to work in the factory or to go to school, when to go to church? And the enjoyment of many other things depends upon knowing accurately what moment we should be on hand. You should learn never to be late, but always to be prompt. Suppose that, with an audience of six hundred people, the preacher should be five minutes late. Each person would then have lost five minutes. This, for the entire six hundred present, would have been equal to more than forty-eight hours for a single person—more than two days and two nights.

But now what is it that makes time valuable? It is the use that we can make of it. David wanted to know about it, so that he could apply his heart unto wisdom. The man who does nothing with his time, in the eyes of others, is worth nothing; but the busy man always finds that his time is very valuable. It is strange, also, that when you go to idle people and ask them to do anything they always say they haven't time, so that the expression has come to be used that "if you want anything done go to a busy man." The more busy the man is the more likely he is to find time, in some way, to undertake any new form of useful endeavor and work.

Now, I want to ask you, What use do you make of your time? Are you faithful in the use of every moment at home, diligent in doing the work assigned you, looking about you, and doing your own thinking, finding, for yourself, what is to be done, instead of standing around and waiting to be told? Are you diligent in school, always studying your lessons, learning all that you possibly can, remembering that everything that you can learn will at some time be of service to you? If you are employed in a store, or engaged in any other kind of business, are you faithful, using each moment and each hour, remembering that you are not to be faithful simply when your employer is looking at you, but you are to be faithful at all times? As the Bible says, "Not with eye service, as men pleasers" (Colos. iii: 22), but doing everything as unto the Lord. Are you faithful in the matter of attending church, and then when you are in the church, giving your mind to the consideration of the truth which is being presented, rather than allowing your mind to be engaged with the amusements and plays of last week, or the plans and purposes of next week? Are you faithful in the Sunday-school? Do you listen attentively to the lessons which are taught by your Sunday-school teacher? Each minute of the thirty devoted to the study of the lesson is very important, and all of the other moments in the Sunday-school are very important.

I was wondering the other day why the clock should have the long hand point to the minutes, and the short hand to the hours; but after all, it seems very wise that the greater emphasis, and greater importance should be attached to the longer hand. It points to the minutes, as though it were constantly saying to you and to me, look out for these minutes, look out for these small parts of the hour, and the whole hour will take care of itself. The big hand points to the minutes because, after all, they are the important things. It is like the old saying, "if we take care of the pennies, the dollars will take care of themselves." If we will take care of the minutes, the hours will take care of themselves.

If you have never thought on these things, and have been an idler, I want to ask you to "Redeem the time." (Eph. v: 16.)

That is, do not let your time go to waste.   If you are not
a Christian, even though you are very busy and very industrious concerning temporal things, you are really wasting your
time.   We are placed here upon the earth in order that we may love
and serve God.   That is our main business here.   If we are going to
serve Christ, we should study to know His life and His teachings,
and yet some people know very little about the Bible.   Did you
ever stop to think that a man who is thirty-five years old has had
five solid years of Sundays?   And the man who is seventy years
old, has had ten solid years of Sundays?   With ten years given to
worship and the study of God's Word, a man at seventy ought to
know a great deal concerning the teachings of the Bible.   May God
teach us so to number our days that we may apply our hearts unto
wisdom.

QUESTIONS.—How do we measure cloth? Are sugar and coal measured by
the yard? How do we measure land? How do we measure time? How many
divisions of time can you name besides seconds? What was the first instrument
with which time was measured? With what did King Alfred measure the hours?
What was later used for measuring time, after the sun-dial? About how long
ago were clocks first invented? About how long ago were watches first made?
Why did David want to be taught to number his days? Can the idle man or
the busy man more easily find time for necessary duties? Will you always make
diligent use of your time? Why does the larger hand of the clock point to the
minutes? If we take care of the minutes, what will the hours do ?

PLANS.

LIVING WITH A PURPOSE.

SUGGESTION:—Object: Architect's drawings for the building of a house.

MY DEAR LITTLE MEN AND WOMEN: I have here what the architect calls "plans," or drawings for a house. Unless the carpenter and builder had a copy of the plans he is to follow he would not be able to build successfully. He would not know what kind of material he would need. He would not know where to place the doors, or how large to make the windows, and whether to put the dining room on

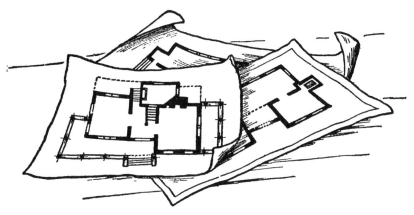

Plans for Building a House.

this side of the house or on the other side of the house; whether the parlor was to be on the first floor or on the second floor. So when a man is going to build, the first thing to be done is to decide what kind of a house he wants, and then to get an architect who is able to draw the plans perfectly, so as to show the size of every door and

307

window and room, and the exact position and place of everything
that is to enter into the building of the house. These plans cost a
great deal of thought and oftentimes much delay in beginning, but
in the end they save both time and expense, and secure the most
desirable results.

Every boy and girl should have a plan, for we are all builders.
We build day after day and week after week, and year after year.
First of all, you should have some great purpose in life, and then
all your other plans and purposes should be made to further and help
the great main object which you have in life.

Once there were two boys who were very intimate when they
were young. They played together, and came to love each other
very much. One was a boy who always had a plan. He had a
plan for studying his lessons; he had a plan which showed what
time he had resolved to get up in the morning; how many hours he
would devote to study; what portions of the day he would give to
play, and how much to work. So each and every day he had his
plans. At the beginning of the year he had his plans for each month
of the year.

The other boy never had any plans. Everything went along just
as it happened. The boy who always had the plans had no money;
his father was poor. But the boy who had no plans had plenty of
money, for his father was rich. These two boys both became mer-
chants, had stores in the same square in a large city. The one who
had the plans always knew what he purposed to do, before the season began. He knew just when to purchase his goods for the spring
trade; he knew when to sell them; everything was done methodic-
ally and with a plan. As the result of his thoughtful plans he soon
began to accumulate wealth, obtained a place of confidence in the
minds of business men, and eventually became one of the most honored and influential men in the city. With the other boy it was not

so. He bought his goods whenever he chanced to see something that he fancied; often bought too much of one thing; had no method in business, and consequently in the course of a few years lost what money he had and died a poor man.

Let me hope that you will always have a plan for everything you do. God is the God of order, and we should also be orderly in all that we do.

These plans of the architect, when followed by the builders, will tell the stonemason, the bricklayer, the millman and the carpenter, the plasterer and the painter, just what each is to do, and all will be able to work in harmony, so as to secure a nice, comfortable and desirable home when the work is completed.

Now, we are all laying foundations in this world, and the perfect character cannot be

Plans for Building a Life.

obtained until in eternity. So when you come to plan for life, do not think that your stay in this world is to be all there is of your life. Let your plans take in eternity. If they leave out eternity they leave out the greatest portion of your existence. If you leave out the idea of eternity you will be like the man who simply lays the foundation and then never builds a house on it, and there, year after year, the foundation stands as the monument of his folly.

But you may desire to know where you can get the plans for a good and noble life—a plan that will include eternity. I will tell you: in the Bible. This is the best book in which to find the plans for a perfect and complete life. Just the same as the man who is going to build a house desires to go and examine other houses, so if you desire to be great and good, you should desire to read the biographies, the story of the lives of great men. I do not mean the fancied stories of lives which were never lived, which are so often told in some kinds of books, but I mean the lives of real men. When you see the difficulties which have been overcome by others; when you see how great and good other people have been, it will help you to be great and good. But after you have studied the lives of all the greatest and best men who have ever lived, and then compare them with the life of Jesus Christ, you will eventually come to see very clearly and distinctly, that after all there has never been but one perfect life lived on this earth, and that was the life of Jesus Christ. So you will readily see that if you desire to use a model which is perfect, you will have to take the life of Christ. You will find it fully portrayed in the Bible, especially in the first four books of the New Testament—Matthew, Mark, Luke and John. This will give you the model of a perfect life and enable you to live so as to make your life glorious while upon the earth, and prepare you for an eternity of happiness and joy beyond this world. Have a plan and live to it, and let your plan include eternity. And may God give you grace to live up to a high ideal, to be noble Christian men and noble Christian women.

QUESTIONS.—What are needed before a house is built? Are all boys and girls builders? Builders of what? Do they need plans? Should we all have a main object in life? What must we use all other plans and purposes for? Which boy in the story turned out the better? What does the story illustrate? Should we have a plan for each thing we do? Does God love order? What foundation are we laying in this life? Should our plans concern only this life? What kind of a builder are we like, if we make no plans for the life to come? Where can we get our plans? What perfect model can we follow?

THE CHRISTMAS TREE.

THE LESSONS WHICH IT TEACHES.

BOYS and girls often think that big people have set apart Christmas as a day for gathering around the Christmas tree, as a time for Santa Claus, for the giving of presents and for having a good time generally. This is not the case. I will tell you why we celebrate Christmas, and particularly the significance and meaning of the Christmas tree. Christmas commemorates the birth of Jesus Christ, the Son of God, who came into this world to redeem us from sin and everlasting death; and the Christmas tree, laden with its many gifts and suggestive of so much joy and blessing, is a symbol of the Saviour. In order that you may best understand the full meaning of the Christmas tree, I must call your attention to the season of the year when Christmas came. You will remember that last summer, when the sun rose at half-past four in the morning and did not set until half-past seven in the evening, the days were very long, and you could see to go about in the evening until about eight o'clock and after. At Christmas time the sun goes down at half-past four in the afternoon, and does not rise until half-past seven in the morning. So you see that the days are about six hours shorter in December than they are in the latter part of the month of June. Christmas occurs at that season when the days are shorter and the nights are longer than at any other period of the year. In the Bible darkness represents sin and unbelief and wickedness; and the daytime or light represents truth and righteousness and godly living. So you will see that the long nights at the Christ-

311

mas period of the year, and the short days, fitly represent the condition of the world at the time when Jesus, the Son of God, was born
in Bethlehem. At no other time in the world's history was there so
much of moral darkness and sin and wickedness and corruption in
the world. Cruelty and crime and wickedness abounded everywhere. If I were to stop and tell you of the condition of society, of
the wrong and the iniquity, which abounded everywhere, you would
be greatly horrified. It was at such a time as this in the world's history, when Jesus Christ, the Son of God, came to this world, that
sin might be banished and righteousness might abound. So you see
that Christmas occurs at that period of the year when the night and
the darkness are the longest of any of the entire year, and it very fittingly represents the condition which existed in the world when
Jesus was born in Bethlehem, as the Saviour of the world. He
came to banish the moral darkness which covered the whole earth.

Not only the time of the year, but also the character of the
Christmas tree suggests something. With the long nights comes
also the cold winter. The earth is wrapped in snow. The trees,
which a few months ago were green and beautiful and in the fall
all laden with fruit, are now all naked and bare, and if you were
to go out into the orchard or forest you could not tell the difference
between a dead tree, and all the others which seem to be dead.
Among all the trees you would only find such as the pine, the hem-
lock, the fir and other varieties, such as are known as evergreen
trees, that would be green and give evidence of life. So you will see
again how the Christmas tree fittingly represents Christ, because
these evergreens, in the field and in the forest, seem to be the only
things that have greenness and life ,while all else around them seems
to be dead and laid in a shroud of white snow.

The custom of setting up a tree at Christmas time and loading
it with fruit and gifts seems to have originated in Germany, and the

Copyrighted, 1911, by Sylvanus Stall.

The Christmas Tree

thought of these people in introducing this custom centuries ago, was that they might teach their children this very lesson to which I have referred.

Now, I desire to call your attention also to the fruit which is so often hung on the Christmas tree. The Bible tells us that a tree is known by its fruit. If you go into the orchard you could tell the apple tree from the pear tree, and you could tell the plum tree from the peach tree. If you did not know them by their leaves, you would at least know them by their fruit. But when you come to look at this tree you find oranges upon it. Now, this is not an orange tree. You find dolls upon it, but it is not a doll tree. Here are a pair of skates, but it is not a skate tree. Here are some candies, but it is not a candy tree. Neither can it be known by the name of any one of these various things which hang upon the tree. But it is a Christmas tree. And all these various kinds of things are properly hung upon the Christmas tree to represent the fulfillment of that promise that, with His Son Jesus Christ, God would also give us all things richly to enjoy.

The gifts hung on Christmas trees are usually presents from one person to another—often not only from parents to children, but from teachers to scholars, and from friend to friend. Now, until Christ was born, there were no Christmas presents. There was no Christmas day celebrated. But the reason we give presents on Christmas day is to remind each other of God's Great Gift to man, the gift of His Son, Jesus Christ, to be our Redeemer and Saviour. With Jesus Christ, God also gave us grace and truth, reconciliation, and pardon and peace and salvation. Man had sinned against God; was living in open rebellion against God. Whatever was good, man hated. He loved to do wickedly. He preferred to serve Satan, rather than to serve God. And Jesus came in order to reconcile men to God—to get them to turn away from sin, wicked-

ness and Satan, and to accept of God's love and pardon and everlasting salvation, and to do that which was right and good and
holy.

If you could travel through the countries where they do not
know of Christ and do not worship Him, and then travel through
Christian countries, where Jesus is loved and honored, you would
soon see what a great difference there is between the two. We
have railroads, steamboats, and telegraphs, and telephones, and
phonographs, and every kind of cloth, and silk, and furs with which
to clothe ourselves for greatest comfort, and when we sit down at
our tables there is no good thing that is produced in any nation
under the sun, that is not available even to those of limited means.

In the heathen countries it is not so. They are still riding in
carts drawn by oxen. Without clothing and without comforts, the
people in Africa are still groping through the bushes and jungles.
And if you go to India and China and Japan you will find that
only in so far as they have been brought under the influence of the
religion of Jesus Christ, do they have even now the material blessings which come with the Gospel.

But there are other blessings which come to us with the preaching of the Gospel. In heathen countries they have no asylums to
care for the orphans, no hospitals for the sick and the distressed and
the dying; no institutions of charity and of mercy; but few schools,
and these only for the rich and the upper classes. So you see that
these things are among the gifts which God has given us with His
Son Jesus Christ, whose birth we celebrate on Christmas day.

Then there are also the spiritual blessings and gifts. God's
grace, communion with God, and the joy and satisfaction we have
in our hearts in knowing that we are the children of God; that Jesus
Christ has redeemed us from sin and death; that we are the heirs
of everlasting life, and of everlasting glory. And the Bible prom-

ises us that in the world to come we shall enjoy everlasting blessedness, and happiness and joy—that we shall dwell forever with Jesus Christ; that we shall be made kings and queens unto our God. The Bible tells us, that it has not entered into the heart of man to think or to conceive of the things which God has in store for those who love Him. If we were to laden this tree with all the richest treasures of the world they could not adequately suggest the great blessings which God has in store for you and for me.

How fitting, then, that we should be glad and joyous on Christmas day!—that you and I should receive not simply these material gifts, but that we should also accept of Jesus Christ in our hearts and receive His spiritual blessings; and so be adopted into the family of God, and be permitted to dwell for ever in His presence on high. May God always bless you in your Christmas joy, and may you be glad not only because you receive the gifts of your parents and friends, but also because God gives to us all, His Only Begotten and Well Beloved Son, Jesus Christ, to be our Redeemer and Friend.

QUESTIONS.—What event does Christmas Day commemorate? About what time of the year are the days shortest and the nights longest? What does the darkness of the long nights represent? Was the world in moral darkness when Christ came? Is He the world's Redeemer? What trees are green in the winter? Whom does the evergreen tree represent? Why? Where did the custom of having Christmas trees probably originate? What do the things on the Christmas tree represent? Did people give Christmas presents before Christ came? What do our gifts to one another represent? With His Son, has God given us other things which we are to enjoy? Where do people enjoy the greatest material comforts and blessings, in Christian or heathen lands? In what lands are the largest spiritual blessings enjoyed?

EASTER SUNDAY.

THE RESURRECTION OF THE BODY.

SUGGESTION :—Objects: An egg and a little chick in a cage, or a toy chick, such as are often available at Easter time may be used.

MY LITTLE FRIENDS: Can you tell me what we commemorate on Easter Sunday? Yes, we commemorate the resurrection of Christ from the dead.

You remember how some weeks ago I showed you a watch-case.* You thought it was a watch, but when I opened it it had no works in it, consequently it was only a watch-case. When I placed the works in the case, then it made a complete watch.

So you have also seen the body of a dead person and you have possibly thought that that was the individual, the person whom you had known; but that which you saw was only the body. The soul, the immortal part, had taken its departure and gone back to God who first placed it in the body. Now, just the same as the works of a watch can keep good time without being in the case, so the soul can exist apart from the body. If you were to take the watch-case and bury it in the ground, that fact would not affect either the existence or the accuracy of the works of the watch in measuring time. So when God takes the soul out of the body we say that it is a dead body, and it becomes necessary for us to bury it out of our sight.

* NOTE—Sermon on Watch and Case, see page 125.

318

The Women at the Sepulchre.

On Good Friday we commemorate the death of Christ upon the cross on Calvary. You remember how, after the crucifixion, Joseph of Arimathea and Nicodemus came and took the body of Christ down from the cross and laid it in a new tomb which Joseph had hewn out of rock in his garden. When this had been done, Pilate remembered how Jesus had said that if He were put to death, after three days He would rise again. Now, Pilate did not believe that Jesus would rise again, but was afraid that His disciples or some friends might come by night and steal away His body and circulate the report that Jesus had risen from the dead; so he placed Roman soldiers around the sepulchre to prevent His disciples from coming near the tomb, or sepulchre where Joseph had laid away the body of Christ. Pilate purposed to prevent the possibility of Christ's resurrection, but in the fact that he placed the soldiers there he secured for all after ages the most positive proof that Jesus did actually rise from the dead. These soldiers were Roman soldiers, and if they had slept while they were upon guard duty, the penalty would have been death. But when the angel came down from heaven and rolled away the stone, then we are told that these Roman soldiers became as dead men.

It is on Easter Sunday that we commemorate this rising of Christ from the grave or sepulchre. Now, can you tell me why it is that on Easter we have these Easter eggs, such as I hold in my hand? I will tell you why it is. It is because while the outside of this egg is like the outside of a vault or grave, yet inside there is a germ of life. If you take a dozen perfect eggs and place them under a mother hen, and have her set on them for three weeks, at the end of that time out of these eggs which seem to have nothing of life in them, there will come forth little chickens, just such as I hold in my hand, only this one is not alive. But it is a very accurate representation of a little chicken a day or two old.

Now, just in this same way if you were to drive through a cemetery and look at a vault, which is the nearest that we have in this country in likeness to the sepulchre in which the body of Christ was laid, you would not suppose for a moment that there would be living people in that vault. While the bodies that are in the vault are dead bodies, yet they have the promise of life, God will some day raise them up, unite again the soul and the body and give them that everlasting life and resurrection glory which Jesus has promised. And as Jesus rose from the dead on Easter Sunday morning, so we have the promise that in the final resurrection the bodies of

Little Chickens Just Out of the Shells.

all who have ever lived upon the earth shall hear the voice of the Son of God and shall come forth; those who have lived Christian lives to the resurrection of life, and those who have done evil to the resurrection of death and eternal punishment.

The egg then is the symbol of life, for out of this seemingly lifeless object there comes forth the living chick; so out of the graves and sepulchres there will eventually come forth the bodies of all who have ever died, and these bodies shall become resurrection bodies. These mortals shall put on immortality, and these corruptible bodies shall put on incorruption; and then the souls and the bodies of all shall be reunited, never again to be separated throughout all eternity.

Perhaps during the past few months or years you may have laid away in the grave the body of some dear little brother or sister, or perhaps of a kind father or mother, or some other friend; if so, the spring season of the year will suggest to you the resurrection. The grass and the flowers which appeared to be dead last fall, and which during the winter have been wrapped in a white shroud of snow, now feel the warm breath of spring, and life and beauty are coming forth out of the sepulchre of the winter.

Soon all the trees will put forth their leaves and then beauteous blossoms and sweet fragrance will tell of the spring time as the resurrection period of the year.

So at Easter time we properly turn to the cemeteries where rest the bodies of our loved ones and know that the long winter of death and decay shall eventually give place to the promised resurrection of life and beauty. On that Easter morn the bodies of our loved ones shall be raised up, the soul and the body shall be reunited, and we shall see them and know them as they are.

Now, just how God shall gather again all the scattered parts of these bodies that were buried in the sea, or have decayed back to earth in the ground, we do not know. But our ignorance does not change the fact. I do not understand how at first God created man out of dust of the earth, nor do I know how the bread and meat and food which I eat each day nourish my life and become part of my own body. I do not know how, out of the same handful of earth, either an apple or a flower might grow. I know that it is so, but the *how* I do not know; nor does my ignorance prevent or hinder God from accomplishing it. If each day I eat food which by some strange power which God has placed within me is changed into bones in my body, to hair on my head, to nails on the ends of my fingers, to teeth, and eyes and ears and thus becomes a part of myself, why should I question, or desire to know how God is able to quicken in the grave the power to make the body to live again. If in the beginning God only spoke and worlds came into being, I know that when He shall command these bodies to rise from death and the grave they also will hear His voice and obey.

I am sure that no boy nor girl here would want that, on the morning of the resurrection his or her body should refuse to obey God's voice when He shall command the dead to come forth from their graves in life and beauty. You will want to obey Him then, but should you not also desire to obey Him now? When God tells you in the Bible what He wants you to do, are you obedient? Do you do as He commands? If you are disobedient now, then in the morning of the resurrection you might even desire, rather to remain in your grave, so that you should not have to look into the face of Him whom you have disobeyed and offended. If you want to awake on that final Easter morning in the likeness of Jesus and be forever with Him in glory, remember that you must obey God now as Jesus did when He was upon the earth. If we would be like Jesus in glory, we must strive to be like Him in all that we do, and I trust that you may think of this daily. At all times when you are uncertain what it is your duty to do, ask yourself this question: "If He were in my place, what would Jesus do?" And then act and do as nearly as possible as you think Jesus would do under the same circumstances.

QUESTIONS.—What does Easter commemorate? Is a dead body actually the person you knew? What has become of the soul? What do we commemorate on Good Friday? Of what are Easter eggs the symbol? What does the shell represent? What does the inside represent? Will the bodies of all who have died be raised some day? Who tells us this? What will God do with the risen bodies? What will become of the good? What of the wicked? Do we know how God will gather the scattered parts of the body? Does it make any difference whether we know how or not? Is anyone likely to refuse God's summons on the Judgment Day? Do we always obey Him now? When in doubt what question should we ask ourselves?

Joseph in the Pit.

CROWNS.

THE CHILDREN OF THE KING.

SUGGESTION:—Objects: A crown of leaves or paper, or of both.

BOYS AND GIRLS: I have to-day two or three crowns, and I want to talk to you about those who are children of the King.

First of all, I have here a crown which is made of leaves. This was the first kind of crown ever used. Three thousand years ago or more, those who excelled in

A Crown of Leaves.

strength, or running, or wrestling, or in any of the games which were common then, received a crown like this, which was placed upon their heads. This was regarded as a very great honor. Afterward, the kings of the earth began to use crowns. Their crowns were made of gold and set with costly jewels. These they wore on state occasions to indicate their high rank and position. Here is a crown made of gilt paper and set with

A Jewelled Crown.

a few silver-paper stars, meant to represent the crowns which kings and queens wear. While this crown is only made of paper, the crowns of kings and queens are made of gold, set with many costly stones. Besides the larger jewels in the crown of King George V. of England, there are also sixteen sapphires, eleven emeralds,

325

nearly three hundred pearls, and some twenty-eight hundred very costly diamonds, and it is estimated to be worth many millions of dollars.

Now suppose that we had gathered into this room the children, the boys and girls, of all the kings and queens of earth. Suppose also that they could all understand English, and that none of them knew that they were the sons and daughters of kings and queens, and that it was my delightful privilege to tell them how great and rich and powerful their parents are; and then I were also permitted to tell them, for the first time, w h a t beautiful crowns their parents own. Suppose also that after exciting their curiosity about these things, I should have the crowns of all the kings of earth placed on a long table at my side, covered with a beautiful cloth, and after

The Crowns on a Table.

telling them about the crowns, I should uncover this table with all these crowns of gold, studded with jewels. Don't you suppose that the eyes of all those boys and girls would sparkle with curiosity and delight?

But now, suppose that it were my privilege to do more than to show them the crowns. Suppose that I were permitted also to tell them that they were heirs to these crowns, and that after their fathers and mothers, the present kings and queens, had died, they were to become kings and queens, and were to receive these crowns as their own. Suppose that, more than this, it were my privilege to pick up the crown of Denmark, and then calling some little boy to me I were to hand it to him, and tell him that he was to keep it, and that some day it would be placed upon his head, and he would be King of Denmark. And then I should take the crown of Sweden, and calling another girl, I should give her that crown, and tell her that she should keep it, until some day it would be placed upon her head, and she should be Queen of Sweden. Suppose that in the same way I should take the crowns of Germany and Russia, and Austria, and Italy, and Spain, and the great crown of England, and all the crowns of all the nations of the earth; and calling the boys and girls by name, should have them come forward and receive these crowns, to be kept until they should be placed upon their heads, when they should be Kings and Queens, ruling in great pomp, and splendor, and honor, and power. Do you not think that it would be a very happy hour to these boys and girls, when all these great thoughts should be disclosed to them for the first time, and they should look upon such costly crowns, and receive them into their own hands, as their very own?

Now, boys and girls, while you have been listening to me, you have possibly not thought that what I have told you is really being fulfilled in your own hearing to-day, for the Bible tells us, "I will be a Father unto you, and ye shall be my sons and daughters, saith the Lord Almighty." (2 Cor. vi: 18.) Then, in another place, it also says, "Beloved, now are we the sons of God, and it doth not yet appear what we shall be." (1 John iii: 2.) So you see that it is my privilege to-day to talk, not to the children of earthly kings, whose glory is only temporal and whose honor is always uncertain, but I am permitted to talk to the children of the King of kings. (1 Tim. vi: 15; Rev. xix: 16.) The Scriptures not only tell us that God "is the only Potentate (the only powerful one). the King of kings," but it also tells us that He "hath made us unto our God kings and priests." (Rev. v: 10.) The same great book also tells us, not only, that we shall be kings and priests unto our God, but that we "shall reign forever and ever." (Rev. xxii: 5.) When a king dies he ceases to be king upon earth, but when God shall make us kings and queens and crown us in Heaven, we shall never die again, or cease to be kings and queens. The Bible tells us very clearly that our Father in Heaven is King over all earthly kings; greater than any of them; greater than all the kings of earth put together; a million times greater; yes, millions and millions of times greater; so much greater that the two do not compare in reality, but earthly kings simply suggest to our minds something of our great Heavenly King. God, this great King, created us and we were His children. But our first parents sinned and rebelled against Him, and refused to recognize Him as Father and to obey what He wanted them to do. But God loved them and us as a tender Father, and sent His only-begotten and well-beloved Son, Jesus Christ, to reconcile us; to tell us that God the Father loved us; that He was willing to forgive us, and that He would still accept us and make us kings and priests unto Himself, would crown us with glory, would give us dominion and make us kings and priests forever in Heaven. So you see that there can be no mistake about our being sons and daughters of the Lord Almighty. We are not only His children, but He has promised us crowns of glory and thrones of dominion and power.

If you and I were in England to-day and could walk into the Tower of London, where they keep the crown and the jewels of the royal family, and we could learn the value of these costly jewels, and crowns and scepters, it matters not how rich we might be, I am sure we would have to despair of ever being able to purchase these costly crown jewels. They are estimated at many millions of dollars. Now, if an earthly crown, which can only be retained for a few years, is so valuable, how much more valuable are the everlasting crowns, such as God gives, and which are to be ours for all eternity? And if we are not able to buy such an earthly crown, how much less are we able to purchase or buy a heavenly crown? The heavenly crowns are so valuable that we could never hope to buy them, therefore God gives them to us because He loves us.

More than two hundred years ago a man by the name of Colonel Blood attempted to steal the crowns and the crown jewels of England. He was not altogether successful, but was arrested before he escaped with them. But do you know that there are many who would steal your crown, and my crown of everlasting glory, if they possibly could? Therefore, God tells us in the Bible, "Hold that fast which thou hast, that no man take thy crown." (Rev. iii: 11.) So you see it is very important that we should be constantly on our guard. The King of England has soldiers to watch day and night, lest any one should steal his crown. And so also you and I need to be constantly on our guard, lest wicked people and sinful influences should rob us of our heavenly crown.

Not only are crowns sometimes stolen, but sometimes they are also lost. About fifty years ago some people were digging in France, and they found eight costly crowns, all lying close together, having been lost or hidden away in the earth. Four of them were very costly and very beautiful, while the others were smaller crowns. The first four were for the king and the queen, and the prince, and one other of the older children, and the other four crowns were for the younger children of the king's household. Yet you see that the father and mother and all the children lost their crowns. I trust that no parents here, or children either, would prize their heavenly crowns so lightly as ever to lose them.

There are thousands of people who would be willing to put forth any effort, or to pay any costs, if they could only obtain an earthly crown, and yet the Bible tells us that these people do it "to obtain a corruptible crown; but we, an incorruptible." (1 Cor. ix:

25.)   Now, by a corruptible crown is meant one that, like this crown made of leaves, will fade and fall to pieces, and decay, and thus pass entirely away.   Even a crown of gold, studded with costly jewels, would thus also eventually perish.   The crown which God gives to us is an imperishable crown, which never fades, and never passes away.   And therefore the Scriptures say, "And when the Chief Shepherd shall appear, ye shall receive a crown of glory that fadeth not away."   (1 Peter v: 4.)

Since the Bible teaches us these truths so plainly, "What manner of persons ought we to be, in all holy conversation and godliness?"   (2 Peter iii: 11.)   What more appropriate words could I say to you in closing, than that which God says to us in the blessed Book in which He has revealed all these things, "Wherefore, beloved, seeing that ye look for such things, be diligent, that ye may be found of him in peace without spot, and blameless."   (2 Peter iii: 14.)

QUESTIONS.—What kind of crown was first worn?   Because crowns of leaves were so perishable, of what were crowns later made?   What can you tell about the crown of the king of England?   If the crowns of all the kings of earth could be brought together, would people desire to see them?   If the children of earthly kings were present and we told them for the first time that they were the children of kings and gave them the crowns which they were eventually to own, would they be likely to be pleased?   Are you the child of a King who is the King above all kings?   Has He promised you a crown?   Will your crown be perishable?   How long will it last?   Can you quote any of the passages of Scripture which tell of our being the children of the King of kings?   Could the crown of an earthly king be bought?   Is there money enough in the world to buy a crown of everlasting life?   How then is this crown to be obtained?   Who once stole a crown and the crown jewels of England?   Was he successful in getting away with them?   Who tries to steal our crown of everlasting glory?   Is he ever successful?   Can you tell about the eight crowns which were found hidden away in the earth in France?   In what book are we told that our crown is to be imperishable and unfading, and to be ours forever?   What exhortation is contained in the last sentence of the last sermon in this book?

THE END.